Southwell's Sphere
The Influence of England's Secret Poet

D1236023

Other Books of Interest from St. Augustine's Press

Rene Girard, *A Theater of Envy: William Shakespeare*

Ralph McInerney, *Some Catholic Writers*

Ralph McInerney, *Shakespearean Variations*

Michael Davis, *Wonderlust: Ruminations on Liberal Education*

Catherine O'Neil and Zbigniew Janowski: *Agamemnon's Tomb: A Polish Oresteia*

Nalin Ranasinghe, *Socrates and the Gods: How to Read Plato's* Euthyphro, Apology, *and* Crito

Joseph Pearce (editor), *Beauteous Truth: Faith, Reason, Literature and Culture*

Michael Platt, *Seven Wonders of Shakespeare*

David K. O'Connor, *Plato's Bedroom: Ancient Wisdom and Modern Love*

Denise Schaeffer (editor), *Writing the Poetic Soul of Philosophy: Essays in Honor of Michael Davis*

Joseph Pearce, *Death Comes for the War Poets: A Verse Tapestry*

Josef Pieper, *Enthusiasm and Divine Madness*

Josef Pieper, *Don't Worry about Socrates*

Seth Benardete, *Achilles and Hector: The Homeric Hero*

Peter Kreeft, *If Einstein Had Been a Surfer*

Roger Scruton, *Perictione in Colophon*

Remi Brague, *The Anchors in the Heavens*

John von Heyking, *Comprehensive Judgement and Absolute Selflessness*

Barry Cooper, *Consciousness and Politics*

James V. Schall, *The Praise of 'Sons of Bitches'*

Frederic Raphael and Joseph Epstein, *Where Were We?*

Southwell's Sphere

The Influence of England's Secret Poet

Gary M. Bouchard

St. Augustine's Press
South Bend, Indiana

Manufactured in the United States of America.

1 2 3 4 5 6   24 23 22 21 20 19 18

Library of Congress Cataloging in Publication Data
Names: Bouchard, Gary M., 1961- author.
Southwell's sphere: the influence of England's secret poet /
Gary M. Bouchard.
South Bend, Indiana : St. Augustine's Press, [2016]
Includes bibliographical references and index.
LCCN 2016012545 | ISBN 9781587318221 (paperback)
LCSH: Southwell, Robert, Saint, 1561?-1595
--Criticism and interpretation.
Southwell, Robert, Saint, 1561?-1595--Influence.
English poetry--Early modern, 1500-1700--History and criticism.
Christian poetry, English--Early modern, 1500-1700
--History and criticism.
Christianity and literature--England--History--16th century.
Catholics--England--Intellectual life. | Catholics in literature. | BISAC:
RELIGION / History. | RELIGION / Christianity / Literature & the Arts.
LCC PR2349.S5 Z56 2016 | DDC 821/.3--dc23 LC record available at
https://lccn.loc.gov/2016012545

¥ The paper used in this publication meets the minimum
requirements of the American National Standard for Information Sciences -
Permanence of Paper for Printed Materials, ANSI Z39.48-1984.

St. Augustine's Press
www.staugustine.net

Table of Contents

Introduction

It must have been a curious sight that the shepherd beheld as the sun came up over the English Channel just east of the village of Folkestone in Kent on the morning of July 17, 1586. Gazing from a bluff above a secluded beach, far from the harbor where ships typically anchored, he watched a large Flemish man bearing one and then another companion upon his shoulders from their small boat, through the shallow waves, onto the dry sand. He could neither have known nor imagined that the younger of the two passengers being carried onto the shore in this fashion was a nobleman returning to his native land for the first time in fifteen years; nor that this nobleman's mother had been a child companion of England's queen; he could not conceive that this same young man being transported upon his pilot's back was a first cousin of the illustrious Copley family, who could number among his kinsmen no lesser Sirs than John Coke, Francis Bacon and William Cecil.

As for the young, gentlemen-clad priests being hoisted onto their native soil like clandestine cargo, their very act of stepping upon this beach was an act of treason. They were shrewd enough to suspect that the shepherd looking on that morning was one of Walsingham's spies, and they were resigned to the possibility that the inevitable violent end they anticipated in their native land might come even sooner than they had imagined.

As it turned out, the shepherd was only a shepherd, and the two Jesuit priests whom he saw inelegantly deposited upon their native shore at the break of day were stepping into an adventure, the tenure and severity of which they could hardly have anticipated. For unlike their notorious predecessor, Edmund Campion, these two priests would remain un-apprehended in their homeland for many years. The younger, Father Robert Southwell, would travel and work clandestinely as a missionary priest for six years before being captured, and his companion, Father Henry Garnet, would not be caught and executed for two full decades.[1] The failed Babington Plot and Spanish Armada and the resulting severities notwithstanding, they managed to travel in disguise under false names; passing themselves off as gentlemen by day and traveling at night; preaching in prisons and bringing the sacraments to covert or defiant Catholics; hiding in priest holes, behind false walls, beneath floors and privies; narrowly escaping capture, and residing for extended periods of isolation in a kind of luxurious house arrest.

Their talents were considerable and complementary. Robert Southwell was a writer and Garnet had worked in Tottel's Print Shop before fleeing to the continent a decade earlier. Garnet set up an underground press and Southwell wrote—poems, pamphlets, treatises, letters, homilies, meditations and translations. He would converse with and console the likes of his cousin Anthony Copley, the musician William Byrd, and garner the attention of the Earl of Southampton. But in stepping upon the shore that morning he could not have comprehended that he was stepping into the midst of England's greatest literary renaissance. Nor in the end could he appreciate that his religious zeal, his determined faith, his Ignatian meditative style, his European tropes, his prolific literary efforts, his make-shift printing press, his dramatic death and his un-silenced voice would impact the writings of some of the most important English literary figures of that age.

It is my goal in the chapters ahead to elucidate that impact more fully than has been done heretofore by considering Robert Southwell's influence upon English poetry generally and examining the effect of his life and work on five major English poets in particular: Edmund Spenser, George Herbert, John Donne, Richard Crashaw and Gerard Hopkins. In the course of this study I consider as well the influence of Southwell's writings on the so-called University Wits, on William Alabaster and on Michael Drayton.

1   Southwell and Garnet's Jesuit superior in England, Father Weston, the only Jesuit in England upon their arrival, would be captured soon after their arrival and Garnet would replace him in his role. Less sought after than his gentleman and poet companion, Garnet managed missionary efforts within England until his capture and death in 1606 in the wake of the Gunpowder Plot. In his book *Saint Robert Southwell and Henry Garnet: A Study in Friendship*, Philip Caraman, S.J. offers a sympathetic and insightful look into the shared adversity and steady companionship of the two priests.

Introduction

I undertake this project at a time when Robert Southwell the covert priest is beginning to step out of the shadows, and when his poetic and rhetorical voices are beginning to emerge from four hundred years of relative silence, the kind of silence that prompted the novelist Graham Greene to ask some years ago "Isn't there one whole area of the Elizabethan scene that we miss even in Shakespeare's huge world of comedy and despair? The kings speak, the adventurers speak . . . the madmen and the lover, the soldiers and the poets, but the martyrs are quite silent." Peter Millward among others has pointed out in recent decades that the martyrs are indeed there in Shakespeare's world, and not so much silent as silen*ced*.[2] And as with the silenced martyrs in Shakespeare's plays, so too with the voices of martyrs like Shakespeare's distant cousin, Robert Southwell, who made his way cautiously through the complex and varied Elizabethan scene, and whose own voice has been twice silenced: first by the conventional and all-too-literal means of imprisonment, torture and execution, and then by centuries of benign neglect on the part of literary critics and the fashioners of anthologies who, even in the current zeal to attend to the marginalized, leave the likes of Southwell all but voiceless in the margins.[3] Recently, however, a growing number of literary scholars are beginning to listen to and appreciate the varied and impactful eloquence with which Southwell spoke and wrote in the Elizabethan world in which he navigated.

2 Graham Greene posed his by now familiar question in his introduction to *The Hunted Priest*. Millward and others have pointed out that in making this observation Greene had not noticed such martyr figures in Shakespeare as Cordelia in *King Lear* and Lavinia in *Titus Andronicus*. Recently, Millward has pointed to recusant implications of these plays as well as *Love's Labours Lost*, *Macbeth* and *Merchant of Venice*. See "Shakespeare and the Martyrs" in Recusant History, vol. 31, No. 1, May 2012. As noted by Millward and here in this introduction the work of John Klause is the most thorough and convincing on this topic.

3 The *Norton Anthology* offers as good an example as any. Robert Southwell breathes there upon one thinning page, represented of course by "The Burning Babe" because Ben Jonson offered it such exceptional praise.

3

One dark irony in apprehending Southwell's voice and helping to bring his work to light is that the powers that permitted or forbade tongues like Southwell's from speaking are named in the very title by which we might assign him literary status. There is after all something of a morbid irony in calling Southwell and his recusant companions *Elizabethans*. By itself the title is still more regal than any other by which one can be fixed upon an English timeline. Any blackened chimney sweep might be a Victorian, but *Elizabethan* is a title that— even after the sophisticated, corrective historicism of the past several decades—we still somehow imagine to have been won at a pageant. This, after all, is Gloriana's Court and Shakespeare's England, which, black death, secret police and grotesque public executions notwithstanding, still can't quite seem to have the merry stretched out of it— not even by the 1590's "new[est] kind of torture, no less cruel than the rack"[4] from which hung Southwell's body for extended periods

4   "Huomo gli racconto c'haueuano una noua sorte di tormento non men" from Fr. Garnet's *Italian Letters*, p. 117a as quoted by Pierre Janelle, *Robert Southwell, the writer; a study in religious inspiration* (NY: Sheed and Ward, Inc., 1935) p. 66. Introduced by Topcliffe, the notorious priest-hunter and Elizabeth's chief torturer, "the manacles," as they were known, "were iron gauntlets, fitted high up on a pillar. The prisoner who was to be interrogated had his wrists inserted in them, and was left hanging, sometimes for several hours" (Flynn, 17). Fr. Garnet reports that "Southwell was hung up against the wall by the wrists, sharp-edged armlets being used for the purpose"; and, as the ceiling was too low for his feet to dangle freely, they "were tied up to his girth behind, which increased his suffering not a little" (Garnet's letter quoted in Janelle, 66). He was left in that posture as long as seven hours on end. After a while he would faint, and it was necessary to "run up and give him some brandy to drink, which having taken he recovered his senses and spewed out a great quantity of blood" (Garnet's letter quoted in Janelle, 66). One description of the new kind of torture was supplied by Sir Robert Cecil who visited his cousin in prison and reported that "he had seen Robert Southwell, being thus suspended, remain as dumb as a tree-stump; and it had not been possible to make him utter one word" (Garnet's letter quoted in Janelle, 66).

of time in two different prisons before his inevitable tri-part execution in 1595.[5] One calls Southwell an Elizabethan only by naming, in effect, his executioner. As Arthur Marotti has observed bluntly: "English nationalism rests on a foundation of anti-Catholicism" ("Remains," 37).

An observation like Marotti's, while it may be stark and even impolitic, is no longer impossible. The voices of the Elizabethan martyrs have not grown any louder with passing centuries, but in recent years historians and literary scholars have begun to listen more astutely to that voice than ever before, and some of the things they have heard are quite astonishing. Almost two decades have passed since Alison Shell first referred to Robert Southwell as "the invisible influence."[6] Since that time more than just the contours of his influence have begun to emerge. One may even identify during the past two decades a modest Southwell revival to which Frank Brownlow's excellent 1996 Twayne series book, *Robert Southwell,* pointed the way. In addition to a steady output of insightful articles offering historical and literary analysis, several notable books in recent years have helped us appreciate Southwell's place in English literature.

Scott Pilarz, S.J., *Robert Southwell and the Mission of Literature* (Ashgate 2004), alerted readers to the inseparability of Southwell's work from his Jesuit mission and his mission's inevitable transforming end. Anne R. Sweeney's *Robert Southwell, Snow in Arcadia: Redrawing the English Lyric Landscape, 1586–1595* (Manchester 2006), made a provocative case for understanding "Southwell as the nexus of much of the most profound thought of his age" (285). John Klause's *Shakespeare, the Earl and the Jesuit* (Fairleigh Dickinson 2008), offered a compelling and thorough response to Greene's question about the absence of the martyr's voice in Shakespeare's huge world of comedy and despair. Southwell's voice is there, Klause demonstrates in line

5   First in Richard Topcliffe's own private quarters and afterwards the Gatehouse prison. Southwell would spend most of his confinement in the Tower, his last days during his trial being in Newgate.

6   In her book *Catholicism, Controversy and the English Literary Imagination, 1558–1660* (Cambridge, 1999), Shell made a strong case that Southwell has been overlooked by critics for the past several centuries.

after line of the two poets' works, and he patiently teaches us where to look and how to listen.

The executed Jesuit, it turns out, haunts the pages of *Hamlet* every bit as much as Hamlet's murdered father. And in a book published the same year as Klause's, Gary Kuchar shows us "the ghost of Robert Southwell" in, among other places, Shakespeare's *Richard II*. In *The Poetry of Religious Sorrow in Early Modern England* (Cambridge University, 2008), Kuchar skillfully examines "the cultural work performed by the poetry of tears . . . popularized by Southwell" (31). Each of these scholars offers not only provocative insights about an author whose work has been largely neglected for the better part of four centuries, but also makes persuasive claims for his influence upon English literature. [7]

Additionally, significant archival work on the printed texts and manuscripts of the Elizabethan Catholic underground has been undertaken by scholars like Earle Havens, Mark Rankin, Robert Miola, and Elizabeth Patton, among others. This work is beginning to illuminate not just the contours of that secretive world as revealed in its prolific book and manuscript culture, but also the place of people like Robert Southwell within the clandestine commerce of words in which they trafficked. And now ten years after Professor Sweeney joined with Professor Peter Davidson to edit a new critical edition of Southwell's *Collected Poems* that presents his poems as they first appeared (Carcanet Press Limited, 2007), Davidson has committed himself to the much more ambitious work of bringing forth in the coming years the complete works of Robert Southwell from Oxford University Press. As a result of all this scholarship, Robert Southwell—even as he steps out of the shadows and into the realm of popular culture as an integral featured character in the recent mini-series *Will*—is more visible today than at any time in history, certainly more so than during his clandestine years in his native England.

7   Three other significant recent works contributing to the growing conversation about Robert Southwell and the English Recusancy include Sarah Covington's *The Trail of Martyrdom* (U. Notre Dame Press 2003), Susannah Brietz Monta's *Martyrdom and Literature in Early Modern England* (Cambridge U. Press 2005), and Sophi Read's Eucharist and the Poetic Imagination in *Early Modern England* (Cambridge U. Press 2013).

In her own assessment of Southwell's impact, Anne Sweeney went so far as to claim that Southwell was "the source of a kind of lyric poem that would lead not just to the works of Donne and Herbert," but "to Milton, to Shelley and beyond" (284). This claim, though bold, may be credible. Sadly, Professor Sweeney succumbed to her own battle with cancer before she could fully pursue the many insights she had discovered as a relatively young Southwell scholar. My modest hope here is to take up her enthusiasm and in a measured way help to further the conversation that continues to garner new perspectives and voices with each passing year.

The poets upon whom I focus the majority of attention in the pages ahead are not intended to comprise an exhaustive list, and may even appear at first somewhat arbitrary if not unlikely. Edmund Spenser and John Donne, though Southwell's nearest chronological contemporaries, would have both harbored decidedly ill feelings towards him. Spenser, when he regarded Southwell at all, viewed him as a seditious traitor to the Elizabethan state that he cherished with unwavering loyalty and that he worked tirelessly to fashion mythically in his great epic poem. Donne, raised as a secret Catholic, was the only one of the five who might actually have encountered Southwell personally, but he would come to reject "the pseudo martyrdom" of extremists like Southwell as dangerous and misguided, and he famously exercised venomous satiric attacks upon the Jesuits. That his brother Henry lost his life for harboring a priest in his room, that two of his uncles were Jesuits, and that their sister, Donne's mother, remained determinedly Roman Catholic into her dotage, which she spent with her son, who was by then the Dean of St. Paul's, all suggests the complicated personal and familial entanglements Donne had with the ancestral Catholicism that he rejected. George Herbert, who became an Anglican priest decades after Southwell's lifetime, would devote himself as a poet exclusively to the composition of religious verse, a prescription urged by his controversial Catholic predecessor with whose works he demonstrates more than just a passing acquaintance. Richard Crashaw elected a life in exile rather than to live in opposition to the Roman Catholic Church to which he was drawn by theological certitude and an aesthetic extravagance that he may have discovered first in the work of Southwell. Gerard Hopkins, an English Catholic convert two-and-a-half centuries removed from Southwell's world, acknowledges him nonetheless as his only predecessor to share the peculiar combination of Jesuit priest, poet and Englishman.

In his dedicatory poem to *Saint Peter's Complaint*, "The Author to the Reader," Robert Southwell asks "heavenly sparkes of wit" to "License my single penne to seeke a pheere." It is not entirely clear in this line whether the poet is addressing a divine muse, his literary contemporaries, or his readers, or perhaps all three. A similar tri-part ambiguity resides in the word *"pheere."* The poet seeks a poetic peer to join him in his worthy enterprise of turning English verse towards "Christian workes." But his spelling of the word as "pheere" suggests that he is seeking to do more than just enlist comparable well-intentioned talent to his cause. He seems to long for a *"fere,"* a companion in his daunting and dangerous undertaking. Finally, and most optimistically, Southwell expresses his vision of a *sphere* of divinely inspired poets and poetry. My use of Southwell's richly loaded quibble in the title of this book invokes all three of the above meanings. I recognize the poet's determined desire for other poets to follow his lead. I acknowledge the daunting and lonely nature of his companionless artistic struggle, and ultimately I assert Robert Southwell's improbable success in shaping in his life and work, and ultimately his very public death, the sphere of influence which he sought.

While Southwell is increasingly regarded as a central player in the vibrant English Recusancy, artistically, he is more often presented within the sphere of other, more major poets— as one of the "metaphysicals" or seventeenth century devotional poets (though he was killed five years before the seventeenth century began). In the pages ahead Southwell is deliberately treated as the central figure in a curious Ptolemaic sphere of other poets, each of whom he impacted differently. Many writers might be regarded within this sphere, Shakespeare chief among them. Southwell's influence upon Shakespeare having been convincingly elucidated by John Klause and others, I focus here upon other poets whose "sparkes of wit" we can appreciate differently by recognizing Southwell's effects upon their work. I make the case in the forthcoming chapters that Southwell's life and writings instructed William Alabaster, provoked Edmund Spenser, prompted George Herbert, haunted John Donne, inspired Richard Crashaw and consoled Gerard Hopkins. While none of these men was Southwell's companion, and while it would have made little sense for any of them to have acknowledged him as a peer, each of them, I suggest, authored some important poetry that may be best understood and appreciated within the sphere of this improbably influential English poet.

Surely it is no coincidence that, except for Spenser, all of these poets were, like Southwell, ordained ministers. The particular personal, political and religious complexities of each of their lives notwithstanding, what they most shared in common with Robert Southwell was their poetic vocation, and more specifically, the writing of devotional Christian poetry. Within the confines of artistic form—verse patterns, lines, stanzas, words and conceits—the more controversial and less edifying machinations of one's life do not vanish or lose their relevance, but they are often diminished or subsumed in the enterprise of successful artistic expression. Thus where one work of art informs another much might be overlooked, if not forgiven. It is here at the nexus of his poetry and that of his fellow poets that Robert Southwell, who remained alive by making himself invisible, becomes visible. Here at this intersection is where the present study originates, and where I join the growing conversation with the simple proposition that Robert Southwell was a minor poet with a major influence.

Chapter 1
Southwell's Miscellany:
Reforming the English Poetic

The advantage of the new kind of torture devised by Richard Topcliffe and tried upon Robert Southwell when he was arrested in 1592 was that, unlike the rack, it left no visible marks on its victims and hence would not provoke the pity of a weak-spirited jury during a defendant's trial. Just so with the marks that Robert Southwell left upon English literature. Though most certainly there, they are not readily apparent and have gone largely unnoticed by juries of literary scholars for the past four centuries. There are, as we shall see, various and complex reasons for this, but at the heart of Southwell's relative obscurity as well as the scarcity of his representation in anthologies of English literature is the deliberate invisibility in which he lived his life in England. Regarded for a time as public enemy number one in Elizabeth's realm, he concealed himself sometimes quite literally underground, traveled in the disguise of "Master Cotton"[1] and was never—either waking or sleeping—out of imminent danger. So well did Southwell achieve his vital invisibility that when Richard Topcliffe, the notorious priest-hunter who had pursued him for years, finally apprehended him, he knew from a description of Southwell provided to him by an informant that he had got his man, though he had never seen him

---

1   A wonderful glimpse into the gentlemanly disguise of Southwell and his confreres is furnished by Scott Pilarz, who cites a critique of Jesuit clothing by the Elizabethan, John Gee: "If, about Bloomesbury or Holborne, thou meet a smug young fellow in a gold-laced suit, a cloak lined thorow with velvet, one that hath gold rings on his fingers, a watch in his pocket, which he will value above 20 pounds, a very broad-laced band, a stiletto by his side, a man at his heeles, . . . then take heed of a Jesuit" (*Foote out of the Snare*, 127).

before.[2] People like the Bellamy family, in whose home Southwell was arrested, welcomed priests like Southwell onto their property at great personal risks.[3] Others associated with him only with the most scrupulous caution and concealed any evidence of having done so. To those who hunted him as well as those to whom he ministered, Southwell remained effectively invisible.

As in life, so too in death. None of the early modern authors treated in the forthcoming chapters or any other poets influenced by the works of Robert Southwell could derive any benefit from having their lives or works associated in any way with him; for all of them such an association would have been regarded at the very least as a political and personal embarrassment, and in the case of Donne it could have been the fatal blow to an already hampered professional career. Like the marks upon his body, therefore, the marks that Robert Southwell left upon English literature were in many cases deliberately concealed. As a result, his literary influence is best understood and appreciated as a subverting and subverted force. In elucidating Southwell's literary influence in this chapter, I will contemplate its complicated, subversive nature; first, however, I will consider two other aspects of his literary impact that distinguish his influence from that of the majority of his English peers; namely, that it was decidedly intentional as well as astonishingly successful.

Before turning to a discussion of Southwell's influence, though, it is first necessary to regard the young priest as an historical literary figure in England between the time of his arrival in England in 1586 until

2   "The slim straight build, the auburn hair, the famous eyes with their arched brows, the finely cut lips set in a slight smile that might be called mockery if it were not so mild and courteous; and not the description only, but a certain air of something undefinable, something absolute, proclaimed that this was the man" (Devlin, 281).

3   "The Bellamy household had been one of the oldest and safest of Jesuit resorts in England. Persons had met the family during his short visit twelve years earlier. Campion had been there and it was the household to give Weston shelter. Both Garnet and Southwell had visited it a number of times" (Philip Carman, S.J., *A Study in Friendship*, 74). Jerome Bellamy had been arrested for concealing conspirators of the Babington Plot and was executed in 1586.

the year of his execution and the rapid publication of his poetry in 1595. As we follow him from his arrival on the shores of his homeland, we see how integral the written and printed word was to his mission, which, while decidedly religious, was surprisingly literary.

His Mission

A first order of business upon coming to England for Southwell and his co- missioner and afterward superior, Henry Garnet, was to establish an underground printing operation. Only ten years earlier, Garnet had been in the employment of Tottel the printer who had had an assistant named Whalley, whose name Garnet now assumed. Garnet established lodging in London, but moved his press regularly from one house to another to avoid capture. Within a year of their arrival "Whalley" and "Cotton" were able to operate the press well enough to publish a variety of books, never making any reference to Rome or giving any indication of the press's true location (Caraman, 35). Ten years later, soon after Southwell's execution in 1595, the press was seized by royal authorities who confiscated "a large stock of many divers books." Following this seizure, Garnet reported to Rome for the first time about the secret press, and offered a description of its early successful publishing operation in London: "We equipped at our expense a press which in a short space of time filled the kingdom from end to end with catechisms and other books of devotion" (Caraman 35–36).[4]

In his book *Robert Southwell and the Mission of Literature, 1561–1595: Writing Reconciliation*, Scott Pilarz treats Southwell as "a first generation Jesuit," professing in the order only twenty years after its founder's death. Pilarz gives renewed emphasis to Southwell's essential Jesuit mission "to labour for the salvation of soules" (*Humble Supplication*, 11). While he overstates the degree to which previous critics have misapprehended or understated the relationship of the priest's writings to his mission,[5] Pilarz emphasizes that Southwell was from

4   From a letter of Henry Garnet to Claudio Aquaviva as quoted in Caraman's *A Study of Friendship*, pp. 35–36.
5   Pilarz regards the emphasis of Louis Martz on the meditative qualities of Southwell's verse, and Rosemund Tuve's emphasis on sacred par-

start to finish "a company man" whose intentions reflect absolutely those of the Society of Jesus: "to winne soules" (*Humble Supplication* 4). He reminds us that "Southwell's motivation for writing has everything to do with his understanding of the mission of the Society of Jesus," that he "writes as a pastor, not a polemicist, and he is confident that his literary efforts will help souls by promoting reconciliation" (43, 46). Southwell and Garnet's superior in Rome, Mercurian, Pilarz notes, had instructed his missionaries to "avoid all controversy and politics" (42), a worthy, but ultimately impossible instruction for English missioners, as their very presence was against the law and therefore an inherently political act which would be highlighted by their Elizabethan accusers who wished to prosecute them as traitors.

The missioner Jesuits sought to minister to recusant Catholics, as well as to win back converts. Under the circumstances, writing and printing were for Southwell and Garnet the only substitute they had for a public pulpit. If stealth was their *modus operandi*, writing was their most significant medium, and Southwell—in devotionals, meditations, epistles, sermons and poetry—the mission's prolific and persuasive author. What we may regard as his literary efforts are inextricable from his religious mission, which sought to comfort and catechize his Catholic readers, and to convert those readers who were not Catholic, even if, and perhaps especially if, they were members of his own family.

Besides the underground press, another significant means by which Southwell's words were propagated was through the private circulation of manuscripts, a circulation which relied upon substantial connections that he fostered with persons of literary interest and influence. There is the obvious case of his first cousin Anthony Copley whom he called "my Anthony," and the less obvious connections to the likes of William Byrd and Shakespeare's patron, "the most

ody and Brownlow's emphasis on his martyrdom all as potentially reductionist. Pilarz's own emphasis upon the poet's primary missionary intentions is neither discarded nor contradicted by the pioneering work of these authors. Pilarz's assertion that Barbara Lewalski ignored Southwell for the purpose of highlighting the dominance of the Protestant aesthetic has been pointed out by Alison Shell as well as others.

illustrious and leading Catholic in England, and a great supporter of
the faithful" (Devlin, 14). Based upon genealogies, Devlin posited that
Southwell's oldest sister and oldest brother had married a nephew and
a niece of Henry Wriothesley, the second Earl of Southampton, making
Southwell twice the Earl's cousin by marriage (Devlin, 15), but John
Klause has carefully checked genealogical records and finds no evidence of this (*SEJ*, 39 and note 4). Familial connections or no, however, Southwell's long estrangement from his country did not leave him
a material or intellectual vagabond. As Father Southwell he enjoyed
the company of his fellow Jesuits. As "Mr. Cotton" he was received
with a wink and a nod into some of the more illustrious estates in England, where, serving as secret chaplain to such households, he was afforded, in this sort of luxurious house arrest, ample time and
opportunity to carry out his mission of writing. Consider, for example,
his seldom mentioned translation from the Italian of the Spanish devotional work *A Hundred Meditations on the Love of God*. This
lengthy prose work represents a significant investment of time and
thought into several hundred pages of translation that saw only a very
private and limited circulation.

What we are to understand from this brief glimpse into the fundamental aspects of his day-to-day work is that while Father Southwell
the outlaw priest remained largely invisible to the English public, his
propagated works, both in manuscript and in illegal print, enjoyed a
significant, albeit cautious, circulation among England's population
of recusant Catholics and their sympathizers,[6] making him something

6   Of the works of Southwell printed after his death, we know a great
    deal. Of what circulated before his death, we can be less certain. See
    Nancy Pollard Brown's "Paperchase: the Dissemination of Catholic
    Texts in Elizabethan England" in which she remarks: "To trace the
    dissemination of Roman Catholic texts during the period of the penal
    laws of the sixteenth century is to enter unchartered territory. If it is
    difficult to reconstruct the movements of priests and to identify their
    helpers except in occasional glimpses, when records of pursuivants'
    raids or spies' reports provide momentary flashes of light, it is equally
    tortuous to follow the precise movements of books and manuscripts.
    The copying of manuscripts and the printing of illicit books followed
    the Catholic Church underground, as in the case of other religious

of a celebrity capture when Richard Topcliffe finally apprehended him in 1592.[7] This understanding of Southwell's literary habits and enterprises that has come to be shared by contemporary critics contradicts a traditional image, shared by Hopkins and many others, of a tortured and isolated prisoner scratching out his poems and prose in the dank, disease-infested prisons of London. Southwell would endure the worst of such treatment and conditions, but those years of torment came after his years of literary creation. During his years as a prolific author of English prose and poetry Southwell was never for a moment, either at work or rest, free from the weight of sudden discovery or capture, and the resulting violence which would follow. Even so, as "Mr. Cotton" he experienced with a certain frequency the accommodations and fare afforded an English gentleman. Southwell had access to the most popular as well as the most erudite contemporary poetry and prose in England, as well as from the continent, and the emergent English literati of his day, from the bohemian university wits to more sober and staid poets like Michael Drayton, likewise had access to his circulated work. He heard the most recent gossip of the court, as well as the rumors among the rabble, and was more carefully attuned than most to the political tenor in England and in Europe. Most importantly, he enjoyed the attention, as well as the occasional company, of an attentive and learned audience of devout readers.

His Intention

The first and most important aspect of Robert Southwell's literary influence is that it was deliberate. That is, while his primary mission was to win souls through his own writings and the administering of sacraments, he was also intent upon curbing the pagan excesses in writing

> groups the Government sought to suppress. As the century progressed and the number of works multiplied, the setting-up of secret presses in England and the importation of books printed abroad in no way replaced the tradition of manuscript copying. The problems of supply and distribution were always critical, and scribes worked indiscriminately from manuscript copy or printed text" (120).

7   Upon capturing Southwell, Topcliffe reported to the Queen that he "did never tayke so weightye a man."

to which English souls were exposed. Southwell crafted his poetry with the intention that it would not only offer consolation and instruction to England's Catholic population, but that it would serve as a moral corrective and literary model for other writers. He makes his literary reformation intentions clear in the verse dedication that he placed before *Saint Peter's Complaint*, but is never more explicit about the manner in which he regards his verse as a corrective model for other poets than in the dedicatory epistle he intended for another group of poems. The epistle, addressed "To my worthy good cousin, Master W.S.", is itself an example of Southwell's fine prose style. I quote here only those parts most pertinent to understanding the author's determination:

> Poets by abusing their talent, and making the follies and fayninges of love, the customary subject of their base endeavors, have so discredited this facultie, that a Poet, a Lover, and a Liar are by many reckoned but three wordes of one signification. But the vanity of men cannot counterpoyse the authority of God, who delivering many partes of Scripture in verse, and by his Apostle willing us to exercise our devotion in Himmes and Spirituall Sonnets, warranteth the Arte to be good, and the use allowable (*Poems*, 1).

Whether these words addressed to "W.S." are directed to Southwell's distant cousin William Shakespeare has been the subject of much critical conversation for nearly a century,[8] with many people having noted the similarity between Southwell's declaration that "a Poet, a Lover,

---

8   A. B. Grosart, Southwell's nineteenth-century editor, first suggested in his 1872 edition of Southwell's poems that there was a personal connection between Southwell and William Shakespeare, indicated by the dedication to "W.S." His suggestion was developed in the twentieth century by Southwell biographer Christopher Devlin who, with better evidence in hand, endorsed what Grosart had conjectured nearly a century before. "Vague though this dedication [W.S.] is," he wrote, "it is the only documentary contact between Robert Southwell and any actual person in that literary world which he hoped to convert. It is vague because there is no known W.S. among his cousins-german (except William Shelley who had been many years in close

and a Liar are by many reckoned but three words" and Theseus's declaration in *A Midsummer Night's Dream* that "The lunatic, the lover, and the poet / Are of an imagination all compact" (V1, 7–8). When he complains of the "unworthy affections" to which poets "have wedded their wils," it is the salacious wills of both poets and their readers that are being indicted in this complaint. But unlike the Puritan polemicists who would have poetry banned altogether, Southwell points to the great good to which poetry has been put by pagan poets as well as the Old Testament authors, and he cites the example of "Christ himself" who affirmed poetry's goodness "by making a Himme, the conclusion of the Last Supper, and the Prologue to the first Pageant of his Passion" (*Poems*, 1). Such examples ought to be imitated by English poets, Southwell insists, but instead:

> the Divell . . . possessed . . . most Poets with his idle fancies. For in lieu of solemne and devout matter, to which in duety they owe their abilities, they now busy themselves in expressing such passions, as onely serve for testimonies to how unwoorthy affections they have wedded their wils (*Poems*, 1).

Not content merely to chastise his contemporaries, Southwell provides in the verse that follows his preface many examples of how they might

imprisonment) and therefore the word 'cousin' must be taken in its looser sense" (260). Devlin noted that this verse dedication was written not just in the identical stanzaic pattern as *Saint Peter's Complaint*, but in the identical stanzaic pattern as Shakespeare's *Venus and Adonis*, and suggested that it was intended for the "Dear eie" of Shakespeare's patron Southampton and by extension his "*will*" who by "stilling Venus's rose" had fashioned the "paynim toye" whose sexual content was such that, when it came to print in 1593, wrinkled copies were purportedly found concealed beneath the vice-ripe bed pillows of many a delighted Cambridge and Oxford student. Richard Wilson has made much of the Southwell connection, though as I indicated in the Preface to this book, the most thorough and careful recent scholarship is that of John Klause, *Shakespeare, the Earl and the Jesuit.*

better put to use the poetic talents that they have heretofore been abusing:

> And because the best course to let them [poets] see the error of their workes, is to weave a new webbe in their owne loome; I have here layd a few course threds together, to invite some skillfuller wits to goe forward in the same, or to begin some finer peece, wherein it may be seene, how well verse and vertue sute together (*Poems*, 1).

I may not be the most skillful poet, Southwell admits, but I know how to fit virtue to verse. I can use the "loome" of contemporary poets, replete with identical stanzaic and metrical forms, motifs and favorite expressions, and weave into that loome a new web of devout and divine argument instead of "follies and fayninges." It would of course be an exaggeration to state that Southwell's short preface and accompanying verse were to late sixteenth and seventeenth century lyric poetry what *Tottel's Miscellany* was to the 1570s and 80s. We ought, however, to recognize nonetheless that it was against the conventional Petrarchan content brought to England in the pages of *Tottel's* that he was writing. The poetic conventions and forms in *Tottel's,* which had fostered an entire generation of English poets, effectively comprised the "loome" upon which Southwell proposed to weave a new "webbe."

It is also important to recognize that what the young priest-poet attempts to inaugurate here is far more than merely an aesthetic argument. The weaving that Southwell proposes and then demonstrates is as startling for its ambition as for its earnestness; for his proposal to turn poetry's use to "solemne and devout matter" cannot be isolated from the much larger loom of the Elizabethan empire and the dauntingly powerful fabric with which all poets were expected to weave. Queen Elizabeth was, after all, England's monarchical Petrarchan mistress, and one to whom, in Southwell's view, poets had, with "unworthy affections . . . wedded their wils." For Southwell, the deploying of pagan images, motifs, hyperbole and pageantry in the worship of a private or public mistress—particularly by a people who had smashed statues and white-washed church walls in order to rid their land of idolatry—was not just a misuse of poetry, but an error begot of the devil. As Anne Sweeney observes, Southwell identified "the lack of moral truth and cosmic order" in "the English poetic landscape," and was deliberately writing against the Elizabethan project of displacing the Virgin Mother Mary with the Virgin Mother Elizabeth, an enterprise to which Spenser and other poets had contributed prolifically with "idle fancies" (164).

For most readers today, the words of Southwell's preface sound like mere puritanical ranting, but to his contemporaries, we should understand, these were fighting words. It was to be sure far more than just damasked roses in women's cheeks or "unworthy affections" that were at stake in the verse that had shaped the English literary landscape since the publication of *Tottel's Miscellany* in 1557, and Southwell knew it. Elizabeth ascended to the English throne one year after *Tottel's* debuted and with his assault upon "idle fancies" Southwell was, in Sweeney's words, "pour[ing] cold water on the perpetual May of courtly love" (165). He was proposing, in effect, a re-writing of the English poetic landscape. As Sweeney describes it,

> [Southwell] was creating a topographical resistance-poetic of sorts, attempting to re-draw the imaginary landscape of the English national poetic agenda as he had tried to redraw the internal landscape of the English subject, to widen and deepen its sense of agency whilst at the same time emphasizing its smallness in the face of cosmic absolutes (165).

Such an ambition seems all the more unfathomable when we consider that his proposed literary reform was but one part of Southwell's mission efforts to which he was quite decidedly and literally devoting his life. And though he was acquainted with many of the "skillfuller wits" whom he invites to imitate him, including obviously "W.S.", it is doubtful that the young priest could have imagined the success of his bold proposal or foreseen the immediate and posthumous popularity of his poetry, as well as its influence upon more skillful and prolific poets of the next century.

Even so, changing the course of English literature was Robert Southwell's professed intention and a mission that he pursued with the same missionary zeal as proselytizing to recusant families. He wrote, not to establish himself as a poet (drawing attention to himself would have only hastened his eventual capture), but to offer his lyrics as models for a new kind of English verse. This, so far as I can tell, makes Southwell unique among his contemporaries, and places the volumes of his verse that proliferated after his death among the most important publications in England since Tottel's treasured exemplar of lyric poetry rolled off the press on the eve of Elizabeth's realm.

His Success

As Robert Southwell sat in prison in the Tower for nearly two years deprived of any means of writing, thoughts of inspiring a one-man literary reformation must have been the furthest thing from his weary mind. His eventual appeal to his cousin Robert Cecil for a trial that he knew would lead to a prescribed guilty verdict and traitor's execution reflects his resignation to the inevitable end of his mission in his native England. The Queen and her cabinet would have much preferred to let the young Jesuit languish quietly in the Tower in the hopes that, like others there, he would slowly fade from people's memories. Elizabeth knew from her experiences with Father Campion and Mary Queen of Scots just how much life a death could bring to a person, and she did not wish to fashion any more martyrs for Catholics to adore in England or abroad. The logic in Southwell's appeal for justice, however, was inescapable and he was soon granted a trial, a predictably theatrical event that placed him in debate with learned Anglican clerics in anticipation of the jury's forgone unanimous finding of guilt.

When Londoners began to assemble to see Southwell the condemned traitor being dragged through the winter streets to Tyburn, the authorities' worst fears were realized. They recognized that their attempts to divert people's attention away from this event had failed. The crowd of onlookers included many who came for the sheer spectacle, some who came to jeer at a notorious enemy to their Queen, and others, like the old fellow who cried out in encouragement as Robert Southwell passed by on the road to Tyburn, "God in Heaven bless and strengthen you." How many people's sympathies were represented by this man's actions would of course be impossible to say. Southwell's eloquent confession upon the scaffolding in which he declared himself a Roman Catholic priest and Jesuit and renewed his loyalty to England's Queen is reported to have moved the hangman who allowed the condemned priest to linger at the end of the rope long enough, so as not to experience consciously the remainder of the macabre proceedings. The predictable irony of the event was that no sooner had he been hanged and his body quartered[9] than Robert Southwell once more had life—this time on the printed page.

Within a month of his execution there followed a proliferation of some of his poems off London presses, indicating a popular demand for his poetry, born in part no doubt from a sympathetic response of the London crowd to Southwell himself.

> The first edition of *Saint Peter's Complaint With Other Poems*, appearing probably in March, was followed by a second edition before some of the type for the first edition had been distributed. When Gabriel Cawood secured the copyright in April and started his series of editions, he may have been confident that he had obtained the rights to a

9 Relative to other such events, Southwell's execution was not bad. When the sheriff held up Southwell's head and declared "Traitor," he received no reply from the crowd, so shouted: "I see there are some here who have come, not to honour the Queen but to reverence a traitor" (Caraman, 114). Far more gruesome was the execution of William Harrington, the young priest found in Henry Donne's lodgings, who, when he was executed in 1593, fought back with his executioners. After finally being pinned down, he had his genitals cut off and thrown onto a brazier and his intestines removed and burned before his eyes. John Carey, to the consternation of many critics, compared the public atmosphere of this age to that of Nazi Germany: "The number of Catholics actually executed was, by the standards of twentieth-century atrocities, quite small. Between the passing of the new anti-Catholic legislation in 1585 and the end of Elizabeth's reign, a hundred priests and fifty-three lay persons, including two women, were put to death. The method used to dispatch the victims amounted, however, in many cases to makeshift vivisection, so it atoned in terms of spectator interest for its relative rarity" (*John Donne: Life, Art and Mind*, Oxford University Press, 1991, pp. 17–18).

commercial success. The other compilation of poems, *Moeoniae*, was issued by John Busby in three editions all dated 1595, and even if the date does not accurately indicate the time of the appearance of the later editions, it points to the enthusiasm for the poetry in that year (McDonald and Brown, *Poems*, lv).

By 1636 *Saint Peter's Complaint With Other Poems*, accompanied by the dedicatory epistle, had been printed in London no fewer than eleven times. Southwell's *Mary Magdalen's Funeral Tears*, which had been published for the first time in 1591 prior to his capture and reprinted in 1592 and 1594, likewise remained very popular. There would be no fewer than seven more printings of this work in the generation after Southwell's execution.[10] This sudden and comparatively abundant publication of Southwell's works following his death rendered the poet an audience that he himself could not have anticipated and which, except perhaps at his execution, he had never known while living. The commercial success of his works indicates that his readership went well beyond devout, covert Catholics to include pious Anglicans. Indeed, the many reprints of these editions suggest that Southwell's meditative verse was part of a new literary style of which he was one of the primary innovators. The swiftness with which Southwell moved from marginalized to mainstream is startling. Frank Brownlow first alerted contemporary readers to the significant popularity of Southwell's works by drawing attention to John Bodenham's *Belvedere*, or *The Garden of the Muses,* published in 1602, seven years after Southwell's death and a year before Queen Elizabeth's:

> This large collection of quotations from contemporary poets is a rough guide to the fame and popularity of the poets represented. Drayton has the largest number of quotations in the book (269), followed by Spenser (215), Shakespeare (214), and Lodge (79). Southwell shares the

10 Altogether, fourteen editions of *Mary Magdalen's Funeral Tears* were published between 1591 and 1827. Vincent Leitch notes the frequent evidence that Southwell's work was influential upon works on Mary Magdalen that followed during the English Renaissance.

fifth place with Daniel; both are represented by 75 quotations. In Southwell's case the quotations are all from the two small books, *Saint Peter's Complaint* and *Moeoniae* (Brownlow, *Southwell* 126).

The popular appeal of Southwell's works to pious as well as curious readers of the late sixteenth and early seventeenth centuries is irrefutable and, based upon the conventional version of English literary history on which most of us were schooled, rather remarkable. Here is an English poet publicly executed as a traitor seven years earlier, whose verse is being counted by one seventeenth-century estimate as among the six most popular Elizabethan writers. Yet, if not for the chance recording of a private remark of Ben Jonson to William Drummond, in which he purportedly praised "The Burning Babe" as better than anything he himself had written,[11] Southwell would likely have long since vanished utterly from the English canon. Before proceeding to examine the influence these popular printed works had upon other poets, therefore, it is imperative that we try to understand the seeming disparity between his posthumous literary popularity and his near disappearance from the pages of English literature.

His Subversion

If Southwell's works were well regarded by readers of that day and many of his contemporary poets, why do we have only Ben Jonson's one superlative word of endorsement? Significantly, Jonson's praise was spoken in a private conversation and recorded by his fellow poet later. It is reasonable to surmise, based upon the prolific printings, many others spoke of Southwell's work in private. It is likewise probable that if, like Jonson, they spoke in order to praise the dead poet's

11 Ben Jonson's remark to William Drummond of Hawthornden that "Southwell was hanged, yet so he had written that piece of his The Burning Babe he would have been content to destroy many of his," is well known and chiefly responsible for the continual anthologizing of the one Southwell poem. Hence the hanged poet hangs presently in the likes of the *Norton Anthology* upon the gossamer-thin claim of one peculiar poem.

work, they most assuredly did so in private and with more guarded prudence than did Jonson. For in death, as in life, Robert Southwell was a dangerous man to know. His body of poetical works, with its accompanying implorations and embedded instructions on how to write sacred verse, was a textual body inseparable from the fresh memory of his political and religious body, recently drawn, hanged and disemboweled before an unusually sedate and sympathetic crowd at Tyburn. Though time would come between Southwell's execution and the many subsequent editions of his works, so too would stirring accounts (both oral and written) of his heroic life and death as well as plenty of anti-Jesuit propaganda. Southwell's writings would likely be promoted as the sacred remains of a martyred priest or dismissed as the pious drivel of a Romish pseudo-martyr,[12] with little or no objective "literary" middle ground. In any case the assembling of his poetical works in concert with the public dismemberment of his body created at the very least a complicated mixed message.

In his provocative essay "Southwell's Remains: Catholicism and Anti- Catholicism in Early Modern England," Arthur Marotti makes the case that for readers in the early modern world "the corpse of the author and the corpus of his work were in closer imaginative proximity" ("Remains," 54). If this was generally true, we can only imagine how inseparable would be the corpse and corpus of an author whose quartered body parts were burned and publicly defiled by executioners and sought after as relics by others. Southwell's writings themselves could amidst such drama easily come to be regarded as a kind of relic. As Marotti notes, "despite confessional differences and the atmosphere of polemical viciousness within print culture, the literary remains of a Catholic author could be both preserved and venerated ("Remains," 53). Nor apparently was this a phenomenon that would subside after a few months or years. Consider the startling description of Southwell's writings offered by printer William Barret[13] in the

12 While the term pseudo-martyr may not have been original with John Donne, his polemical tract by that name fixed it in the English lexicon as a way describing Catholics executed for a cause not worth dying for, and unworthy of the title of martyr.

13 Marotti ascribes these words to William Leake, but Janelle (p. 316) and Early English Books Online confirm that it was William Barret.

dedication to an edition of the poet's writings in 1620, twenty-five years after his execution. Speaking as though he had made his way about the gruesome remains at Tyburn, Barret tells his patron that he "first collected these dismembered parcels into one body and published them in an entire edition" ("Remains," 53).

It is not an exaggeration therefore to point out that a person owning a copy of Southwell's writings might regard him or herself or be regarded by others as possessing a relic, making it a kind of contraband that, though not eagerly displayed, had unusual commercial value. Hence, while one might purchase and read a volume of Southwell's poetry in London soon after his death, as many apparently did, one would likely exercise care in choosing to whom one spoke of having done so. As for England's poets—the bold claim of Ben Jonson excepted—most of them, we can imagine, would be more cautious than the average reader in not wanting to be caught possessing, copying from, or so much as alluding to the literary relics of an executed traitor and Jesuit. As for following Southwell's implorations to weave sacred verse in the secular loom by directly imitating his many fine examples, it seems that an aspiring or established poet would enter upon such literary exercises with a caution which might make Harold Bloom's anxiety of influence look like a bad case of Freudian nerves. As Shell points out, one might copy Southwell's poetic examples with great success, but one would not likely speak of having done so:

> Simply from reading what Elizabethan poets have to say about their mentors, one would assume that the turn towards religious poetry at this date [1595–96], was spearheaded almost entirely by Edmund Spenser, Guillaume Salluste du Bartas and the spirit of Philip Sidney. It is not that Southwell is never mentioned at all since a number of contemporaries praise his style; but it is as if a martyred Catholic could not escape an ideological miasma of a kind which did not prevent his being read or imitated by non-Catholics, but which may well have impeded their overt acknowledgment of him as an example (59).

Decades after the Elizabethan era when poets like the young George Herbert or the ordained John Donne put on the garb of religious poets, they were mindful of the established Protestant poetic that now preceded them, but conscious too, I would contend, that religious poetry in England was originally a Roman habit, and that there was a politically complex and violent history accompanying that habit.

The predicament that these poets faced in fronting their immediate English literary predecessor in the religious lyric is one that still lingers even today. For, whether one would accept or modify Marotti's proclamation that "English nationalism rests on a foundation of anti-Catholicism" ("Remains," 37), the fact that a Jesuit missionary should have spawned what became arguably the most enduring form of lyric in the seventeenth century is a literary irony that many might rather forget than celebrate. Yet, it is precisely because of his circumstance as a subversive practitioner of poetry, his "counter" presence and inevitable execution that, I believe, Southwell's influence is best understood in more than narrow, literary terms. Southwell's legal and cultural marginalization is the first thing one must acknowledge in any consideration of his literary influence. For to acknowledge the particular influence of Southwell upon poets of sixteenth- and seventeenth-century England without considering the impact upon those same poets of his covert Catholic life and resulting public death affords one, at best, an incomplete understanding of his influence. The paradoxical life of this young gentleman who moved in secret among some of his most influential countrymen before being publicly hanged and disemboweled cannot be separated from any literary influence that he might have had upon these same men. Here is where the current critical context can be especially instructive.

One of the most enduring and important legacies of New Historicism is, I think, an understanding of history and historical artifacts, not as inanimate raw material or data, but as animate, politically charged elements that invigorate any subsequent "text" in which they reoccur. An Elizabethan actor costumed in acquired Roman Catholic clerical vestments wears as well all of the significant political messages that that garb signals. What he says and how he looks and moves upon the stage in such a costume may well carry complex and ironic signals to which we may pay attention, but which we will never be able to "read" quite the way his immediate audience did. It is no coincidence that at the same time we have come to appreciate the potential politically charged nature of all inter-textuality, that interest in the English recusancy has been increasing proportionally, and as more light continues to be shone upon this dark underground, Robert Southwell emerges from the shadows as emblematic of the intricate political, religious and literary complexity of the Elizabethan world that has been frequently overlooked before now.

To appreciate this complexity we need only consider Stephen Greenblatt's description of the relation between Edgar's feigned possession in *King Lear* and *A Declaration of Egregious Popish Impostures*:

> In so far as this "material" is taken seriously at all, it is as part of the work's "historical background," a phrase that reduces history to a decorative setting or a convenient, well-lighted pigeonhole. But once the differentiations upon which this model is based begin to crumble, then source study is compelled to change its character: history cannot simply be set against literary texts as either stable antithesis or stable background, and the protective isolation of those texts gives way to a sense of their interaction with other texts and hence to the permeability of their boundaries (165).

The "protective isolation" in which Robert Southwell composed his poetry was always of the most precarious nature, and when we begin to regard seriously the known details of his life, we begin to perceive the permeability of the boundaries between, not just Southwell's life and writing, but of his writing and that of other poets, and between his life and death and the body of literature that followed.

One other familiar critical approach of the past several years offers us an aperture into contemplating the complicated place of Robert Southwell in literary history. In his book *Self-Consuming Artifacts*, Stanley Fish offers a description of an astute reader's coming to terms with the dialectical nature of seventeenth-century religious verse. His explanation may also describe the experience of seventeenth-century poets reading Robert Southwell. "The dialectic presentation is disturbing," Fish says,

> for it requires of its readers a searching and rigorous scrutiny of everything they believe in and live by. It is

didactic in a special sense; it does not preach the truth, but asks that its readers discover the truth for themselves, and this discovery is often made at the expense not only of a reader's opinions and values, but of his self-esteem (1–2).

The dialectician, he observes, functions as a good physician who "tells his patients what they don't want to hear" (3) urging them towards "a conversion" from one way of seeing the world to another, "the way of faith." Fish's most striking insight into the nature of the dialectic is his central thesis, that "a dialectical presentation succeeds at its own expense; for by conveying those who experience it to a point where they are beyond the aid that discursive or rational forms can offer, it becomes the vehicle of its own abandonment" (3).

Just how adequate the physic of Robert Southwell's poetry was to the seventeenth-century poets who came after him is certainly debatable. His demand that poetry be employed for sacred rather than secular purposes certainly told many of his Elizabethan contemporaries "what they didn't want to hear." He regarded it as a form of "preaching the truth," hoping to inspire conversions, but his best verse does in fact invite his readers to discover the truth for themselves. Relying more on piety than wit, and more on image than argument, Southwell's poetry may lack the sort of explicit self-analysis, the "searching scrutiny" of more dialectic presentations such as Donne's "Good Friday 1613" and Herbert's Affliction poems. Even so, Southwell's poetry provoked by Ignatian meditation certainly urges in readers the kind of self-scrutiny from which it sprang. *Saint Peter's Complaint*, in fact, has been read to contain directives for one to achieve perfect contrition in the absence of a confessor.

As human text, the good physician Robert Southwell offers an unusually hard medicine to swallow in the "presentation" of his own good life. His work as subversive, recusant priest and as Jesuit requires, before imitation, "rigorous scrutiny" of many things in which these poets believed. His life is one which they may, in fact, not want to hear, and when rational discourse failed him at his trial—where all the participants are part of something politically larger than themselves and the result predestined—Southwell finally and undoubtedly succeeded at his own expense. Conveying those who regarded his life and work to a point where they were beyond his aid, he was then, in his execution "consumed in the workings of [his] own best effects." True to Christian paradox and true to dialectic presentation, Southwell signified most successfully in his failure. In Fish's words: "a self-consuming artifact signifies most successfully when it fails, when it points away from itself to something its form cannot capture" (4) or, in Southwell's own words as he has Magdalen describe her loss in "Marie Magdalens complaint at Christ's death":

> Borrowed streames refraine their running,
> When head springs are hindered.
> One that lives by others breath,
> Dieth also by his death (9–12).

Lacking the probability of a life charged with inevitable execution for their religious beliefs, those practitioners of religious verse who came after Southwell, I believe, swallowed some portion of the medicine of this good physician Southwell, comprehended the tragic loss of this thirty-four-year-old poet and considered the price of *The Good Life*. In place of a secret life and tortuous death, these poets offer a successful employment of the kind of dialectical poetry Southwell had advocated. Though his poetry is not as apparently self-analytical as Donne's or Herbert's, his confessional soliloquies of Mary Magdalene and Peter, as well as his personal Petrarchan laments like "Sinnes heavie loade," "Life is but Losse" and "I dye alive" document the superficial pleasures of this world and direct poets decidedly in the direction of a new kind of lyrical introspection, prompting a more modern poetry which "fails" in just the right way; fails in the very manner of Southwell's life, bringing poet, poem and reader to a point of inadequacy where the only solution lies outside the poem whose form has failed to capture what it sought to say—because it cannot be said. Each poem is a small martyrdom, an annihilation of the self for something bigger.

His Legacy

It has been over over six decades since Louis Martz first encouraged readers to pay attention to Southwell's poetry for its own sake as well as to consider it as the first sampling of a kind of poetry which had already been assigned two misnomers, "Metaphysical poetry" and "the school of Donne."[14] Calling his landmark book simply *The Poetry of Meditation*, Martz began with Robert Southwell, claiming that he brought to England "the practice of religious meditation, and the conversion of methods of profane poetry to the service of God. In establishing these arts on English soil," Martz claimed,

> Southwell became the first significant writer of a new kind of poetry, a kind which at its best blended religious meditation with Elizabethan lyric. He is a pioneer experimenting with an unstable compound of old and new, producing only eight or nine poems without some grievous flaw. But these few are among the best religious lyrics of the sixteenth century in England; and of those that are flawed, fully half show here and there some irridescence of poetry that we may value. Southwell is a poet, not a mere example of a trend; and our interest in his work must be twofold (*The Poetry of Meditation*, 183).

In his 1983 book *The Emotive Image, Jesuit Poetics in the English Renaissance,* Anthony Raspa focused primarily upon Richard Crashaw and made as substantive and well supported a case as anyone that the Ignatian aesthetic first identified here by Martz flourished in England during the Counter Reformation. This present study concurs with and in some ways extends this view shared by Raspa and others who followed in the direction that Martz pointed, though my

14 The recent shift from the use of the term Metaphysical Poetry to "Seventeenth-Century Lyric" or "Seventeenth-Century Religious Verse" effectively ignores Southwell since he was killed in the last decade of the sixteenth century. As Shell notes, these new literary terms ought to "be treated with caution" because "had he been thought to be an important poet, they would never have been coined, and with the persistent use of these terms, he continues to be written out of the canon" (58). It is doubtful that "Southwell's Sphere" is going to replace any of these terms, but it is interesting that in the nineteenth century Gerard Hopkins referred to this poetry as "Herbert and his school."

consideration of Southwell's influence is broader than just the Ignatian aesthetic elements of his verse. More recently Alison Shell has modified Martz's claim by demonstrating that there was a ripe literary context for the religious lyric when Southwell came to England. "It would be a mistake," she says, "to claim that Southwell single-handedly re-introduced imaginative religious poetry to England after the Reformation." Even so, she argues:

> The posthumous publication in 1595 of *Saint Peter's Complaint* gave sacred verse a definitive new direction, and helped to create a climate in which non-biblical religious poetry became increasingly acceptable. The title-poem in particular inaugurated a publisher-led trend, while the collection as a whole was one of the most important stimuli to the urgent moral debates conducted by English poetic theorists of the later 1590s (58).

In each of the forthcoming chapters, I will be treating poets who resided artistically and personally within the climate of religious poetry that Martz, Shell, Brownlow and others credit Robert Southwell with having created; poets who reside within, as it were, Southwell's sphere. Only one of these poets likely knew Robert Southwell personally and only one other refers to him by name. And while none of them lived as covert a life as Southwell, biographical details in several instances are nearly as murky. To find the marks of Robert Southwell therefore I turn deliberately to the body of their works, sometimes broadly, but more often with intentional focus upon particular poems; and always with an eye to the reformation poetic that this invisible poet successfully inspired with his "course threds," and which may be seen in the finer pieces of the skillfuller wits who went forward well after his own voice was silenced.

Chapter 2
The Sphere's First Tears:
The Wits, Alabaster, and Drayton

The Wits

Robert Southwell made his first noticeable impact upon the writers of his age during what Christopher Devlin has described as one of the most "confusedly creative half decades" in English literary history (1590–95). While Edmund Spenser labored upon *The Faerie Queene* over in Ireland, the fashion of "amatory sonnet-sequences" began to give way in his native country to "the historical series of the Plantagenet Wars" ("Contemporary Poets – I," 170). During these same years emerged works as unprecedented in their content as they were unlikely in their origins: repentance writings from the notorious University Wits. Recalled as much for their bohemian debauchery as their early contributions to the English stage, the Wits' playwriting skills and vibrant personalities shaped the emergent London theatre scene at the beginning of the 1590s.

We can hardly imagine the pious Father Southwell in their unsavory company, and it is quite unlikely that he ever was. Nonetheless, as with his distant cousin William Shakespeare, it is here that we detect the first traces of Southwell's impact upon the English literary world, an impact, in this case, as much evident in dramatic personal conversions as poetic style. When we recall that the plague was casting a fatal shadow upon London during these years we can appreciate that dramatic calls to conversion like the one that Southwell was making were not easy to dismiss as mere pious abstractions or the ranting of an overzealous papist. The plague's gruesome effects, which understandably seemed to foretell an apocalyptic crisis to many, created a ripe atmosphere for at least one thing: the forceful and provocative writings of an author who, in dramatic images and elaborate emotional appeal, urged his countrymen towards personal as well as literary repentance.

Suffering, death and damnation were on people's minds and Southwell delivered a stirring prose consolation, *Mary Magdalen's Funeral Tears,* whose multiple printings (1591, 1592, 1594) and wide circulation indicate the solace that it supplied to an audience wider than just recusant Catholics. This emotive meditation combines Ignatian style mediation, homiletic argument and Euphuistic prose style into an extravagant first-person complaint as a distraught Magdalen arrives at the empty tomb of Christ and experiences the double loss of her dead savior and his vanished body. The work serves, among other things, as an allegory to strengthen the wills of recusant English Catholics facing unexpected injustices, but as the re-printings demonstrate it found readers well beyond these circles. *The Funeral Tears* was the first of Southwell's works to be widely circulated and the only one to be published before his capture and death.

Describing in his prefatory address to the reader his surprise at the speed with which copies of the work were being reproduced without his permission, Southwell remarks that he thought it "should have been an eye-sore to those that are pleased with worse matters" (*Prose Works,* viii). He then deploys the very ornithological metaphor that Robert Greene would soon use to complain of a young upstart crow's unauthorized borrowings:

> Yet the copies flew so fast and so false abroad, that it was in danger to come corrupted to the print. It seemed a less evil to let it fly to common view in the natural plume and with its own wings, than disguised in a coat of a bastard feather, or cast off from the fist of such a corrector as might haply have perished the sound, and imped it in some sick and sorry feathers of his own fancies (*Prose Works viii*).

To preserve the integrity and quality of his work, in other words, the author, with a certain hint of false modesty, says that he found it necessary to allow the work to be published. His metaphor of birds' flight for this instantly popular work is not very far from the actual truth. As Nancy Pollard Brown has reminded us recently, "As soon as the *Funeral Tears* was completed, copies began to be made" ("Southwell's M. Magdalen," 9). So in 1591, five years after his arrival in England, Southwell's first work was published. The subsequent re-printings in the successive years mean that the work yielded economic as well as spiritual profit. The original printing was done anonymously "by John Wolfe for Gabriel Cawood, who submitted either a manuscript or a copy of the printed book to the Stationers' Company and received the copyright on November 8, with"—and here is the rather startling piece—"licence [sic] from Richrd Whitgift, Archbishop of Canterbury" (Brown, 9). *The Funeral Tears* was dedicated to Mistress D.A., signaling either Anne Dacres or Dorothy Arundel, daughter of the recusant Sir John Arundel, who with her sister would go into exile and become a Benedictine nun in Brussels.[1]

As F. W. Brownlow observes, "the *Funeral Tears* is really a story, cast in the form of a homiletic meditation, about a woman's overwhelming love for an infinite object, such a love as could never exceed, because the thing loved is of infinite perfection" (37). Magdalen's compounded loss and layered griefs are cast in tropological extravagance and in fits of weeping that would soon become notorious in the literary world. For recall that Southwell was not simply fashioning a substantial religious meditation for people, but making a determined effort to reform the literature of his native England. That he went about doing both of these things in such an appealing literary style was both his making and unmaking. That is, he attracted the attention of writers who found his work worthy of emulation, which in turn would attract the attention of those who perceived his influence as necessitating his removal. Writing only months after Southwell's execution, his Flemish associate John Deckers observed:

> He wrote his works partly to comfort Catholics and strengthen waverers in the Faith, partly to cleanse the

1   Brownlow follows the lead of Janelle and others in asserting that the dedication is to Dorothy Arundel. Brown argues that Southwell's words "To the worshipfull and virtuous Gentlewoman" would not have been suitably deferential as an address to Anne Dacres, now Anne Howard, Countess of Arundel ("Southwell's *M. Magdalen's Tears*," 6). Klause, however, argues convincingly that the dedication was in fact to Anne Dacres. See "Catholic and Protestant, Jesuit and Jew: Historical Religion in The Merchant of Venice." *Religion and the Arts* 7 (2003), 87

cess-pool of filth in England . . . So graceful and attractive was his style that English critics, themselves no friends to us, and traitors to the Faith, praised it for its soft rich flow of eloquence and its honeyed diction (as quoted by Christopher Devlin in "Robert Southwell and Contemporary Poets – I," 169).

Whether or not Southwell had been, as he indicates, genuinely surprised by the rapid circulation of *The Funeral Tears* and its subsequent publication under the watchful eye of the Anglican Archbishop, he and Garnet must have been ecstatic at this great sign of the success in their mission, a success that as always, Southwell hoped others would imitate. They did, and this "was one of the main reasons why," Deckers surmises, "the heretics picked on him rather than on others, and demanded his death so eagerly" (Devlin, "Contemporary Poets," 169).

In his preface "To the Reader" at the beginning of *Mary Magdalen's Funeral Tears* Southwell makes an explicit reference to the vain work of the University Wits. In a searing indictment of the fruitless manner in which these "finest wittes" have heretofore lost themselves, the young priest makes clear that the complaint is not his alone, but that of persons who matter, persons who would be patrons:

> It is a just complaint among the better sort of persons, that the finest wittes lose themselves in the vainest follies, spilling much Art in some idle phansie, and leaving their works as witnesses howe long they have been in travaile, to be in fine delivered of a fable. And sure it is a thing greatly to be lamented, that men of so high a conceit should so much abase their abilities, that when they have racked them to the uttermost endeavor, all the praise that they reap of their employment consisteth of this, that they have wisely told a foolish tale, and carried a long lie very smoothly to the end (*Prose Works* vii).

Should these wits of whom he speaks wish to do more than "abase their abilities" in fashioning foolish tales and long lies, Southwell offers them an alternative. As he later did in the Preface to *Saint Peter's Complaint*, he makes an explicit appeal to other writers in the dedicatory letter to this stylized prose work, inviting the imitation of those whom he acknowledges to be better writers than himself:

> yet shall I think my endeavors well repaid if it may but woo some pens more skilful, from unworthy labours, either to supply, in this matter, my want of ability, or in others of like piety (whereof Scripture is full) to exercise their happier talents. I know that none can express a passion that he feeleth not, neither doth the pen deliver but what it copieth out of mind; and therefore the finest wits are now given to write passionate discourses. I would wish them to make choice of such passions as it neither would be shame to utter, nor sin to feel. But whether my wishes in this behalf take effect or not, I reap, at the least, this reward of my pains that I have showed my desire to answer your courtesy, and set forth the due praises of this glorious Saint (*Prose Works* vi).

He is satisfied, he says, to have given praise to Saint Magdalen and to have made an effort to please Lady Arundel, but his greater intention is, in his words, to woo more skillful pens than his own, to turn the heads and the hearts of his literary peers to make a better choice. He would have them convert their passions from the praise of ladies (and of Elizabeth herself), to follow his example in praising Magdalen or any of the other many worthy subjects from scripture.

His wooing apparently worked. How responsible *Mary Magdalen's Funeral Tears* was for the rash of conversions that would take place among the University Wits in the wake of its publication we cannot know with absolute certainty, but there are enough traces of his work in some of theirs to suggest that he had succeeded in his aim of getting skillful writers to exercise their happier passions in the service of scripture. In two sequential articles in *The Month* in 1950 Devlin laid out the case for Southwell's influence upon his contemporaries, numbering among those authors who produced a sudden burst of literary repentant tears Thomas Nashe, Nicholas Breton, and Thomas Lodge. Samuel Daniel, William Shakespeare and Michael Drayton, Devlin noted, all produced in the wake of *Mary Magdalen's Funeral Tears* poems in rhyme royal stanzas "whose ostensible theme is the rape of a fair lady, but whose most striking passages are concerned not with rape but with repentance" ("Contemporary Poets – I," 170–71). Devlin sees this sudden spring of repentance-themed writing as originating in Southwell's *Funeral Tears* and culminating in Marlowe's *Dr. Faustus*, and the evidence supporting this literary trajectory is plausible, even as it is punctuated with more intrigue and violence than the Wits were creating for the stage.

Within a couple of short years after the publication of *The Funeral Tears* of course Southwell was betrayed, arrested and imprisoned, a circumstance that could only have added additional layers of intrigue and authenticity to the popular meditation that has suffering as its theme. Thus it is in the politically, religiously and artistically charged, plague-rife atmosphere of the early 1590s that we find the recently captured, unnamed Jesuit at the center of what Devlin refers to as "two of the most sensational literary events of 1592–93, the controversy between Gabriel Harvey . . . first with Robert Greene then with Thomas Nashe," and second "Greene's pamphlet about his death-bed repentance, which was accompanied or followed by other 'conversions' among the University Wits" (265). Greene's notorious pamphlet[2] warned his companions of, among other things, an overreaching "upstart crow" who would topple their own fame.

The only hope, the impoverished and fatally ill Greene admonished his companions, was in repentance. Greene's exhortation, Devlin observes, "may be better likened to a weather-cock than to an efficacious wind" (265), repentance being a popular by-product of the plague. Greene's collaborator, Thomas Lodge, was already reported by this time to be quitting the stage and "turning to Papistry" (Devlin, 265). Even Kit Marlowe—the suspected papist, atheist, and goodness knows what else—is rumored to have been fashioning at the time of his ill-fated death a morality play quite different from his "previous masterpieces on 'atheism'" (Devlin, 265).[3]

2 Some scholars suggest that the pamphlet may have been written by Henry Chettle.

3 Devlin's speculative account of Christopher Marlowe's violent and tragic end and the disposition that led him to it is as plausible as anything I have ever read upon the subject. See pages 316–19 of "Robert Southwell and Contemporary Poets – II," *The Month* (1950).

Greene's untimely death and accompanying warnings, far from bringing a cessation to Gabriel Harvey's invective against him, seem instead to have inspired it. Harvey offered a cruelly unsympathetic account of Greene's death that inspired an immediate and stinging reply from Greene's companion Thomas Nashe. Yet before Harvey could retort, Nashe himself experienced—what else?—a sudden conversion, announcing his repentance in a pamphlet entitled *Christ's Tears over Jerusalem*, which included a particular apology to Gabriel Harvey. Vexed at being poised to continue a rhetorical fight and now having no opponent, Harvey put his pen to work nonetheless, scoffing at Nashe's sudden conversion, and the text that he surmised had caused it, Robert Southwell's meditation on Magdalene's loss: "Now he hath a little mused upon Mary Magdalen's Funeral Tears, and is egged on to try the suppleness of his Pathetical vein . . . I know not who weeped Mary Magdalen's Funeral Tears: I would he that sheddeth the Patheticall Teares of Christ, and trickleth the liquid Teares of Repentance were no worse affected in pure devotion" (quoted in Devlin, 266). In fact, as Devlin points out, Harvey likely did at least have a good idea who had written the *Funeral Tears* since he had described it earlier that year, along with Persons's *Book of Resolution*, as "elegantly and pathetically written" (*Pierces Supererogations*, 1593, 191). Harvey may even have found the marks of Southwell's work upon Marlowe's Dr. Faustus when he complained: "Greene and Marlowe might admonish others to advise themselves: and I pray God the promised Teares of Repentance prove not the Teares of the Onion upon the Theater" (Devlin, 266).[4]

4   Following upon Harvey's hint perhaps, Devlin suggests that the startling line in Marlowe's *Faustus* "See, see, where Christ's blood streams in the firmament" may owe its origins to the floating Christ child in "The Burning Babe." This seems to me unlikely. The coincidences that may have brought Southwell into contact with Marlowe are more intriguing, though they have little to do with literary influence. The two men shared a mutual friendship-acquaintance with Thomas Watson, who was imprisoned at Newgate with Marlowe at the same time that Southwell routinely made visits there. Also, both Southwell and Marlowe, Devlin notes, were being shadowed by Robert Poley.

In Thomas Lodge's *Prosopopeia The Teares of the Holy, Blessed, and Sanctified Marie, the Mother of God* (1596), the author openly acknowledges both the *Funeral Tears* as well as *Saint Peter's Complaint*. The work, as Brownlow observes, is Lodge's response to Southwell's challenge to "better [his] intent." Lodge's repentance and conversion to Catholicism was enduring. He married a Catholic waiting-woman from the household of Southwell's protector the Countess of Arundel, and would become the countess's physician. As for Nashe, "a careful study of [his] *Christ's Tears Over Jerusalem*," claims Devlin, "puts it beyond a reasonable doubt that he had been reading Southwell's *Epistle of Comfort*.[5] That Southwell's work impacted his sudden repentance we have no evidence other than Harvey's angry accusation.

Besides the apparent provocation of the University Wits towards repentance and a sounder way of life, the more farreaching and substantial impact of Southwell's *Funeral Tears* and the pleadings within his prefatory pages may have been, as Devlin suggests, the prompting in William Shakespeare of "a loftier and more metaphysical vein" ("Contemporary Poets – I," 180), a surmise certainly borne out by the work of Klause and others who have found in Shakespeare's work not just the echo of dozens of lines of Southwell's verse, but very often the strain of his thought as well. The more immediate and less enduring impact of the *Funeral Tears* was the several "derivative imitations" by minor poets whose pious complaints fill a veritable well with repentant tears. Alison Shell provides a good summary of the more significant of these works in her *Catholicism, Controversy and the English Literary Imagination, 1558–1660*. She lists among the imitators of Southwell's tears Markham, Breton, Rowland and Ellis, most of whom wrote and published within the Protestant mainstream.[6]

---

5   Devlin offers specific convincing parallels between the two texts. See "Contemporary Poets I," pp. 175–76.

6   These "Southwellian pieces," Shell notes, "tend to be characterized by a combination of two factors: the internalized lament and call to repentance of a figure from the Gospels—Saint Peter, St. Mary Magdalen, St. John—together with prefatory material which repeats Southwell's criticism of secular verse and calls for poets instead to write about sacred things" (80).

William Alabaster

Among minor sixteenth-century poets the most provocative and pro-lific imitator of Southwell's tropological tears was William Alabaster (1567/8–1635). When remembered at all, Alabaster is more likely to be recalled for his dramatic conversions than for his verse. In fact, the religious tensions and controversies of that era could not be better summarized or witnessed in one person than in the astonishing life of Alabaster, a Calvinist-leaning Anglican who, during his seventy-two years, would risk his career and life on several occasions for both the Catholic and the Protestant causes. Consider that Alabaster's sudden and dramatic repentances, of which nobody has an exact count, pro-pelled him from being an aspirant young chaplain to the Earl of Essex in the mid- 1590s to a Roman Catholic exile determined to be a Jesuit, studying where Southwell had learned and taught at the English Col-lege in Rome, to ultimately, by 1614, serving as chaplain to King James himself.

In the tumultuous seventeen years following his initial discovery that "Now I am a Catholique,"[7] which came on the eve of a prosper-ous marriage and career, Alabaster would be interrogated by his Eng-lish overseers, held in light confinement, be deprived of Anglican orders, and then escape to the continent and eventually study to be-come a Jesuit under the guidance of Father Robert Persons. Later he would be imprisoned in the Tower by his countrymen and on the con-tinent by ministers of the Inquisition. He would serve as an informant against Catholic plots, then finally renounce his Catholic beliefs and not only be reinstated in Anglican orders, but made a Doctor of Di-vinity at Cambridge by the command of King James himself. Ulti-mately, Alabaster would settle into a marriage and live out his many remaining years as a faithful, if theologically eccentric, doctor of the Anglican Church, whose preaching, while apparently appreciated by

7 Upon his arrival at the English College in Rome, Alabaster was en-couraged by Father Persons to write an autobiography recording the events leading up to and following his conversion. The result, while certainly a subjectively favorable account of Alabaster's religious jour-ney, offers a valuable window into recusant England and one man's struggles in that tumultuous world.

the King, provoked suspicions of papistry and plain bewilderment from his fellow clergymen.[8]

As fascinating as the events of Alabaster's life may be, his achievement as a poet warrants more critical attention than it has received, which since the publication of his works in 1959 has amounted to very little. As part of the Cambridge literary circles, Alabaster composed Latin poetry, including *Elisaeis*, an unfinished epic on Queen Elizabeth that would be praised by none other than Edmund Spenser, who in *Colin Clouts Come Home Againe* asked rhetorically of Alabaster's poem, "Who lives that can match that heroic song?" Robert Herrick proclaimed of his theological writings that "One only glory of a million / In whom the spirit of the Gods dost dwell." His Latin tragedy *Roxana* was regarded by none other than Samuel Johnson as the best Latin poetry written in England before Milton.[9] So, in addition to his propensity for bipolar religious repentances, Alabaster possessed native literary brilliance. His application of that brilliance in English verse resulted in very mixed results, and ones that concern us chiefly as we consider one of the early impacts of Southwell's works in English literature.

William Alabaster was among the first English poets to utilize the sonnet form in the service of sacred subject matter, and by his own account his sonnets, 77 in all, were fashioned during the months of his first religious crisis between 1596 and 1598,[10] though it is possible

8   Following his conversion to Roman Catholicism, Alabaster, at the recommendation of Fr. Persons, composed an account of his conversion. This autobiographical account extends only to his arrival at the English College in Rome. The remaining events of his life were fairly well documented by others. The account I have provided here relies in large part upon the summary provided by Helen Gardner and G. M. Story in the introduction to his works (William Alabaster, 1959).

9   Quotations here cited from the *Unpublished Works by William Alabaster*, edited by Dana F. Sutton, printed by University of Salzburg in 1988.

10 Describing his time spent in the weeks following his conversion, Alabaster writes: "And I did sett some tymes certayne strife and wager between my present affections and future, my present persuading to devise sonnets now and so full of fyerie love and flaminge ardour to-

that some of them may have been begun earlier. Alabaster's unsettledness on the matter of religion and his growing "tenderness of harte towards Christes Crosse and Passion" and "certain sweet visions"[11] that came to him in his sleep all culminated at Easter in 1597, under the guidance and persuasions of Father Thomas Wright, the same priest responsible for Ben Jonson's conversion. Alabaster's account of the climactic moment of this conversion is worth quoting in full, partly so that the extremes of emotion and reason that comprise his poems can better be appreciated, and also because it offers us an excellent window into the mind and heart of the very kind of person to whom Southwell was directing his own poetry and prose:

> I went to my lodging with this little booke of Mr William Reynaldes[12] in my hand and sitting downe after supper on my beds side; to spend that ydle time, I begane to read the preface thereof, that treated very learnedly and lardgly out of the writinges of protestentes themselfes of their inconstant and deceitfull manner of proceedings. I had not read for the space of a quarter of an howre (if I remember well) but as if those squames [scales] that fell from St Paules boddylye eyes at his [words missing] and understanding so was

wards Christ, that then it sholde serve for a patterne and sample for the tyme to come, to shew upp and conserve my hart in devotion, but on the contrarie parte my future devotions made offer so to maintaine [and] increase the heate and vigour of love and affection in me, that when I should come afterwards to reed over my former sonnets I might wonder at the coaldness of them then gather heate by them" (123).

11 All direct quotes herein are from Alabaster's own account of his conversion in the *Unpublished Works by William Alabaster*, edited by Dana F. Sutton.

12 William Reynolds, brother of John Reynolds (Dr. of Divinity at Oxford) was raised Catholic, converted to be a Protestant and then back to being a Catholic. Alabaster goes to great lengths to bolster Reynolds's reputation since it was his book, as his narrative shows, that pushed him over the edge in his move towards believing as a Roman Catholic.

I lighted upon the sudden, feeling my selfe so wonderfully and sencybly changed both in judgment and affection as I remanded astonished at my trewe state. I fownde my minde wholie and perfectly Catholeque in an instante, and so to be persuaded of all and everie point of Catholique religion together, as I beleved them all most undoubtedly and every point and paccell thereof, though I knew not the reasons of all, not made perhaps sure the arguments of the contrarye parte. Nether did I desyer any perticuler resolution in any other question of controversie, for ai saw most evidently in my inward judgment, that all were trewe and nothing could be false which the Catholique Roman Churche dyd propose to be believed. And feeling this in my selfe upon the sudden with such inward light of evidens as I cold not contradict and w[i]th such force of affection as I cold not resist, I lept up from the place where I satt, and saide to myself, now I am a Catholique, and then fell down upon my knees , and thanked God most hartely humbly and effecteously for so rare a benefit (118).

From this same fire of intellectual and spiritual certainty sprang Alabaster's religious sonnets in the months ahead. He continued writing them after his arrest and during the unsettled months of his confinement that included numerous interrogative discourses with an impressive variety of English bishops and scholars. He may also have continued working on the poems during the months he spent at a safe house under the care of the Jesuit John Gerard before being sent across the channel to Douay. By this time of Alabaster's initial conversion in 1597 Father Gerard's fellow Jesuit Robert Southwell had been dead for two years and was revered among recusant Catholics. In addition to the popular *Mary Magdalen's Funeral Tears*, *Saint Peter's Complaint With Other Poems* had now been printed several times. Alabaster was very likely well acquainted with Southwell's prose and poetry prior to his conversion and Southwell's writings may, as with Nashe and Lodge, even have helped inspire his conversion. If not, these works were likely among the many Catholic works that Alabaster acquired immediately upon his conversion.

After his sudden conversion in his London lodgings, Alabaster returned to Cambridge where he first had the difficult task to "breake of the marriage which I had so earnestly treated and concluded to make." Word that his betrothed "was like to dye of greefe" did not apparently assuage him) (121). "The next thing" Alabaster undertook "was to furnishe myself with prinncepall Catholique Authors which I dyd buying so many books as cost me tow or three and twentie powndes, which ioyning to the furniture I had before, seemed sufficient for the [purpose] I had designed" (121). Twenty-three pounds in the mid-1590s would have furnished Alabaster with a not unsubstantial collection of Catholic reading.[13] It is reasonable to presume that if Southwell's *Mary Magdalen's Funeral Tears* and *Saint Peter's Complaint With Other Poems* were not among "the furniture" that Alabaster had acquired before, they were among his substantial post-conversion purchases. My own view is that Southwell's writings were among those that contributed to Alabaster's increasing "tenderness of harte towards Christes Crosse and Passion" (114) during his unsettled spiritual journey towards conversion prior to 1597. He certainly would have had access to them in manuscript as well as published volumes and it seems quite likely that someone of his Catholic leanings and literary talents would have been drawn to or directed towards them.

In any case, Alabaster's abrupt conversion to Roman Catholicism, followed by a similarly sudden flood of devotional and repentant poetry, certainly suggests his acquaintance with sacred verse, and in England at this time none would have been more compelling to a prospective Catholic convert than the widely circulated and recently published works of Southwell. Additionally, we know that by the time Alabaster was secreted away to John Gerard's safe house he was well

13 Reckoning the number of books that Alabaster purchased for that amount is, in Frank Brownlow's words, "a tricky question because we're talking about black-market books. We know what books like play quartos, bibles or the Shakespeare folio cost—anything between 6d and a pound, but what it would have cost to buy smuggled Catholic books?" (e-mail correspondence 9-12-2012, with permission). We have no way of knowing where Alabaster would have purchased these books, but the price might be considerably higher if the seller factored in the risk cost.

acquainted with the spiritual discipline of the Jesuits. He gave as his reasons for wanting to join the Jesuits the fact that they required obedience, did not allow their members to seek ecclesiastical office and, he reasoned, since they were the most detested by Protestants, whom he now regarded as heretics, they must possess the Spirit of God, which the devil cannot abide (Gerard 141).[14] Alabaster, it is clear, had been paying keen attention to the religious controversies of his country and to the work of the Jesuit mission in England, which included, in Southwell's case, a call to convert the use of poetry from its present pagan idolatry to the worthy praise of Christ. This call would have resonated strongly with a zealous convert who had heretofore followed Spenser's example of using verse to praise in lavish and deifying terms the virtues of Queen Elizabeth.

None of this is to suggest that William Alabaster, in turning to the composition of devotional verse in the throes of his initial conversion, was consciously imitating the poetry of Southwell. Under the circumstances this likely would have been impractical. What the 77 sonnets of Alabaster's *Divine Meditations* do reveal, however, is an acquaintance both with what Southwell had written and with what he had encouraged other poets to do in the prefaces of both *The Funeral Tears* and *Saint Peter's Complaint*. Alabaster may well have regarded himself as "one of the finest wits" when he chose to use the sonnet form in order to weave sacred expression on the most fashionable Elizabethan loom of the 1590s and simultaneously give expression to the powerful emotions and convictions of his personal religious experience. That he chose many of the same topics that Southwell treats in his verse may indicate only their common reliance on scripture and proverbial Catholic themes, and after all Alabaster was a learned theologian prepared to give expression to the most vexing Christian paradoxes. Certain poems and passages in his *Meditations*, however, suggest at the very least a recollection of Southwell's work and indicate that he was indeed answering the Jesuit's appeal to poets with his own innovation.

In the famous epistle preceding Southwell's work, he had offered as justification for the writing of sacred verse the example of Christ

14 For a full account of Alabaster's safe abiding with John Gerard, who himself had just escaped from the Tower, see Gerard's *The Autobiography of an Elizabethan*.

who "himself by making a hymme the conclusion of his last Supper and the prologue to the first pageant of his passion gave his spouse a method to paterne to know the trew use of this measured and footed style" (1). Alabaster begins the second sonnet of his *Portrait of Christ's Death* by asking, "What meaneth this, that Christ an hymn did sing, / An hymn triumphant for an happy fight, / As if his enemies were put to flight / When yet he was not come into the ring? (2, 1–4).[15] The sonnet, which like many of Southwell's poems, reflects upon the author's own possible martyrdom, claims that as Christ by singing before his passion "anticipated with delight / The present pains which should such glories bring" (2, 7–8), we should likewise render thanks "For sufferings beforehand" (2, 14).

Just as Southwell offers a series of poems upon the mysteries of Christ's Incarnation, from conception to circumcision, so too Alabaster offers fifteen sonnets meditating upon the Incarnation. Unlike Southwell's poems, however, which derive their success from their Ignatian focus upon the specific physical elements of scripture, Alabaster's offerings rely mostly on the abstractions of theological paradox cloaked in familiar paradigms such as fountains, streams and firmament. In Southwell's poems the reader shares the poet's concern that Mary, walking "With Pilgrimm foote upp trying hils" ("The Visitation," 3) to visit Elizabeth, may stumble and harm the Prince she bears within her. From Alabaster we get only compacted fourteen-line sermons on the Incarnation. One brief comparison shows the superiority of Southwell in this instance. Alabaster offers haltingly: "Two, yet but one, which either other is, / One, yet in two, which neither other be, / God and man in one personality" (Sonnet 54, 1-3). Southwell by contrast had rendered this paradox with memorable succinctness: "Behould the father is his daughters sonne / The bird that built the nest, is hatched therein" ("The Nativity of Christ," 1–2).

Near the end of his eleven sonnets on The Portrait of Christ's Death, Alabaster focuses upon Saint Peter in a poem that shows his familiarity with Southwell's final and most famous work. Here we may credit Alabaster with succinctness. For though he does not condense the full weight and power and meaning of *Saint Peter's Complaint* into

---

15 All quotations from Alabaster's poetry from *William Alabaster*, ed. by G. M. Story and Helen Gardner, Oxford University Press, 1959.

fourteen lines, he does make commendable use of the Italian sonnet
form to narrate Peter's fateful promise in the octave and then shift in
a sestet of three couplets to a meditation upon his own freshly made
promise and his determination to keep it without falling:

> Though all forsake thee, lord, yet I will die,
> For I have chained my will to thine
> That I have no will left my will to untwine,
> But will abide with thee most willingly.
> Though all forske thee, lord, yet cannot I,
> For love hath wrought in me thy form divine
> That thou art more my heart than heart is mine:
>
> How can I then from myself, thyself, fly?
> Thus thought Saint Peter and thus thinking
> fell, And by this fall did warn us not to
> swell, Yet still in love I say I would not fall,
> And say in hope I trust I never shall,
> But cannot say in faith, what might I do
> To learn to say it, by hearing Christ say so!
> (Sonnet 10)

The paradox offered us in the example of Peter, of course, is that the
more fervently we profess our faith the more we elevate ourselves for
a similar fall from grace, and if Peter betrayed Christ, who are we to
profess that we never will?

Having described the notorious certainty of Peter, Alabaster speaks
his own determined hope, "Yet still in love I say I would not fall."[16]
His final couplet is riddled with an ambiguity that unfortunately is not
an isolated instance in Alabaster's verse. The sense seems to be that
the poet cannot say in faith what he might do in Peter's circumstance,
but hopes he would learn to be faithful by hearing Christ say to him

16 If indeed Alabaster in the exuberance of his recent conversion to
   Roman Catholicism regarded all Protestants as heretics, the 1597 Alabaster would most certainly have regarded the 1613 Alabaster as
   one who had fallen. The irony here then is that Alabaster ultimately
   does not fare any better than Peter whom he hopes to best.

Peter's words, "I shall not deny thee." Near the end of *Saint Peter's Complaint* Southwell offers a more circumspect version of this predicament from the mouth of Saint Peter himself who desires to make amends, but dares not promise to do so: "A poore desire I have to mend my ill; / I should, I would, I dare not say, I will" (761–62).

Another instance of resemblance in the works of these poets may be found in the familiar sorrow of Mary Magdalene upon Christ's death. Alabaster cleverly fashions a sonnet, "Upon Christ's Saying to Mary 'Why Weepest Thou?'" that offers Mary an opportunity to elaborate upon this famous question posed by the angels at the empty tomb. The first quatrain of his sonnet offers a response that echoes Southwell's sentiment that she has died with Christ. First Alabaster: "I weep two deaths with one tears to lament: / Christ, my soul's life, out of my heart is fled, / My soul, my heart's life, from me vanished, / With Christ my soul, and with my soul, life went" (21, 1–4). Now, the more memorable and precedent lines from Southwell's "Marie Magdalens complaint at Christs death": "Selye starres must nedes leve shyninge / When the Sunne is shadowed / Borrowed streames refrayne their runninge / When hed springes are hindered. / One that lives by others breathe / Dieth also by his deathe" (7–12). Alabaster may also have been recalling in the fashioning of this sonnet the several pages of prose that Southwell devotes to this famous question of the resurrection narrative in his *Funeral Tears*. As Brown suggests, Southwell was most certainly writing his Magdalen poem as well as "A vale of teares" at the same time he was working on *The Funeral Tears* (Brown, Southwell's Mary Magdalen." 9).

In fact, while the resemblances above argue for Alabaster's familiarity with the work of the Jesuit poet whom he must have at one time regarded with hostility, the greatest impact of Southwell upon Alabaster seems to have been, just as in the case of the University Wits, a provocation of a flood of weeping provoked by *Mary Magdalen's Funeral Tears*. The innovation of Alabaster was to transport the tears of the famous convert Magdalene to his own circumstances and to use his own voice to weep the pangs of repentance within the confines of the Italian sonnet, a form invented for the profuse sorrow and longing of a first person narrator. As Shell puts it, "Alabaster, the convert, positions the anonymous repentant self inside the text rather than beyond it" (93). By contrast, when the first person pronoun is used in Southwell's verse it is more often than not a familiar saint or recusant hero speaking. Southwell speaks sparingly as "I" in such poems as "Life is but Losse," and does so with a pious, sober and restrained resignation to existential and theological realities. Ignatius's *Exercises* were designed to provoke the deepest personal introspection through scriptural meditations, but the result was not primarily to be the evangelizing of others by way of testimony about oneself. Alabaster, who would be found unsuitable to Jesuit discipline, was a Calvinist-formed convert whose personal conversion experience was nothing if not the opportunity to inspire others to a similar course. As he states in his description of the sonnets' composition: "And these verses and sonetes I made not only for my owne solace, and comforte, but to stir up others also that shold reed them to soew estimation of that which I felt in my self, for which cause my desire was so extreme ardent to impart this my happiness with others that I felt in me the trew force of that St Dionysius Ariopagita saith, *bonum est sui diffusivum*, the nature of goodness is to spredd itself to many" (123). Thus Alabaster fashions the precedence for "the private ejaculations" of George Herbert and others when he authors eight tear-filled sonnets intent upon moving others to conversion, and several others that reflect upon the details of his struggle.

At the start of these sonnets Alabaster sounds very much like the Calvinist he was raised to be: "My sins in multitude to Christ are gone, / Against my soul indictment for to make, / That they his lingering vengeance may awake / Upon my just deserts" (12, 1–4). Then, as if taking his lead from the favorite recusant saint whose tears Southwell had made famous, the poet instructs his tears: "Then run, O run / Out of mine eyes tears of compunction, / One after other run for my soul's sake, / And strive you one the other to overtake, / Until you come to his heavenly throne" (12, 4–7). In the next sonnet the poet meditates for the entire octave upon his soul growing in the garden bed of heaven, concluding that the lack of overflowing love must be for want of rain. So he instructs his eyes at the sestet's start: "then you two characters, drawn from my head, / Pour out a shower of tears upon my bed" (13, 9–10). In Sonnet 14 he offers justification to his tears in the form of an explanation of evaporation: "Doubt not, my tears, how you should so aspire, / When other showers all downwards still do rain, / For they were drawn up from this watery plain, / and therefore to their towers must retire" (14, 1–4). This evaporative cycle of rain is the last desperate hope to which Marlowe's Dr. Faustus commends his damned soul[17] and the one to which Hamlet alludes when he prays that his "too, too solid flesh would melt,/ Thaw, and resolve itself into a dew!" (I, ii, 129–30). But such a consideration spoken here to one's supposed penitent tears seems to put both poet and reader at a distance from the weeping of Magdalen, from the clarion penitent verse of Southwell, and from scripture or the catechism of either Calvinism or Catholicism. So too in Sonnet 16 as he parses the three types of tears that he weeps into those of compunction, those of compassion and those of devoutness. In the case of both sonnets the elaborateness of the poet's arguments signals an intellectual distance from the over-whelming emotions of conversion.

The Petrarchan extravagance of his tropes notwithstanding, Alabaster's own tears were certainly not merely tropological. He was in the conversion that begets these poems forsaking his church, his marriage and his country. Describing the days following his conversion, Alabaster recalls, "And when the floodes of teares came downe uppon me, I could do no lesse but open the gates to let them pass: I was wont often to walke into the fieldes alone, and being then summer ther I wold sett me downe in certaine corne feldes, where I could not be seene nor heard of others" (122). Alabaster's tumultuous circum-stances did not permit such isolation and distress to be "recollected in tranquility," but rather shaped into the kinds of extravagant tropes that we ought to recognize as the earliest intonations of the poetry that would come to be called metaphysical. If it is not recognized as such it is because Alabaster's poetic efforts can often leave the reader more perplexed than edified. In Sonnet 17, for example, an intricately argued metaphor is made in a direct appeal to Jesus, but when the poet instructs "Then weep forth pearls of tears to spangle thee" it is unclear whether he is addressing Jesus or his own eyes and also unclear exactly to what the antecedent "thee" refers.

Among Alabaster's other penitential poems one is worth quoting in full because it offers an impressive blending of what Alabaster

17 "You stars . . . Now draw up Faustus like a foggy mist/ Into the en-trails of yon laboring cloud/ That when you vomit forth into the air,/ My limbs may issue from your smoky mouths" (*Faustus*, V, ii, 155, 157–61).

derived from Southwell and what he innovated himself in sonnet form. The result is perhaps Alabaster's most successful poem and one that we hear echoed in the work of a much more famous poet:

> My soul a world is by contraction,
> The heavens therein is my internal sense,
> Moved by my will as an intelligence,
> My heart the element, my love the sun.
> And as the sun about the earth doth run,
> And with his beams doth draw thin vapours thence,
> Which after in the air do condense,
> And pour down rain upon the earth anon,
> So moves my love about the heavenly sphere,
> And draweth thence with an attractive fire
> The purest argument wit can desire,
> Whereby devotion after may arise.
> And these conceits, digest by thoughts' retire,
> Are turned into april showers of tears.
> (*Sonnet 15*)

The reader recognizes in the opening lines of this sonnet the more familiar declarative opening of Donne's Sonnet 15: "I am a little world made cunningly / Of elements and an angelic sprite" (1–2). One recognizes as well the use of the astrological spheres for the contemplation of the soul with which Donne is so familiarly associated. The brilliance that Spenser and Johnson recognized in Alabaster's Latin verse is on display here in this imaginative, tightly wrought, provocative meditation. It stands, unfortunately, as more of an exception among his other poems. What G. M. Story and Helen Gardner observed a half century ago in bringing Alabaster's works into print remains true. His sonnets are of uneven quality. They often begin well but collapse into ambiguity or forced argument and rhyme.

William Alabaster is a minor figure amidst a retreating constellation of poets. Nonetheless in Southwell's sphere he is a crucially important author to consider; for though, as far as we know, he never took to writing poetry again, these sonnets that he fashioned in the heat of his conversion belong to the poetic tenor that Southwell had modeled, encouraged and inspired. At the same time Alabaster is, as

Story and Gardner observed in introducing him to twentieth-century readers, "a different *kind* of poet" (*William Alabaster*, xxxi). The poetic innovations in his sacred poems anticipate and furnish the earliest examples of the metaphysical style associated with Donne and Herbert.[18] "The continuity of devotional literature in England down to the seventeenth century is easy to over-emphasize," Story and Gardner cautioned in introducing Alabaster to modern readers, "But in spite of the revolutionary temper of the sixteenth century, the persistence of the devotional tradition throughout the period is striking" (*William Alabaster*, xxiii).

And in this instance what we should be struck by is the manner in which Southwell and Alabaster pointed the way to the seventeenth-century devotional poets whose works, when the continuity which Story and Gardner long ago observed is ignored, are apportioned a novelty that they do not deserve.

Michael Drayton

A popular and successful Elizabethan poet, Michael Drayton (1563–1631) offers us an example of Robert Southwell's early influence quite unlike any other. Drayton, who consciously fashioned a literary career that began in the early 1590s and spanned four decades, was no Bohemian in need of a religious conversion. Nor, other than in some unsuccessful juvenilia, did he ever write a religious poem or align himself in any way with the devotional tradition. His models were Philip Sidney and Edmund Spenser and he lived a life even more steadfastly Elizabethan than either of them. Drayton's only interest in Robert Southwell would have been a literary one and as such he offers us a noted instance where we see that, quite apart from Robert Southwell's controversial and provocative place as an outlawed Jesuit in his native country, his poetry was admired as poetry by a literary professional whose own works were the most popular of that age.

18 Some scholars dispute the dating of Donne's devotional poems posited by Gardner, suggesting that some of them may have been written in the sixteenth century. My claim here that Alabaster and Southwell's poems served as a possible influence on Donne does not depend upon a strict dating of Donne's poems as all seventeenth-century creations.

Michael Drayton was the son of a tanner who served as a page in the household of Sir Henry Goodere at Polesworth Hall in Warwickshire. By ten years old, young Michael determined to become a poet and was apparently so convincingly ambitious in this determination that Sir Henry, who had been a friend of Philip Sidney's[19] and whose own son would be a close companion to John Donne, accommodated his young page by arranging in his will for Drayton to be accommodated by the great literary patroness Lucy Harrington, Countess of Bedford. This arrangement permitted Drayton to pursue his career as a poet and he did so with great success and no eccentricities that drew attention to himself. He developed and retained a lifelong affection for and devotion to Henry Goodere's youngest daughter Anne. A marriage arrangement was out of the question and Drayton was by all accounts a complete gentleman in the matter, demonstrating nothing but loyalty to and affection for Anne and her husband. Fittingly, Drayton put his longing to artistic use, converting Anne to his platonic ideal who is the subject of his sonnets, *Idea,* first published in 1594.

Michael Drayton steered his life through the mainstream, prudently unaffected by the controversies of that era that disrupted, enveloped or transformed so many of his peers like Alabaster and Donne. He had no use for the extremism of the Puritans, but also disapproved of the popular use of cosmetics. Apparently tolerant of a wide range of personalities, Drayton was a noted friend of Ben Jonson as well as Samuel Daniel and William Browne. He kept company with Roman Catholics like the Beaumont and Cockayne families, as well as John Davies, and he expressed regret for the destruction of the Catholic monasteries, what his fellow poet Shakespeare memorably described as, "Bare ruined choirs where late the sweet birds sang" (Sonnet 73). Whether Drayton and Jonson were in fact drinking companions of Shakespeare on the eve of the playwright's birthday and untimely death or whether this is mere lore we shall never know. He seems not to have been a reveler, and had little use for shows of extravagance, haughtiness or bigotry. Drayton was forty years old when Queen Elizabeth died and while he instantly set his pen to the praise of the new Scottish monarch, he also grew increasingly nostalgic for what he

---

19   Henry Goodere had in fact been with Sidney at Zutphen and had witnessed his will as well as followed him in his funeral (*Poems,* xii).

regarded as the golden age of Elizabeth. That nostalgia was expressed chiefly in the imagery of the world that Drayton loved most, the English countryside.

Recall from the previous chapter that in John Bodenham's 1602 collection of quotations, *Garden of the Muses*, Michael Drayton had the largest number of quotations in the book at 269, followed by Spenser, Shakespeare and Lodge, and that Robert Southwell shared the fifth place with Drayton's friend Samuel Daniel. What, besides their place on this auspicious list, might a good Elizabethan like Drayton have to do with a clandestine Jesuit like Robert Southwell? One possibility is that the sixain stanza form that Drayton uses in his early pastoral poems published 1593 may be something he admired and borrowed from Southwell's *Saint Peter's Complaint*. The stanza was common in the sixteenth century, but Drayton may have recognized its particular narrative and lyric effectiveness in *Saint Peter's*. If so, it would have been a case not of flattery, but a professional poet using what he saw worked, and what worked best; for the sorrow- wrought shepherd complaining in his poem was the same stanza of the distraught Peter in Southwell's well known poem. Only four of his nine eclogues use the six-line stanza, and of these two are dialogues. The first and final eclogues, however, voice sorrowful lament in six-line stanzas just as *Saint Peter's Complaint* had done.

Resemblances between the two poets' works were first noted long ago by Drayton scholar Bernard Newdigate who noted similarities between *Saint Peter's Complaint* and Drayton's *The Shepherd's Garland* (1593) and *Matilda the Fair* (1594). In *The Shepherd's Garland*, composed in the identical verse form as Southwell's poem, Newdigate observed "passages which suggest both the thought and manner of Robert Southwell" (quoted in Devlin, 269). Devlin finds the similarities between *Matilda* and *Saint Peter's Complaint* "distressing" insofar as the borrowings of a still aspirant Drayton from Southwell "bring out the weakest features of both" ("Contemporary Poets – II" 311). One exception that he cites from each poet is in their correspondent descriptions of shame that precede repentance, in which he believes both poets approach Faustus's famous final speech. Southwell's Peter laments:

> If Adam sought a veyle to scarfe his sinne,
> Taught by his fall to feare a scourging hand;

If men shall wish that hills should wrap them in,
When crymes in finall doome come to be scand:
What mount, what cave, what center can conceale
My monstrous fact, which even the birds reveale?
(*Saint Peter's Complaint*, 511–16)

Matilda's ravisher pleas for such a cave to consume him:

Earth, swallow me, and hide me in they wombe,
O let my shame in thy deep Centre dwell,
Wrap up this murder in thy wretched Tombe,
Let tender Mercy stop the gates of hell:
And with sweet drops this furious heate expel.
O let Repentance just revenge appease,
And let my soule in torment find some ease.
(*Matilda,* Stanza 156)

Devlin finds Drayton's most frequent borrowings from Southwell in his profuse and hyperbolic descriptions of tears and offers several examples before conceding that "Drayton's real model during these years was Edmund Spenser" ("Contemporary Poets – II," 311). Drayton and Southwell are poets involved in very different projects, and where pastoral eclogue is concerned Drayton already has his chosen models in Theocritus and Virgil, and more immediately Spenser whose *Shepheardes Calender* had rearticulated the pastoral formula in English: at Phoebus's descent the landscape will grow cold and a shepherd will step forth and make his complaint against fortune and nature who by way of an unrequited love or unjust peers or both have delivered to the plaintiff unprecedented sorrows. Said shepherd may hang up or smash his bagpipe to signal the futility of song.

Drayton does not veer from this formula in his depiction of the unrequited shepherd Rowland, and but for the sorrow, his and Southwell's poems share little in common. What is apparent in sampling some stanzas from each side by side, however, is that Southwell's skillful verse offered the young Drayton, besides a suitable stanza form, a language and tone of complaint with greater emotional proximity and with less apparent artifice than the pseudo-antique tongue of Spenser's shepherds. Without an eye to any "flagrantly obvious borrowings," but an ear tuned to similarities in language, imagery and emotional tone, we may consider side by side the eighth stanza of *Saint Peter's Complaint* alongside of the eighth stanza of Eclogue I of the 1593 *Shepherd's Garland*, each of which yields a flood of tears. First *Saint Peter's*:

> All weeping eyes resigne your teares to me:
> A sea will scantly rince my ordur' de soule:
> Huge horrours in high tides must drowned bee,
> Of every teare my crime exacteth tole.
> These staines are deepe: few drops, take out no such:
> Even salve with sore: and most, is not too much.
> (43–48)

And then *The Shepherd's Garland*:

> O shepheardes soveraigne, yea receive in gree,
> The gushing tears, from never-resting eyes,
> And let those prayers which I shall make to thee,
> Be in thy sight perfumed sacrifice:
> Let smokie sighes be pledges of contrition,
> For follies past to make my soules submission.
> (43–48)

Now a sorrowfully conceived funeral from each poet. First from *Saint Peter's*:

> A self contempt, the shroud: my soule, the corse:
> The beere, an humble hope: the herse cloth, feare:
> The mourners, thoughts, in blackes of deepe remorse:
> The herse, grace, pittie, love and mercy beare.
> My teares, my dole: the priest, a zealous will:
> Pennance, the tombe: and dolefull sighes, the knill.
> (745–50)

And then from Rowland in the *Garland*:

> Devouring time shall swallow up my sorrowes,
> And strong beliefe shall torture black despaire,

Death shall orewhelme disgrace, in deepest furrowes,
And Justice laie my wrongs upon the Beere:
Thus Justice, death, beleefe, and time, ere long,
Shall end my woes, despayre, disgrace, and wrong.
(61–66)

Rowland's sorrow can only be eliminated by time and death. Ultimately of course, after 792 lines of verse, Peter is redeemed by
penance.

Devlin sees Drayton's poems, together with *Lucrece* and Samuel
Daniel's *The Complaint of Rosamund* as an indication of a change in
poetic taste that accords with the hope that Southwell had expressed
in his preface to *Magdalen's Tears*. "In fables are figured moral truths,
and that covertly uttered to a common good which without mask
would not find so free a passage" (*Prose Works*, vii). This seems to
me little more than a case of Devlin seeing what he hopes to see. Drayton is as conventional an Elizabethan poet as there ever was, a devo-
tee of Spenser, who will eventually in his revisions be even more
successful than his master at converting classical pastoral to the English landscape (in his 1619 version even his forlorn dog, Whitefoote,
wags a cut tail). No covert allegory is embedded in Drayton's eclogues
to offer the reader a profound moral truth. Rowland has been
wronged in love. Rowland complains to fortune and the deities. Rowland despairs.

Neither do I think, however, that Drayton's use of Southwell's successful stanza form for his complaint is utter coincidence. He recognized in Southwell's skillful rendering of *Saint Peter's Complaint* a
poetic model worthy of imitation and put it to effective use. No conversion accompanies the tears that he borrows from Southwell. Rather
than looking for embedded utterances that bespeak a moral allegiance
to Southwell, we should instead recognize Southwell's place in this
small literary world. That someone of Drayton's poetic ambitions and
skill seeking to develop the full potential of his poetic powers found
Southwell's most significant poem worthy of imitation is no little endorsement. By the time Drayton's pastorals were completed in their
first edition, Southwell had been arrested and was marking his time
in English prisons. Ironically, by the time Drayton revised and
reprinted his pastorals early in the next century, *Saint Peter's*

Complaint had already been reprinted multiple times and was enjoying a readership surpassing that of Drayton's eclogues.

As Robert Southwell sat in prison for the last three years of his young life, under the watchful eye of Richard Topcliffe, his deprivations included, among other things, materials with which to write. His brief literary career was finished. Even so, outside of the Tower walls his two improbable literary ambitions were being fulfilled. His works continued to be printed, circulated and read by Catholics and non-Catholics alike, and the "skillfuller wits" who he had hoped might imitate his example were doing so. Thus, from the dark confines of his cell, he continued to "woo some pens more skilful . . . to exercise their happier talents." Had those pens belonged only to Nashe and Lodge and Alabaster, or represented only the slight borrowings of Michael Drayton, my present project need not have been undertaken. In fact though, by the time of his imprisonment the young priest's writings had caught the attention not just of these men, but of young William Shakespeare and other authors whose skills and reputations either had or eventually would far surpass those of Southwell's in the decades and centuries to come, leaving him in the ever dimming shade of anonymity and near obscurity. Finding Southwell's marks in the works of these poets not only brings light to that still darkening shade in which Southwell has resided, but illuminates as well our understanding of some of this era's greatest poets.

Chapter 3

Southwell's Clout: Reforming Edmund Spenser?

In retrospect 1595 would turn out to be one of the more important literary years in the Elizabethan era. Besides the debut of Shakespeare's *Richard II*, there was the first London publication of works by Guillaume Salluste du Bartas, the French Protestant writer who offered a defense of divine poetry. More significant was the first appearance in print of Philip Sidney's *Defense of Poetry* as well as the publication of Spenser's *Amoretti and Epithalamion*. And even while readers anticipated the second installment of Spenser's *Faerie Queene*, London would witness a most curious literary phenomenon, which began with an event that would seem to be anything but poetic: the gruesome public execution in February of Father Robert Southwell for high treason. Southwell's public hanging, drawing and quartering was a well-attended and well-documented spectacle, and, as we have seen, the dismembering of the priest's body was followed more or less immediately by the assembling and proliferation of his poetical works, beginning with *Saint Peter's Complaint*, whose commercial success suggests that its printing was, in Alison Shell's words, "designed to capitalize" on his execution. "Southwell's biographers agree," she notes, "that there was a race to get the book out" (62). His execution, though not a deliberate, macabre publicity stunt was, in fact, another miscalculation of the Elizabethan authorities who in rendering him death brought Southwell to literary life.

The most curious aspect of Southwell's posthumous commercial success is not the poetry, the printers, or the poet's gruesome end, but the audience of readers ready to purchase and read the verses of an author identified in the volumes as "R.S." Many, if not most of those purchasing the books would have recognized them as the creations of the notorious executed Jesuit priest. Some of these customers were certainly covert Catholics and others may have had strong Catholic sympathies, but these groups alone would not have been large enough to beget the kind of commercial success that ensued. Rather, as Shell points out, "the majority of Southwell's large audience, certainly at the beginning, must have been Protestants aware of Southwell's religious persuasions and Southwell's fate; and the poems' instant and continued popularity argues that a large section of the reading public was prepared to buy, and to go on buying, the works of a papist who had died a traitor's death" (63). This curiosity of the market-place confounds some of our traditional assumptions about this era. We may puzzle at the seeming inconsistency of Elizabethan officials or ponder the degree of Catholic sympathies. What seems clear in any case is that there was, in current speak, a market for religious verse, Catholic or otherwise. Printers were capitalizing on this market and it seems likely that Southwell's poetry, now being promulgated for the first time in print, was actually increasing the value of that market (Shell, 66).

Returning from Ireland that year as England's most celebrated national poet, Edmund Spenser, we may imagine, would have found the popular demand for religious poetry perplexing, if not disconcerting. He had come to London to oversee the publication of the second installment of his great epic poem, as well as an exceptional cycle of love sonnets and other verse. The apparent and sudden fervor for devotional verse was a trend that Spenser might have ignored altogether—if not for the prefatory epistle and verse at the start of one of these books that accused English poets of doing little more with their talents than fashioning pagan toys. Southwell was "accusing most mainstream poets of profanity, in an all-embracing condemnation of the effects of the Protestant poetic" (Shell, 68). The very poetry that Spenser brought to London in his saddle bags—the best of its kind—was being castigated by a dead, Jesuit priest. And his critique was selling.

It was enough to make a loyal Protestant poet wonder what was in the London water. Spenser had most certainly heard of Robert Southwell and would have regarded him as another Campion, an enemy to his country, his Queen and himself. The Jesuits were a dissembling, treacherous malignancy and those who would heed his latest books of *The Faerie Queene* would be offered an allegorical cure. Readers need only behold in his figure of Malengin (Guyle) in canto 9 of Book V, the shape-shifting, disguised missionary priests who came from their holes to stir up falsehood and sedition. Elizabeth Heale, in her 1990 article "Spenser's Malengine, Missionary Priests and the

Means of Justice," offered a convincing reading of the Malengin figure as representing the sort of guileful Jesuit priests like Edmund Campion and Robert Persons who began making their way to England in the 1580's, posing a threat to the Queen and her Protestant realm. Following Heale's lead, Cyndia Clegg made a convincing case in her 1998 essay "Justice and Press Censorship in Book V of Spenser's *Faerie Queene*" that the figure of Malengin "can be associated with the Jesuit mission in several respects" (251). Clegg points to Malengin's dissembling, shape-shifting character, his elusive nature, the fact that he resides in a hole (i.e., priest hole), as well as his ultimate violent end at the hands of Talus. "Pursued," she notes, "Malengin colors and counterfeits, transforming himself into first a fox, then a bush, a bird, a stone, and a hedgehog. In his final transformation, as a snake, he falls prey to his pursuer's 'yron flayle'" (253). The predictably ruthless destruction of Malengin at the iron hands of Talus, Clegg notes, has been pointed to as one more instance of "the problematic nature of Justice in Book Five" (253), but, she argues, the violent action in this case would have appeared as a reasonable or at least recognizable form of justice to Spenser's contemporaries who, Clegg argues, would have recognized in Spenser's allegory just who Talus was flailing. Malengin in his final incarnation has morphed into a serpent, an emblem in the sixteenth-century Protestant imagination of the papist enemy; so when Talus leaves "all his bones, as small as sandy grayle broken" and "did his bowels disentrayle" (V, 9, 19, 4–5), Spenser's audience would recognize, Clegg suggests, the just punishment for the crime of high treason administered upon Jesuits like Robert Southwell. In defending such punishments in the wake of the execution of Campion and his companions, Lord Burghley had referred to the Jesuits as a "kind of vermin . . . suffered to creep by stealth into their realm" (*The Execution of Justice in England*, 1583, as quoted by Clegg, 254). Burghley had urged the Queen to bring justice to the Jesuit vermin "by the sword as by the law" and in Talus's crushing and disemboweling of Malengin Spenser offers his readers a graphic allegorical depiction of this policy.

More recently, Jennifer Rust has taken Heale and Clegg's readings a step further and offered a provocative interpretation that Malengin is in fact an allegorical representation of the one Jesuit priest most troublesomely on Spenser's mind in the early 1590's while he was constructing Book V: Robert Southwell. In her essay, "Malengin and Mercilla, Southwell and Spenser: The Poetics of Tears and the Politics of Martyrdom in *The Faerie Queene*, Book 5, Canto 9," Rust argues that the violent death of Malengin is not merely an archetypal representation of a conventional hanging, drawing and quartering, but a depiction of Southwell's own grisly end. "The resemblances between these two deaths is ultimately more than coincidental," she claims "insofar as canto 9 assembles an allegorical representation constellation that both cites and contests Southwell's poetic and political legacy as a Catholic missionary in post-Reformation England" (186). Rust suggests that "the ghost of Southwell appears not only in Malengin's grisly end but also in the numerous details that link him to the figure of the Jesuit missionary" (186). Specifically, she claims, Spenser deploys an allegorical parody of "Southwell's most prominent contribution to sixteenth-century English literature," the "trope of the weeping woman as an emblem of penitent devotion" (188). Just as Spenser's old Cambridge friend, Gabriel Harvey, had dismissed Thomas Nashe's sudden conversion as insincere by disparaging the sudden emotive effect of *Mary Magdalen's Funeral Tears*, so in this episode of his epic poem, Rust claims, Spenser depicts "a parodic reiteration of Southwell's Magdalene weeping in front of Christ's tomb" in the figure of "Samiant weeping before Malengin's cave" (191). In an even more complexly layered reading Rust also discusses the affective weeping of Mercilla in this canto. The scene, conventionally read as a representation of Queen Elizabeth's weeping at the execution of Mary Tudor, Rust sees as paradoxically alluding to Southwell's Magdalene.

Rust's readings of Spenser's canto 9 as conjuring and critiquing Southwell's popular poetic of tears has important implications for the claims of influence I am making in this chapter. First, of course, we are presented with the very real probability that Spenser was mindful of Southwell not just as the latest Jesuit enemy, but of Southwell as a disruptive literary presence, propagating a Catholic aesthetic that needed to be thwarted. The kind of parody that Spenser offers of Magdalene's weeping certainly suggests that he had firsthand knowledge of the *Funeral Tears*; that he did not simply rely upon the word of Harvey or follow the caustic pamphlet wars, but read Southwell's meditation himself, including the upbraiding of poets for their "vainest follies" and "idle phansies." Finally, as Rust points out in her explication, canto 9 demonstrates "Spenser's potential intervention in the literature of tears" (191).

Having already had the sort of "agonistic reaction"[1] to Southwell's work that begets the guileful serpent in Book V, we may imagine that beholding the proliferation of the executed Jesuit's verses in print and observing the apparent demand for religious poetry would only have deepened his resolve against this religious and literary enemy. At the same time, Spenser would have been shrewd enough, I believe, to recognize that Southwell was an enemy who, even in death—or perhaps especially in death—could not be ignored. Given the Jesuit's posthumous publishing success, "it would be hard to imagine," Shell argues, that Spenser did not read at least some of Southwell's poetry. And having done so, it would have been difficult to ignore the affronting challenge it presented to Protestant poets like himself who demonstrated what she calls "a crucial hesitancy surrounding religious poetry: a widespread willingness to admit that poetry was an acceptable means of celebrating divine subject-matter, but in practice, a reluctance to break out in any direction that might lead to accusations of idolatry" (72–73).

Spenser had not only kept, as it were, the walls and naves of his poetry pure from any kind of conventional religious subject matter or imagery that might suggest idolatry, he had made mocking sport of such papist idol worship throughout his epic poem. Paradoxically, however, as the title of his great epic poem proclaims to the ages, he had joined with his fellow English poets in propagating a whole new kind of idolatry, effectively swapping one virgin queen for another. Besides contributing lavishly to the cult of Elizabeth, he and his contemporaries had deployed Petrarchan conventions without restraint in the idealization of female beauty. Now the English literary establishment of which he was arguably the champion was being confronted by a papist insurgent who proclaimed to English poets and their readers: "Give not assent to muddy minded skill / That deems the feature of a pleasing face / to be the sweetest baite to lure the will" ("At Home in heaven," 31–33). What

---

1   "The term" says Shell, "is Harold Bloom's," noting that Bloom "does not list theological dissent among the reasons for poets to disassociate themselves from their predecessors." FN 54, "Catholicism, Controversy and the English Literary Imagination, 1558–1660."

was the poet who had inherited "Sidney's mantle of Protestant exemplarity" (Shell, 72) to do with this upstart moral crow whose pious cawing only grew louder after his extermination? How was the poet who had staked out the moral high ground in English poetry and declared it firmly Protestant, to respond to this challenge which Southwell issued?

That challenge would have been especially awkward for Spenser since in 1595 he published *Amoretti and Epithalamion*, Petrarchan masterpieces which, with far less of the ironic humor that exudes from Sidney's *Astrophil and Stella*, unapologetically deem "the feature of a pleasing face / to be the sweetest baite to lure the will." Shell offers sonnet 72 as a specimen, though any number of verses might do:

> Oft when my spirit doth spread her bolder wings,
> In mind to mount up to purest sky,
> It down is weighed with thought of earthly things
> And clogged with burden of mortality,
> Where, when that sovereign beauty it doth spy
> (Resembling heaven's glory in her light),
> Drawn with sweet Pleasure's bait it back doth fly
> And unto heaven forgets her former flight (1–7)

Caught here in the very act that Southwell so reviled, Spenser as a Christian neo-Platonist could, Shell suggests, defend such verse as representing the way to the Divine through earthly beauty, a position that Southwell the priest and poet had considered and rejected:

> If picture move, more should the paterne please,
> No shadow can with shadowed thinge compare,
> And fayrest shapes whereon our loves do ceaze:
> But sely signes of gods high beautyes are.
> Go sterving sense, feede thou on earthly maste,
> Trewe love in Heav'n, seeke thou thy sweete repast
> ("Lewd Love is Losse," 7–12)[2]

2   In each stanza of this poem the poet offers different metaphors for the hazard of earthly worship, including "barren soil," "the fly . . . with the flame," and "self-pleasing souls, that play with beauty's bail, / In shining shroud may swallow fatal hook.

These lines demonstrate the two fundamental points of view in an inherent debate between Southwell and Spenser that never took place. If it had, Spenser would have found himself ironically in the place not of Piers, the good, Puritan-leaning, Protestant minister in the "May Eclogue" of his *Shepheardes Calender*, but Palinode, the loose May-dance-loving Catholic priest in that eclogue. The uneasy neo-platonic ground upon which the Protestant poets stood found them condemning papists' devotions to so-called holy images while simultaneously devoting their own poetry to the worship of sacred human images, to their "mistress' eyebrow," as Shakespeare has Jacques describe it. In any case, since no actual debate of this kind ever took place between these two viewpoints, no resolution was ever reached. The question of whether "the fayninges of love" constitute a neo-platonic ascent towards the divine or a simple abuse of one's talent would continue to ripen and would, as we will see, preoccupy the aesthetic of George Herbert.

Meanwhile, there is Edmund Spenser, returned to his native London in the mid-1590s having accomplished what he had set out to do a decade and a half earlier. He had written England's great national poem with his Queen at its center. His achievement in epic poetry, on display in thousands of rhyming stanzas, allegorical figures and intertwined, morally complex narratives, may not have fashioned English gentlemen, but it did establish his reputation as this era's greatest English poet. He had paused from his monumental effort only to apply his poetic virtuosity to the lyric form. He was now preparing to bring into print a masterful sonnet cycle as well as the latter half of *The Faerie Queene* in whose final book he nods at his own fame with the rhetorical inquiry: "Who knows not Colin Clout?" The famous parenthetical rhetorical question, which harkens his readers back to the 1570s when the author of the self-conscious, gloss-ridden pastoral eclogues was fashioning himself as England's great national poet without having composed a single word of his imagined epic poem, is worthy of all of the smugness that it contains. The Colin Clout of *The Shepheardes Calender* had limped out of that poem on a walking stick, encrusted with hoary frost and crow's feet that furnished him the conventional excuse of old age, lest he fail to fulfill the proposed epic poem that his October Eclogue forecasts. The Colin Clout walking in London in the mid-1590s required no more literary excuses, but he did now have real crow's feet and white hairs to go with his well-deserved fame; and unless his poetic ambitions were beyond the bounds of all reason, he also recognized that his greatest literary output lay in his past, even if the full appreciation of his literary achievements remained ahead. Where his reputation was concerned, therefore, there was still substantial self-fashioning to be done, especially as the last luster of the glorious monarch to whom he had dedicated his talents began to seriously fade. Colin Clout, having come home again, now faced a familiar artistic question: Where to next?

In an irony nearly too poignant to imagine, the poetic remains of a disentrailed Jesuit Malengin may well have pointed the way that Colin would go next. Whatever animosity Spenser might have felt privately towards Southwell and his unlikely posthumous literary success, his public response was not the polemical kind rendered in Book V of *The Faerie Queene*, but a more measured response that from a professional literary standpoint might even be regarded as calculated. He certainly would have recognized that Southwell "was constructing a model of poetic virtue alternative to that imputed to Sidney" (Shell, 70), but he wisely did not choose to bring any more attention to Southwell by entering this debate. In response to the Either/Or dichotomy issued by Southwell—uncorrupted religious verse or nothing—Spenser offered up in his next published work, *The Fowre Hymnes*, a highly stylized Both/And. Whatever fever this dead Jesuit was stirring in the hearts of others, I would argue that he pointed Spenser towards a gap in his otherwise illustrious literary resume. Spenser had yet by 1595 to write a straightforward religious poem. So now he did.

Whether or not one accepts Rust's interpretation of the Malengin episode therefore, any other pertinent connection between the poetical works of Spenser and the verse of Southwell necessarily brings us to what Spenser wrote after 1595, itself an unresolved question that has fostered a critical debate which we must, of necessity, engage. So it is then that we turn to Spenser's *The Fowre Hymnes*, a complicated grouping of poems with their own history of critical debate. Whether and to what extent Spenser was impacted by the poetry of Southwell

2   All quotations from Southwell's poetry throughout this text are from *Collected Poems*, edited by Peter Davidson and Anne Sweeney, Carcanet Press Limited, 2007.

depends first and foremost upon when the *Hymnes* were actually composed. The reverse is likewise true. To the extent that we recognize Southwell's impact in the *Hymnes*, we also gain insight into how and when they were composed. Ultimately, I find that a careful assessment of Southwell's verse and Spenser's *Hymnes* together suggests that Spenser in his *Hymnes* may well have been responding to the sudden popularity of Southwell's religious verse, and more out of professional necessity, I think, than hostility. Informed by Anne Sweeney's argument that Southwell's verse introduced to England a more personalized intensity, I find Spenser's poetic response to Southwell's poems to be, not so much agonistic as inadequate.

At the crux of the critical debate concerning Spenser's *The Fowre Hymnes* is the relationship of the first two hymns composed in honor of earthly love and beauty and the second two hymns composed in honor of heavenly love and beauty. Where one comes down in this debate depends, in large measure, on whether he or she is willing to take the poet at his word when he tells Lady Margaret, Countess of Cumberland and Lady Marie, Countess of Warwick, in his dedicatory epistle that the first two hymns were composed "in the greener times of my youth" (690).[3] Having discovered that some corrupt young readers have been moved to "sucke out pyson" (690) from these hymns, an effect which has displeased one of his patronesses, Spenser decided, he says, to "call them in." Alas, however, these verses have been too widely distributed, so he "resolued at least to amend, and by way of *retractation* to *reforme* them, making in stead of those two Hymnes of earthly or naturall loue and beautie, two others of heauenly and celestiall" (690, all italics mine).

Many critics recognize in the poet's proposed retraction, a commonplace convention, and find the four hymns so well unified in form, image and narrative as to suggest persuasively that they were all composed at the same time, between 1595 and 1596. These readers regard the dedication as a clever bit of rhetorical posturing, designed to draw attention to the contrast between the two sets of hymns. One practical difficulty with reading the dedicatory epistle as a fiction, however, is

3   All quotations from Spenser's Fowre Hymnes are taken from *The Yale Edition of the Shorter Poems of Edmund Spenser*, edited by William A. Oram.

that it requires that the poet's patronesses shared in the lie that is being presented. This seems both peculiar and improbable. Some critics have shown convincing biographical evidence that Margaret Russell's life became "a pilgrimage of grief" when she was betrayed by her husband. These critics argue that the movement of the hymns from a celebration of romantic love to a celebration of spiritual love would have fulfilled her personal longing for divine consolation.[4] In other words, there were apparently good professional reasons for Spenser to compose two hymns that effectively retracted his earlier verse.

One need not believe, in any case, that the first two hymns were written decades earlier in order to acknowledge that there is a profound shift in theme between the two sets of hymns. Given the poet's claims in the epistle, as well as his sharp self-reproach at the beginning of *The Hymn of Heavenly Love*, it seems possible, even likely, that something other than just time came between the composition of the first two hymns and the composition of the second two; it seems probable, in fact, that what the poet says in his dedication is at least an approximate version of the truth. What intervened between the two sets of hymns may simply have been, as the poet says, the complaint of one of his patronesses, who was disillusioned with the extravagant promises of cupidity, and, like many London book buyers in 1595 apparently, seeking spiritual consolation in verse.

The other event that may well have intervened between the composition of the two sets of hymns is the execution of Robert Southwell and the subsequent proliferation of *Saint Peter's Complaint with Other Poems*. Spenser's two hymns in honor of Love and Beauty, after all, represent vividly everything against which Southwell objected in the dedications of his own verse: the use of poetry for unrestrained, profane adoration of Cupid and Venus. Recall again Southwell's familiar complaint:

> Poets by abusing their talent, and making the follies and feynings of love the customary subject of theire base endeavors have so discredited this facultye that a Poete, a

4   See Russell J. Meyer's paper, "Webster, 'Two by Two or One by Four, the Structural Dilemma of Spenser's *Fowre Hymnes*'," presented at Kalamazoo in 1982.

lover and a lyer, are by many reckoned but three wordes of one signification. For in lieu of solemne and devoute matter, to which in dutye they owe their abilities, they now busy themselves in expressing such passions as onely serve for testimonies to howe unworthy affections they have wedded their willes.

(*Collected Poems*, 1)

And again, in his dedicatory poem, he declares in his prefatory verse to *Saint Peters Complaynt*:

Still finest wits are stilling Venus Rose.
In paymin toyes the sweetest vaines are spent:
To Christian workes, few have their talents lent (16–18)

If Edmund Spenser read these words, which were now proliferating around London, he may, given his most recent compositions, have been chastened, or mildly embarrassed, or perhaps just outraged. It is hard to imagine, however, given "the follies and feynings of love" which he had brought to London to be printed, that he would have been indifferent. For, at the very least, he would have recognized that he was possibly out of step with a trend. His long absence in Ireland may well have reinforced this notion and his patroness's complaint might also have been a reminder.

Whatever the case, Spenser resolved to write for the first time a straightforward religious poem, *A Hymne of Heavenly Love*. And he began the poem with a self-remonstrance that resembles Southwell's own language, using the word "follies" twice in his explicit recanting of his "paymin toyes" against which the poet-priest had complained:

Many lewd layes (ah woe is me the more)
In praise of that mad fit, which fooles call loue,
I haue in th' heat of youth made heretofore,
That in light wits did loose affection moue.
But all those *follies now I do reproue*,
And turned haue the tenor of my string,
The heauenly prayses of true loue to sing.

And ye that wont with greedy vaine desire
To reade my fault, and wondring at my flame,
To warme your selues at my wide sparckling fire,
Sith now that heat is quenched, quench my blame,
And in her ashes shrowd my dying shame:
For who my passed *follies* now pursewes
Beginning his owne, and my old fault renewes
(8–21, italics and emphasis mine)

As in the case of the dedicatory epistle to the *Hymnes*, critics have pointed out that such a recantation as this one is a convention traceable back at least to Petrarch. Yet, we may need to be reminded here and elsewhere that just because something is conventional—be it a singing shepherd, a pining lover or a repentant poet—does not mean that it is therefore an utterly insincere fiction. The line between the "I" and the poet in any work of literature is necessarily indiscernible, but it does not follow that because something is tropological that it is not also real.

Certainly, if Spenser truly wished to reprove himself for his former follies and did not wish his readers to warm themselves at his wide sparkling flame, he would have quenched those flames himself by not publishing (or perhaps, in this case, not republishing) the first two hymns to love and beauty. At the same time, Spenser says in the closing couplet of these first three stanzas that whoever now pursues his past follies is only beginning follies of his own, as well as renewing the poet's ("my") old fault. If this warning had come at the beginning of *The Fowre Hymnes*, it would have been peculiar enough to be regarded as a clever marketing ploy along the lines of: "I have here published these four hymns. Please, whatever you do, don't read the first two, as they may provoke your sin and foster mine." This caution is really no less peculiar coming as it does after the fact, in *media res*, as it were, of the published work. Presumably readers of *An Hymn of Heavenly Love* have arrived at this poem after reading the first two of *The Fowre Hymnes* and are being told now by the author that they really ought not to have done that. The whole predicament is confoundedly Spenserian, and any reader of *The Faerie Queene* has experienced dozens of such moments of delightful or frustrating ambiguity when the narrator intrudes to editorialize upon his narrative. Here between the two sets of *Hymnes* is but another instance of Spenser being Spenser, and more like the Queen who governed this age than the zealous Jesuit who had called for absolute reform, this well-established Protestant poet is having it both ways.

William Johnson has observed insightfully that most readers interpret the word retraction in Spenser's dedicatory epistle to mean "'withdraw' (from *retractus*, past participle of *retrahere*). But the word makes much more sense in its other meaning, derived from *retractare*, to undertake anew" (431). What the poet undertakes anew in the stanzas that follow the above retraction is the perfect counterpoise to Spenser's first hymn, which had lavishly celebrated the divine origins and powers of Cupid. Here in this hymn Spenser presents a very conventional overview of the Gospel story, with some neo-platonic overtones in its treatment of Christ's origins as inspired by the Gospel of John. The hymn as a whole is a rather unspectacular account of salvation history as God's redemptive love is shown manifest in man's fall and Christ's subsequent birth, death and resurrection. The poetry itself is good, if somewhat forgettable. Framed to make references back to the *Hymne in Honour of Love*, it is nonetheless free of the trappings of elaborate allegory or learned allusions, and in the end may be described, with the exception of its evident poetic virtuosity, as rather *un*-Spenserian. The hymn is scripturally sound and theologically instructive, and certainly pious enough to satisfy any of the real or imagined qualms of a patroness who desired Spenser to depict Christian rather than pagan truth. If the recounting of God's redemptive love in Christ is somewhat perfunctory, this does not mean that the *An Hymne of Heavenly Love* is not a sincere articulation of the poet's own Christian beliefs.

In any case, Spenser could be satisfied that he had laid claim to the trend of religious poetry without ceding the territory to Catholics. He demonstrated to his readers that they need not turn to the dangerous musings of a dead papist to find divine verse. A devout Protestant like himself could write a devotional poem, and here he had done so. He followed this hymn with *An Hymne of Heavenly Beauty* to counterbalance his elaborate hymn to Venus. This praise of Heavenly Wisdom continues his "retraction" with a devoutly Christian tone, and as Sapience is a biblical entity, Spenser's capacity to write religious poetry is still on display. Even so, as Divine Wisdom is an allegorically feminine figure, Spenser is also on more comfortable poetic ground here, more able, as it were, to be Spenser.

Shell believes that *The Fowre Hymnes* offer an "agonistic reaction" to Southwell because, taken together as published in the volume, they seem to make the case that the Neoplatonic, allegorical extravagance of the Protestant poetic need not yield to the moral strictures insisted upon in Southwell's call for reform. In other words, the *Hymnes* demonstrate that pagan toys can reside alongside of conventional Christian piety to form a comprehensive truth about love and beauty. Insofar as *The Fowre Hymnes* are a response to Southwell, however, I do not think that response is necessarily an agonistic one. In the first place, I am proposing that whether or not Spenser composed the first two hymns in the greener days of his youth, he did write them before Southwell's execution and the subsequent publication of his poems in 1595. I believe further that Spenser's *An Hymne of Heavenly Love*, with its opening stanzas of self-remonstrance, shows that Spenser did in fact recognize Southwell's clout. Had he chosen to publish just the hymns to earthly love and beauty, particularly on the heels of *Amoretti* and *Epithalamion*, he might have found himself out of sync with the interest in and demand for religious poetry. On the other hand, had he published only the hymns to heavenly love and beauty, he would have been acknowledging and even verifying Southwell's clout. By publishing all four hymns together Spenser pleases his patronesses and satisfies his readers that it doesn't take a traitorous Jesuit to write a religious poem. At the same time, he retains in the work as a whole all things Spenserian: Neoplatonic extravagance, elaborate allegory, multiple allusions, yoked opposites and rhetorical ambiguity. By putting pagan extravagance on display within the same binding as conventional religious verse, he counters Southwell's severe call for poetic reform. If Spenser regarded this response as a victory of sorts, he might also have been self-consciously aware of how strangely things had changed since he had published *The Shepheardes Calender* a decade and a half earlier. For, as I have noted, here in this current literary moral exchange he casts himself in the role of the more libertine Palinode, while on the other side, inhabiting the persona of the more pious Piers was, not an uncompromising Calvinist pastor, but a dead Roman Catholic priest.

Whatever his literary or political intent in his *Fowre Hymnes*, ultimately, Spenser's project meets with only limited success, and, relative to the kind of poems Southwell had fashioned and which were now proliferating posthumously, Spenser's work may even be said to have failed. Few readers then or now acknowledge the *Fowre Hymnes* as among Spenser's greatest achievements. Rather, they are mostly overshadowed by the exceptional quality of his other works. And while the straightforward *Hymne of Heavenly Love* is unlike anything Spenser had ever written, it also demonstrates that Spenser did not really grasp the new poetic force that people were attracted to in Southwell's verse, a force that was much more than simply the choice of a religious subject matter. Anne Sweeney puts it this way: "Southwell was more than a copyable poet in the way that the form or style or phrasing of a Surrey or a Sidney could be copied: his status as both priest and martyr turned the actual process of creativity around from upthrusting creative ambition to an authoritative interpretation of the Divine creativity as it descends humanwards" (286). The new intensity in "personation" identified by Frank Kermode as characteristic of the early seventeenth century, was, Sweeney claims, already being done by Southwell in his first-person meditations of Magdalen and Peter. "Where Wyatt and Sidney had introduced into English the eloquently disappointed lover," Sweeney says, "Southwell, trained as he was in the recounting of real emotion, had introduced the language of the honest but incoherent heart" (Sweeney, 152). Sweeney makes a persuasive case that a new poetic was emerging in the 1590s, one of psychological meditation of the kind we associate with Donne and Herbert, as well as Hamlet and an array of other Shakespeare characters. It was Robert Southwell's verse, not Edmund Spenser's, Sweeney claims, that was at the front of this new poetic force.

To understand the difference between these two poets that Sweeney describes, it is helpful to consider a sample passage from each. Whether or not he is deliberately heeding the instructions of Robert Southwell's dedicatory epistle, Spenser in his *Hymne of Heavenly Love* is certainly weaving a new pious web on the well-worn loom of the Petrarchan convention. Here he describes Christ's crucifixion:

> And that most blessed bodie which was borne
> Without all blemish or reprochfull blame,
> He freely gave to be both rent and torne
> Of cruell hands, who with despightfull shame

Revyling him, that them most vile became,
At length him nayled on a gallow tree,
And slew the just, by most unjust decree.
O huge and most unspeakable impression
Of loves deepe wound that pierst the piteous hart
Of that deare Lord with so entyre affection,
And sharply launching every inner part,
Dolours of death into his soule did dart;
Doing him die, that never it deserved,
To free his foes, that from his heast had swerved.
(Stanzas 22, 23)

The Petrarchan threads on this old loom are as predictable as they are familiar. The cruel hands, the despiteful shame, and love's deep wound in the
pierced and piteous heart. Even when he is average, however, Spenser is superior to most poets and these stanzas are indicative of the quality of his
Hymnes as well as his capacity to succeed in yet one more genre, the religious lyric. The distinction which Sweeney makes between what Spenser is
writing and the new personal intensity that was emerging is evident, however, as soon as we turn from the third-person voice and familiar imagery
of these stanzas to a passage from Southwell's *Saint Peter's Complaint*:

Give vent unto the vapours of thy brest,
That thicken in the brimmes of cloudie eyes:
Where sinne was hatch'd, let teares now wash the nest:
Where life was lost, recover life with cryes.
Thy trespasse foule: let not thy teares be few:
Baptize thy spotted soule in weeping dewe.

Flie mournfull plaints, the Echoes of my ruth;
Whose screeches in my freighted conscience ring:
Sob out my sorrowes, fruites of mine untruth:
Report the smart of sinnes infernall sting.
Tell hearts that languish in the sorriest plight,
There is on earth a far more sorry wight. (7–18)

Those familiar with this poem know that the intensity of the speaker's
anguish never relents. It is not a pious meditation upon Christ's

sacrifice, but the sustained cry—tears, sobs, screeches, stings and sorrows—of the disciple who has betrayed him in that sacrifice. It is this voice, not Spenser's, that anticipates Donne's *Holy Sonnets* and Herbert's *Temple*, as well as, paradoxically, the laments of the most provocative epic character in English poetry, Milton's Satan. That "Southwell's poems met a need for imaginatively engaging religious verse, different from mainstream English poetry of the 1590s" (63), as Shell claims, is clearer today than ever before. However, early attempts at erasure of Southwell's influence from people's memories undoubtedly made it less so in the years after his execution.

Rust speaks persuasively of Spenser's own attempts at the erasure of Southwell in canto 9 of Book V where, she argues, "the palimpsestic vision of Mal overwriting Bon emblematically alludes to Southwell as a literary figure in the process of being 'raced' out of English national discourse" (195). As she notes, however, the sympathies of the author seem conflicted in this treatment of the poet. Nonetheless, Rust claims, Spenser's overarching project in incorporating Southwell's poetic paradigm was to "appropriate the spiritual rhetoric of a religious antagonist to reinforce a myth of Tudor sacred sovereignty . . . while simultaneously attempting to efface or overpower the very source of this rhetoric" (203). If such a project seemed allegorically possible before 1595, it must have seemed far less realistically so in the wake of the posthumous proliferation of Southwell's works immediately following the violent public erasure of his person.

Shell points to one particular example, however, that would suggest that the project Rust imagines Spenser to have undertaken had at least some success. She points to an instance where Southwell's place as the innovator of the poetics of tears is actually accredited to Edmund Spenser. If Southwell's name had no other literary associations by the turn of the seventeenth century, he certainly would have been known as the author of *Saint Peter's Complaint*, which had been printed several times by then, and as the author of the prose treatise, *Marie Magdalens Funeral Tears*, which had circulated for several years before being published in 1591. Both works, as Gary Kuchar observes, "were praised, imitated and satirized throughout Elizabethan and Jacobean England" (*Religious Sorrow*, 46). This makes all the more astonishing Gervase Markham's apparent deference to Edmund Spenser in his prefatory verse to his 1601 *Marie Magdalens Lamentations, For the Losse of Her Master Jesus*:

> If you will deigne with favour to persue
> Maries memorial of her sad lament,
> Exciting Collin in his graver Muse,
> To tell the manner of her hearts repent (f.A4b quoted in Shell)

Spenser, via his familiar pastoral pseudonym, is here invoked by Markham as the innovator of the poetry of tears that Southwell had pioneered.

To be fair, Markham's invocation of the recently departed and revered Colin Clout might have been merely an earnest misperception on his part. However, if it was an act of deliberate erasure of Southwell or, as in the case of contemporary book jacket endorsements, a marketing ploy to bolster his own verse, both efforts failed. Nobody today recalls Gervase Markham or his *Lamentations* (Shell in her discovery even referred to him as an anonymous author), and nobody in the seventeenth century, neither those who continued to fashion tears poetry nor the best writers of English devotional verse, regarded Edmund Spenser as its innovator.

Only nine years after Markham's publication, a seventeen-year-old George Herbert declared his intention to compose only religious poetry, and in doing so, as we shall see in the next chapter, he referenced lines from Robert Southwell. Later on, as a mature poet defending the unambiguous truth expressed in his religious poems, Herbert critiqued that other kind of poetry that relies on Neoplatonic exposition, depictions of imaginary landscapes, and elaborate allegorical transference of meaning:

> May no lines passe, except they do their dutie
>   Not to a true, but a painted chair?

> Is it not verse, except enchanted groves
> And sudden arbours shadow course-spun lines?
> Must purling streams refresh a lovers loves?
> Must all be vail'd, while he that reades, divines
>   Catching the sense at two removes?

Shepherds are honest people; let them sing
Riddle who list, for me, and pull for prime:
I envie no man's nightingale or spring;
Nor let them punish me with losse of ryme,
   Who plainly say, *My God, My King.*
   (Jordan I, 3–12)

Who knows not—here in these unflattering lines—Colin Clout? The
singer of a kind of song whose time has passed. The stark final line of
the poem, on the other hand, fulfills prescriptively the very call to poetic reform for which Robert Southwell had called years before.

In her consideration of the poetry that came after Southwell, Anne
Sweeney presses with a sort of urgency beyond religious lyricists like
Herbert and makes the astonishing claim that

> Milton, who evidently preferred Southwell's to Spenser's
> rhetorical vision, borrowed his early baroque imaginative
> universe-scape. In his visually rich portrayal of Biblical fig-
> ures in a drama of his own devising, Milton was inheriting
> from Southwell's rhetoric the pedagogic imagery of the
> Roman churches, not Spenser's anxiously non-idolatrous
> allegories (283).

A claim this bold will undoubtedly stir debate, and since it lies beyond
the scope of my own study, let me simply note in light of the small sample I have offered above that *An Hymne of Heavenly Love* is no *Paradise Lost*; nor, though it recounts in summary form much of the same
theological thought and events of salvation history, could it be. For Milton's poem depends upon a force of internal meditative thought and
voice that the very best of Spenser's poetry does not approach. People
may certainly dispute the unnerving suggestion that Milton inherited
his poetic voice in part from a martyred Jesuit of the latter sixteenth
century, but in any case readers of Southwell know that the "baroque
imaginative universe-scape" that Sweeney identifies is certainly present
in his poems. Spenser in his poetic maturity either missed this new poetic
strain or disregarded it as excessive and idolatrous.

What we ought to recognize with renewed clarity today is that
two rival poetic styles and voices were emerging in England in the

middle of the 1590s. One of those voices was, paradoxically, growing louder, after having been silenced. Another voice was wearing thin, having sung the greatest songs of that generation. Critics for centuries have recognized and acknowledged this dichotomy, though with the prominent exception of Louis Martz, most until recently have associated the two styles with Spenser and Donne. In the mid-1590s, however, John Donne was in his mid-twenties and while he may have written some of his religious poems he was still a long way from being the innovative devotional poet we now recognize him to be.[5] A more accurate and honest description of the change in literary styles that was taking place in England in the 1590s would, it seems to me, be Spenserian and Southwellian, and with no intended slight to honest singing shepherds, it is to the echoes of this latter pastor that I attune my ear in the chapters that follow.

5   The dating of Donne's poetry will likely remain an unsettled subject of scholarly discourse. Evidence for the later dating of his devout poetry is conjectural, and as A. J. Smith has observed, "there is nothing to suggest that the nineteen sonnets [that comprise "Divine Meditations"] make up a single body of work written over a short period of time."

Chapter 4
Poetic Pheres: Southwell and George Herbert

In his improbable and ambitious literary reformation, Robert Southwell was seeking company. He had in Henry Garnet as good a spiritual
and strategic companion as one could desire. He moved among recusant Catholics in homes and prisons where he was sustained by friends
and acquaintances whose faith and courage in the face of persecution
must surely have served as inspiration to his own mission. Still, what
he lacked and what he sought in those like his cousin Anthony Copley
were peers who would join him in his determination to marshal poetry
towards sacred ends. In his familiar verse preface to *Saint Peter's Complaint*, "The Author to the Reader," the poet priest demonstrates his
despondency at the current state of things:

> So ripe is vice, so greene is vertue's bud:
> The world doth waxe in ill, but waine in good.
>
> This makes my mourning muse resolve in teares,
> This theames my heavy penne to plaine in prose.
> Christes Thorne is sharpe, no head his Garland weares:
> Still finest wits are stilling *Venus* Rose
> In paynim toyes the sweetest vaines are spent:
> To Christian workes, few have their talents lent (11–18).

Some have speculated that the lament of this preface has a specific target, such as Shakespeare. Whether Shakespeare was the intended
"will," the "Deare eie that daynest to let fall a looke" (1) upon these
words, and whether he ever actually did so are questions worthy of
continued consideration, but even if that was the case, his eye was not
the only one Southwell was seeking to catch. The poem represents a
more general, earnest and unfulfilled desire. In his enterprise of religious poetry Robert Southwell was seeking poetic company.

In the opening line of this poem's final stanza the poet's yearning
is explicit: "*License my single penne to seeke a pheere.*" As I noted in
my Introduction, the word "pheere" is rich in its connotations, suggesting the desire for a "fere" or companion who shares his particular
religious and poetic fervor; a "peer" at least one but perhaps several
English poets, men whom Southwell would have recognized as more
talented and less constricted than himself, who by turning their talents
to "Christian workes" could change the course of English literature.
Together, the line suggests, they might comprise a sphere that could
fulfill Southwell's far-flung vision.

So emphatic is he in this desire that as this final stanza of the poem
continues one can hear an invocation to a heavenly muse:

> *You heavenly sparkes of wit, shew native light:*
> *Cloud not with mistie loves your Orient cleere,*
> *Sweet flights you shoot; learne once to levell right.*
> *Favour my wish, well-wishing workes no ill:*
> *I moove the Suite, the Graunt rests in your will (20–24).*

If one follows the syntax carefully here and observes what the heavenly
sparks of wit are ultimately being asked to accomplish, it becomes
clear that Southwell is addressing not abstract divine muses, but English poets whom he urges to be more English by shining their "native
light." Alluding to the familiar lost bark at sea in Petrarch's sonnets,[1]

---

1 Thomas Wyatt's famous rendering:

My galley, chargèd with forgetfulness,
Thorough sharp seas in winter nights doth pass
'Tween rock and rock; and eke mine en'my, alas,
That is my lord, steereth with cruelness;
And every owre a thought in readiness,
As though that death were light in such a case.
An endless wind doth tear the sail apace
Of forced sighs and trusty fearfulness.
A rain of tears, a cloud of dark disdain,
Hath done the weared cords great hinderance;
Wreathèd with error and eke with ignorance.

Southwell would have English poets shine through, unclouded by misty love. Rather than flying in flights of fancy, he would have them be straight shooters—"*learne once to level right*"—who might guide their countrymen to Christ. That Shakespeare was impacted by the poetry of Robert Southwell now seems very apparent and the specific nature and instances of that impact have been meticulously well documented by John Klause.[2] Southwell's influence on Shakespeare's work notwithstanding, however, it seems just as clear that neither Shakespeare nor any of his contemporaries became the kind of peer that Southwell was seeking in the above verse.

To claim that George Herbert became the English poetic peer that Southwell was seeking is to speak with anachronistic hyperbole since Southwell had been dead for fifteen years when the pious, young George Herbert composed his first surviving poems. Besides being a generation removed from one another, there are other pronounced differences in their lives. One was a clandestine Roman Catholic priest during the reign of Elizabeth, the other a member of a prominent Anglican family in the Jacobean realm. Southwell lived his years in England in constant danger of apprehension. The closest Herbert came to the potential violence of religious controversy was as a schoolboy at Westminster in 1605 when he and his classmates must have been awed by their immediate proximity to the infamous Gunpowder Plot. His older brother Edward in fact had avoided his obligations in parliament that day because of premonitions he had received in dreams the night before. The drama of such potential terror could only have codified the enmity Herbert would have felt towards the Roman Church, and it seems fairly certain that he himself would never have regarded a Jesuit priest who was at the heart of the recusant movement as a peer.

Allowing for all of this, there are I believe enough similarities in the two men's lives and in their use of poetry as a means of proselytizing, to suggest that George Herbert, both in his professed intentions and what he actually accomplished, was the very kind of "heavenly

> The stars be hid that led me to this pain;
> Drownèd is Reason that should me comfort,
> And I remain despairing of the port.

2   *Shakespeare, the Earl and the Jesuit.* Readers may wish to begin with Klause's excellent articles on *The Merchant of Venice* or *King John.*

spark of wit" and "native light" that Southwell had been seeking two decades earlier. Whether or not Southwell might have imagined an Anglican priest as the instrument of his proposed literary reformation, George Herbert was mindful of Southwell's professed desire that English verse be put to Christian use and he was also well acquainted with the poetic examples of this project that Southwell had fashioned. As Sweeney and Davidson, among others, have pointed out, "the numerous editions of Southwell's poems which appear in the 1590s and in the early decades of the seventeenth century are sufficiently censored to have passed as books for Anglican or even Calvinist devotion" (Collected Poems, 146). Louis Martz, in "looking over the whole range of [Southwell's] work, good and bad, poetry and prose," identifies "five strands by which he is firmly tied to the religious poets of the following century." Among them are "his campaign, by precept and example, to translate the devices of profane poetry into the service of religious devotion" and another, which he calls a consequence of this campaign, is "the kinship between his poetry and George Herbert's" (*The Poetry of Meditation*, 184). That kinship is evident in the very first poems that Herbert wrote.

In 1610 an earnest seventeen-year-old Herbert sent a letter to his mother, enclosing two sonnets as a "New-year's gift." In the letter he declared explicitly what the two poems themselves exhibited: "For my own part, my meaning (*dear Mother*) is in these Sonnets, to declare my resolution to be, that my poor Abilities in *Poetry* shall be all, and ever consecrated to Gods glory" (Walton, 268). As Herbert biographer Amy Charles has observed, the letters also show us a "young student and poet taking himself very seriously, scorning secular poetry, dedicating his verses to God" (72). We might dismiss the young man's sanctimonious self-seriousness as the expressions of youthful arrogance if, in the decades to follow, he had ever veered from his pledge; but Herbert, like his improbable literary predecessor, who at that age was pestering his superiors to allow him to become a Jesuit, speaks with an unusual earnestness and determination which his life and work go on to fulfill. In doing so he may well have found that he himself was without a peer. Not that he did not enjoy the company of other pious Christian companions at Cambridge, but the idea of writing exclusively religious verse to counter what he regarded as the foolish pagan uses to which poetry had been put harkens back to the familiar dedicatory epistle of Southwell's, which the young Herbert had likely read more than once:

> For in lieu of solemne and devout matter, to which in duety they owe their abilities, they noe busy themselves in expressing such passions, as onely serve for testimonies to how unwoorthy affections they have wedded their wils . . . And because the best course to let them [poets] see the errour of their workes, is to weave a new webbe in their owne loome; I have here layd a few course threds together, to invite some skillfuller wits to goe forward in the same, or to begin some finer peece, wherein it may be seene, how well verse and vertue sute together (*Poems*, 1).

God willed us, Southwell insisted to his readers, "to exercise our devotion in Himmes and Spirituall Sonnets" and the young George Herbert took up this charge with particular literalness, and he did so, practically speaking, with as little poetic company as Southwell.

Far from indicating "poor Abilities in *Poetry*" Herbert's two earliest poems clearly show Herbert to be one of "the skillfuller wits" whom Southwell had hoped might go forward in his new web. The sonnets take up with vehemence the very complaint that the young Southwell had made some eighteen years earlier in his epistle and in his prefatory verse to *Saint Peter's Complaint*. Herbert writes:

> My God, where is that ancient heat towards thee,
> Wherewith whole showls of Martyrs once did burn,
> Besides their other flames? Doth Poetry
> Wear *Venus* Livery? only serve her turn?
> Why are not Sonnets made of thee? and layes
> Upon thine Altar burnt? Cannot thy love
> Heighten a spirit to sound out thy praise
> As well as any she? Cannot thy Dove
> Out-strip their *Cupid* easily in flight? (1–9)

Besides reiterating the same gospel of Southwell's literary reformation, Herbert's rhetorical questions, "Doth Poetry Wear *Venus* Livery? only serve her turn?" echoes Southwell's very complaint about poets' misplaced devotion, even to the italicizing of the goddess's name: "Still finest wits are stilling *Venus* Rose."

It was Herbert's editor, F. E. Hutchinson, who first pointed out the similarities between Herbert and Southwell in the above passages from the two poets. It seems unlikely that Herbert would have imagined Southwell to be among the "showls of Martyrs" who "once did burn" with "ancient heat towards thee" and the allusion "Besides their other flames" might even be meant to reference the Protestant "martyrs" set ablaze by Bloody Mary. However, Southwell's muse-like plea that his talented readers might best the vain efforts of other poets, "*License my single penne to seeke a phere / You heavenly sparkes of wit, shew native light: / Cloude not with mistie loves your Orient cleere,*" is not only echoed by Herbert in his second sonnet but improved upon. After complaining of the ingredients that Southwell attributes to "mistie loves"—"*Roses* and *Lillies* speak thee; and to make / A pair of Cheeks of them, is thy abuse. / Why should I *Womens eyes* for Chrystal take? (l. 6–8)—Herbert then declares: "Such pooer invention burns in their low mind, / Whose fire is wild, and doth not upward go / To praise, and on thee Lord, some *Ink* bestow" (l. 9–11). Both poets, burning with "that ancient heat," desire "heavenly sparks of wit" which would send their singular pens upward to seek an eternal sphere. Both poets also insist that such heavenly sparks would not originate from an imaginary female muse. Southwell's complaint in this regard, "Ambitious heades dreame you of fortune's pride: / Fill volumes with your forged Goddesse praise" (*Complaint*, 31–32), is echoed by Herbert into a rhetorical question: "Cannot thy love / Heighten a spirit to sound out thy praise / As well as any she?" (I, 6–8).

Southwell's clever punning upon the word "pheere" while not duplicated by Herbert is implied in the content of these two sonnets, which are addressed to God, offered as gifts to his mother and serve as a critique of the general sphere of English poets. The strategic sense in this is clearer when one considers that Magdalene Herbert was much more than merely the young Cambridge student's mother. A literary patroness of some reputation, she was among other things a friend and supporter of John Donne. Donne was a regular visitor in the Danvers household in both London and Chelsea and a great admirer of Mrs. Herbert. Her mutual high regard for him, as well as his familiar presence among the family makes it almost certain that the young Herbert would have looked to the elder Donne for guidance in matters both poetic and non-poetic. Professor Charles surmises that the acquaintance between George Herbert and Donne likely began in Herbert's childhood (119). Charles's further observation that their relationship "must have deepened over the years when Herbert followed Donne's example in writing devotional verse" (119) reflects a commonplace understanding about Donne and Herbert which presumes a poetic influence without necessarily offering any specific internal evidence of the fact. How early Donne authored religious poems of the kind that Herbert would have seen and desired to imitate is impossible to say with certainty since the dating of Donne's devout poems remains a question among scholars, though it seems plausible that by 1610 the young Herbert may have taken his cue from the elder Donne in composing his own religious sonnets to his mother.

However, in comparing Donne's poems with Herbert's earliest offerings one finds little resemblance beyond the sonnet form and the fact that the content of all the poems may be categorized as religious. Donne's poems are individual meditations whose discoveries rely as much upon intricacy of argument and virtuosity of wit as spiritual revelation or religious devotion. As Frank Brownlow observes, "Donne was writing stylized love poems to Mrs. Herbert and the countess [of Bedford] at the same time that he was writing them equally stylish religious poems" ("John Donne," 5). Brownlow challenges the conventional notion that Donne's religious poems represent his own steps to the temple, that is, that they are expressions of a resolved piety and harbingers of his eventual ordination to the priesthood. The "obligation [of priesthood]," he notes, "lay well in the future when he was writing his religious sonnets. In those days he was still a clever layman with hopes of state employment writing for an aristocratic circle of people who counted on him to produce witty, unexpected turns of thought, whether the subject was religion or love" (5).

Interestingly, George Herbert was addressing the very same audience as Donne in sending the two New Year sonnets to his mother. It is not altogether improbable that the young man was in some fashion competing for his mother's attention, or at the very least alerting her to his own poetic talents, but at sixteen he could not presume to approach the daunting word play, syntactical intricacy or reasoned virtuosity of Donne's religious sonnets, nor is there anything in his two sonnets to suggest specifically that he was attempting to imitate Donne's religious poems or that he had in fact even read them. Donne offers individual, internal spiritual meditations. The young Herbert makes two general and emphatic complaints to God about the hollow worldliness and lack of Christian content in English poetry.

If we listen and take seriously the questions that Herbert asks in his first sonnet—questions that ought not to be dismissed as merely rhetorical—we certainly do not hear the voice of a young poet who has read the *Holy Sonnets* of John Donne. Or, if he has read them, he seems to have found them to be an unsatisfactory response to his concern that English poetry has not been used to glorify God. "Why?" he asks in prayer, "are not *Sonnets* made of thee?" (l. 5) And again, "Cannot thy love / Heighten a spirit to sound out thy praise as well as any she?" Cannot thy *Dove* / Outstrip their *Cupid* easily in flight? (l. 6–9). And then anticipating the aesthetic criticism he makes in "Jordan I," he asks, "Will not a verse run smooth that bears thy name!" (11) Of the several capitalized and italicized words in the poem, *Sonnets* seems to me the most provocative since it seems to be referring not merely to a poetic convention, but to the works of poets who have relied for inspiration upon "no braver fuel . . . than that, which one day, Worms, may choose refuse." (13–14)[3] Given a choice of whether the young Herbert was unaware of Donne's religious sonnets or dissatisfied with their content, I would select the former case, as there is little in what we know of Herbert's character to suggest that he would be brash, precocious, or discourteous enough to give offense of this kind to either his mother or the elder poet whom she admired.

What all of this suggests therefore is that, at least in his earliest offerings, Herbert was not looking to John Donne as an example of how to write religious verse. Rather, the overt literary critique and call to poetic conversion contained in these two poems, sent to a woman who was not only his mother but an influential literary patroness, suggest that Herbert's purposes were the same as Southwell's had been two decades earlier. The specific echoes within the poems that I have

3   Herbert may have in mind in particular of *Astrophil and Stella* and *Amoretti*, both brought to print in the 1590s and Shakespeare's *Sonnets* printed a year before Herbert wrote these poems.

identified above certainly reinforce this idea. Herbert may well have been aware that Donne was now writing some divine poems, but it is not to align himself with Donne that these two sonnets were written. He is not merely experimenting with a renowned literary form or imitating an elder poet. Rather, these first literary offerings amount to a sincere religious commitment to which he was calling others. Aspiring as he was in his youth to a sparsely populated poetic and religious sphere, the young Herbert may well have felt that he did not have a peer. The long dead priest and poet of *Saint Peter's Complaint* offered, if not a peer, at least precedence.

Years later, in the poem "Jordan (II)," recalling his earliest attempts to write religious verse Herbert describes his failed attempts to use "quaint words" and "trim invention":

> When first my lines of heav'nly joyes made mention,
> Such was their luster, they did so excel,
> That I sought out quaint words, and trim invention;
> My thoughts began to burnish, sprout, and swell,
> Curling with metaphors a plain intention,
> Decking the sense, as if it were to sell (1–6).

The luster of heaven's joys was such that the inexperienced poet automatically resorted to what his Elizabethan predecessors had done, employing fancy diction ("quaint words") to decorate the sense as for sale. With his thoughts burnishing, sprouting and swelling, he curls his plain intentions with metaphors. If this poetic predicament and youthful blundering sound familiar it is not just because they are tropological, but because Herbert is indulging in a very specific bit of sacred parody. In documenting here in "Jordan (II) his own early attempts to compose religious verse, he deliberately mimics the language and narrative of Philip Sidney's artful and ironic rejection of poetic imitation in his opening sonnet of *Astrophil and Stella*, where the lover recalls unsuccessfully "studying invention fine" to find "fit words." Sidney's Astrophil describes himself "turning others' leaves" only to find that "others' feet were strangers in his way" (l. 7, 11). Herbert in his second stanza declares that he "blotted what I had begunne; / This was not quick enough, and that was dead" (l. 9–10). Sidney is rescued from proverbial pen biting by his muse who intervenes to tell him famously "look in thy heart and write" (l. 14). Herbert is similarly rescued, not by a muse but by an anonymous friend:

> But while I bustled, I might heare a friend
> Whisper, *How wide is all this long pretense!*
> *There is in love a sweetnesse readie penn'd:*
> *Copie out only that, and save expense* (l. 15–18).

The comic genius of Sidney's poem is contained in his elaborate pretense of rejecting poetic precedence and arriving at pure originality ("look in thy heart") even while having fashioned a brazenly conventional sonnet. Herbert imitates Sidney's maneuver in his apparently autobiographical poem, but in the instruction he receives in the poem's whispered climax he is actually told to copy, not other poets' quaint words or curling metaphors, but the sweetness in love that is already penned. The love of course is God and more specifically Christ. Write *this* sweetness, the anonymous friend whispers to him, and that will be sufficient "to clothe the sunne" (l. 11).

It seems quite certain that the friend who guides the young Herbert away from the poetic extravagance of curling metaphors would not be John Donne, nor, though Herbert employs the familiar Southwellian metaphor of weaving in his final stanza—"So did I weave myself into the sense" (l. 14)—is the young poet rescued from his writer's fit by Robert Southwell. The anonymous friend who rescues Herbert, like Sidney's intervening muse, would seem to be one of his private making, an invention urging him to avoid invention. Any serious reader of Herbert understands that the aesthetic declarations of the Jordan poems notwithstanding, the plain diction of his poems is nonetheless wrought with plenty of ingenious invention, curling metaphors and, as in the case of "Jordan (II)," a self-conscious awareness of and inevitable imitation of the English poets like Sidney who came before him. Yet where religious poetry was concerned, Herbert had few examples and though it would have been imprudent to ever mention his name, the verses of Southwell pointed the way.

The most recent critic to contemplate the poetic similarities in Southwell and Herbert is Anne-Marie Miller-Blaise who in her article "Priests and yet Prophets?" draws attention to the shared prophetic voice in the shorter lyrics of the two poets. Observing that Herbert "probably began writing his religious poetry quite a few years before he became a rector, then a priest" (114), and that Southwell in his religious lyrics "is speaking from within the ecclesiastical hierarchy of the Catholic Church" as well "as a double exile calling the nation of his birth back to its original faith" (118). Miller-Blaise claims that both men would have regarded their poems as having a prophetic intent, which she defines as witness to the Truth and calling others to that Truth. "Southwell and Herbert," she claims, "each in their own personal style and within the aesthetic limitations prescribed by their confessions, use the voice of the prophet, if not the rhetorical tools of prophesying" (123).

Of Southwell's prophetic voice, Miller-Blaise observes that the "pleading voice" in many of his poems, especially those that depend upon the trope of apostrophe,

> corresponds to a general invitation to repentance and conversion through the acknowledgement of the mysteries of the lives of the holy family. In certain poems, the speaker exhorts the soul, his soul, every one's soul. Voice stands out on its own, prophetically, calling "faire soule" out of "exile" and back to the blazing light of heaven ("At home in heaven)" (119).

Of Herbert, Miller-Blaise notes, "The voice in *The Temple* allegedly oscillates between the private voice of spiritual dejection or joy, and the voice of the priest and preacher, both of which extend out to the communal liturgy of the Church" (117).

Miller-Blaise supports her case by offering an explication of Southwell's "Burning Babe" and Herbert's "Redemption" in which she points out the similar parabolic narrative progression of both poems. Although neither poem is, strictly speaking, a case of prosopopoeia, she admits, "one definitely has the sense, as one reads them, that there is a person speaking. This persona happens to tell a tale of an experience or a vision designed to become a revelation for the reader, and can therefore be regarded as prophet-like" (119). In Herbert's poem the speaker, personified as a tenant in an indefinite time and place, seeks his rich Lord to grant him a suit and after two stanzas of searching in heaven, great resorts, cities, theatres, gardens, and parks discovers him among ragged thieves and murderers, where "straight, *Your suit is granted*, said, and died" (14). The reader, like the teller of the tale, witnesses Christ's death a second time. "The whole poetic parable," Miller-Blaise notes, "is like a prophecy in retrospect" (120). It is also a parable entirely of Herbert's own making. In Southwell's more famous poem, Herbert had been furnished an example of how to fashion such a parable, a tale beyond the bounds of scripture, but true to the scriptural truth, and a tale where Christ himself speaks that truth. The speaker in Southwell's narrative witnesses the weeping Christ child aflame in the air and unlike the brief line of the dying Christ in Herbert's "Redemption," here Christ speaks for the majority of the poem, and where Herbert's poem offers a biblical moral teaching, Southwell's poem is a startling vision whose imagery, as Miller-Blaise notes, is more Petrarchan than biblical. As in Herbert's poem, Southwell "rehearses a story of redemption or forgiveness that has already been written" and uses "a certain number of rhetorical qualities" (Miller-Blaise, 122) that Herbert would also deploy.

More than specific rhetorical tropes and a means of displaying Christ's spoken redemption, Southwell's "Burning Babe," as well as his other poems, provided Herbert something more crucial, namely an example of how to write the prophetic poem: how to bear witness to the truth of the Gospels within the aesthetic confines of poetry which heretofore had been deployed in honor of Venus and her trappings; how to speak as a sinful "I" that can nonetheless bear witness to divine truth. This latter predicament is something that Herbert would always struggle with, most notably in "Windows," but the "I" of Southwell's poems had offered him a model. As Miller-Blaise explains, in the case of both poets:

> a visionary, individual "I," is quite often endowed with the function of speaking to the community through his own experience. But this "I" never exceeds the space that is drawn out for him by the Scripture of the Church; this "I" can never prophesy, at least in the shorter lyrics, anything that has not been written (in the Bible or in doctrine) (123).

While it is not Miller-Blaise's intention to speak of Southwell's possible influence upon Herbert, her choice of "Redemption" and "The

Burning Babe" as representative "prophetic" poems is instructive not just for seeing how Southwell may have offered Herbert an example, but also for demonstrating the significant aesthetic departure that the Anglican Herbert made from his sixteenth century Roman Catholic predecessor. While both poems accomplish a similar parabolic instruction about Christian redemption, and each features Christ as the central figure that instructs the "I" and thereby the reader, they are, from an aesthetic standpoint, dramatically different literary artifacts that offer a stark contrast between Catholic baroque and Anglican plainness. The imagery of Herbert's poem is largely conventional and abstract. We don't really see heaven or the cities, theatres, gardens and parks of the speaker's search. They are each one word that combined convey the idea that he searched far and wide in very nice places. Even the thieves and murderers are brief biblical tropes whose brief cameo concludes one line later with the poem's end. Christ's place among the lowly, his redeeming death and words are the point of the poem. Our senses remain virtually unengaged. In Southwell's famous poem the effect is the opposite. It is difficult, and for many an honest reader impossible, to get past the startling image of the floating, burning, weeping infant Jesus to hear what he is saying. One can imagine that for Herbert, as for many readers, the image of the "newly borne" Christ declaring "In fierie heates I frie" was simultaneously compelling and repelling. The metaphysical vision in his final words would only compound this response: "So will I melt into a bath / To wash them in my blood" (14). Such visual excess may have seemed to a pious Anglican like George Herbert to be the very reason that church interiors had been painted and purged during England's religious reformation. And yet, at least one of Herbert's poems suggests that he did not altogether escape the divine flames of Southwell's famous poem.

When the "pretty babe all burning bright" of Southwell's poem explains for the startled viewer what he is witnessing, each portion of the dramatic icon is assigned meaning: "My faultless brest the furnace is the fuell wounding thornes / Love is the fire and sighs the smoke the ashes shame and scornes / The fewell Justice layeth on and Mercy blowes the coals / The metal in this furnace wrought are mens defiled soules (9 – 12). In Herbert's "Love II," Love is the fire and the poet speaking to immortal love offers what would be a suitable response to Southwell's unusual flaming icon of the infant Christ:

Immortal Heat, O let thy greater flame
Attract the lesser to it: let those fires,
Which shall consume the world, first make it tame;
And kindle in our hearts such true desires,

As may consume our lusts, and make thee way
Then shall our hearts pant thee; then shall our brain
All her invention on thy Altar lay,
And there in hymnes send back thy fire again, (l. 1-8).

Herbert's sonnet is not an imitation of Southwell's "The Burning Babe"
so much as an implicit acknowledgment of the power of the image
Southwell had conceived and a spoken response to that representation
of Christ. The fact is that without an image like Southwell's imprinted
in our minds, we see nothing in Herbert's poem. As with "Immortal
Love" in the companion sonnet that precedes it, "Immortal Heat" is a
theological abstraction. The flame is both pentecostal and purging in
effect, but the promise in the poem that "Our eies shall see thee" is just
that. As with the sparse story of "Redemption" we witness a predictable contrast between the two poets, Southwell offering dramatic
sacramental imagery and Herbert emphasizing the efficacy of the word.

As she emphasizes the prophetic voice in these two poets, Miller-
Blaise questions, "whether these poets actually speak as priests from
within their poetry" (114). Indeed, while Southwell's sacramental min-
istries were all performed covertly and Herbert was only an ordained
priest for the last few years of his life, the liturgical imagery is common
to both their poetry and a place where we do indeed hear them "speak
as priests." Herbert's *Temple* is sometimes just that, a sacred place of
sacramental worship, and where sacramental imagery in verse was
concerned Southwell offered him poetic precedence that was otherwise
quite scarce. Consider the following similarities between the two poets'
respective temples.

Amidst a meditation on the Blessed Sacrament, Southwell offers his
English Catholic readers a brief catalogue of sensory liturgical elements
that some of them may have experienced only in their memories:

To ravishe eyes here heavenly bewtyes are,
To winne the eare sweete musicks sweetest sound,

To lure the tast the Angells heavenly fare,
To sooth the sent divine perfumes abounde,
To please the touch he in our hartes doth bedd
Whose touch doth cure the dephe, the dumm, the dedd
("Of the Blessed Sacrament of the Aulter" 31–36)

Southwell is effectively providing here in verse the physical liturgical elements to which many in his audience may not have had any access without considerable risk. The homes of some of the wealthier recusants we know did contain chapels with all of the accompanying accoutrements to accommodate a formal Mass.[4] However, we can be certain that in other households when a dining room was secretly converted into a makeshift chapel to accommodate a secret Mass, the occasion did not afford the decorated church interior ("heavenly bewtyes"), incense ("divine perfumes"), or well-rehearsed music ("sweet musicks sweetest sound") that Southwell here conjures for his readers in verse.

Herbert has no such covert need to bring liturgy to life in words, and yet, like Southwell before him, he is intent in "The Banquet," to bring his Temple to sensory life:

O what sweetnesse from the bowl
   Fills my soul,

Such as is, and makes divine!
Is some starre (fled from the sphere)
   Melted there,

As we sugar melt in wine?
Or hath sweetnesse in the bread
   Made a head

To subdue the smell of sinne;
Flowers, and gummes, and powders giving

4   Devlin notes that when the musician Richard Bold hosted Fr.'s Weston, Garnet and Southwell at Hurleyford, William Byrd was there, and that Bold retained "in his house a chapel, a choir, and all sorts of instruments" for such occasions (114).

All their living,
Lest the enemie should winne? (l. 7–8).

In both instances the ordinary sinfulness of the worshipers is overcome through the senses. In Southwell's poem the sacrament ravishes eyes, wins ears, lures tastes, sooths s[c]ent, and pleases touch.[5] In Herbert's more Anglican stanzas the ingredients are more simple and more personal—"my"—though no less enticing or triumphant. "Lest the enemie should winne," the sweetness of the bowl fills the speaker's soul and the smell of sin is subdued, not by incense (a vanished papist ingredient), but by the sweetness in the bread. Southwell's verse is cumbersomely catechetic, Herbert's by far more lyrically enticing.

As in the above passages, when one finds similarities in selected passages of the two poets, one also finds that Herbert has typically improved lyrically upon any thoughts and images that he may have derived from Southwell. Since he regarded his verse as but one extension of his priestly mission and intended his audience to be as broad as possible, Southwell's poetic fault typically lies in saying too much. Consider this unedifying paradox in a couplet from "Of the Blessed Sacrament of the Aulter": "Twelve did he feede, twelve did their feeder eate, / He made, he dressed, he gave, he was their meate" (11–12). Here the delicacy vanishes and the too obvious metrical pattern renders a kind of cacophony in the completion of the heavy-handed catechism. Herbert would use these very same two words as the end rhymes in the couplet that ends his poem "Love (III)" in which Jesus personified as the hostess of an inn invites the hesitant sinner to partake: "You must sit down, sayes Love, and taste my meat / So I did sit and eat" (17–18). If Herbert is borrowing from Southwell here, he is doing so with better effect, the imbalance of the lines and the simplicity and directness of the invitation startling the reader into the loving offer of the Eucharist.

5   Recusant Catholics' experience of the Mass in a makeshift home chapel certainly would not have enjoyed the scent of incense, the bold singing of hymns, or any other liturgical ingredients that might attract attention or which could not be easily hidden away in the event of a raid. Southwell is therefore giving his readers in poetry an experience they could not have in life.

Southwell's extravagance of imagery is again on display in another treatment of the Eucharist, "Christ's bloody Sweat":

Fat soyle, full springe, sweete olive, grape of blisse,
That yeldes, that streames, that powres, that dost distil,
Untild, undrawne, unstampde, untouchd of presse,
Dear fruit, clear brooks, fayre oyle, sweete wine at will:
Thus Christ unforc'd preventes in shedding bloode
The whippes, the thornes, the nailes, the speare, and roode.

This poem would have been appealing to Herbert, if only because the dramatic force of its repetitive monosyllables make it so un-Elizabethan. The compressed thought of the final couplet is made clear in the understanding of "prevents" in its old sense of "anticipates." Thus Christ's agony in the garden is but a precursor to the much worse agony, given emphasis in the five monosyllabic iambs of the stanza's final line. The line is echoed in a couplet from Herbert's "Good Friday" where two of the iambs are repeated identically: "That when sinne spies so many foes, / Thy whips, thy nails, thy wounds, thy woes" (25–26). In Herbert's "Affliction II" he describes the prepayment for our sins that Christ made upon the cross. In doing so he executes a pun that reverses Southwell's notion that Christ was "untouched of presse": "Thy crosse took up in one, / By way of imprest, all my future mone" (14–15). In this same poem Herbert echoes the title of Southwell's poem, noting that if all of humanity's tears were combined "They would discolour thy most bloody sweat" (10). Southwell's essential idea of Christ being turned into a sweet and saving wine may be heard in Herbert's more famous poem "The Bunch of Grapes" where Herbert again insists that Christ was indeed pressed: "But can he want the grape who hath the wine? . . . But much more him I must adore / Who of the laws sowre juice sweet wine did make, / Ev'n God himself, being pressed for my sake" (22, 26–28).

Robert Southwell was determined to show that the popular poetic techniques and conceits of his day could be easily converted to religious purposes. This sacred parody, as we have come to call it, yielded several poems whose stanzas are transparently Petrarchan. In his poem "I Die Alive," for example, Southwell writes "I live, but such a life as ever dies, / I die but such a death as never ends" (5–6). Herbert repeats this very sentiment from St. Paul's epistle in "Affliction II," but avoids the worn-out tone of Petrarchan complaint. The result is a couplet that is both more enigmatic and more powerful: "Though I in a broken pay / Die over each houre of Methusalems stay" (4–5). In "Man's Civill Warre" Southwell again presents a conventionally Petrarchan image of spiritual anguish: "My hovering thoughts would fly to heaven / And quiet nestle in the skye / Fayne would my ship in vertues shore / Without remove at Anker lye / But mounting thoughts are haled downe / With heavy poyse of mortall load" (l. 1–6). Herbert's version of this very predicament in "Affliction IV" retains the violence and the weight, but avoiding the familiar Petrarchan image of the tossed ship, introduces a metaphor far more startling, effective and therefore memorable: "My thoughts are all a case of knives, / Wounding my heart / With scatter'd smart / As watering pots give flowers their lives" (8–11).

The provocative image of thoughts inflicting physical wounds is in fact anticipated by another Southwell poem, "Dyers Phansie turned to a Sinners Complaint," where Southwell writes: "O thoughtes, no thoughtes but woundes / Sometyme the seate of joy / Sometime the store of quiett rest, / But now of all annoye" (45–48). This poem, while it retains Petrarchan tone and imagery ("As one that lives in shewe, / And inwardly dooth die"), contains as well a personal tone that makes it far more than mere conventional sacred parody. It seems, perhaps for this reason, that it may have served as a particular influence upon Herbert. In the poem's opening stanza Southwell's speaker describes himself as "Hee that his myrth hath lost / Whose comfort is to rue, / Whose hope is falne, whose faith is cras'd / Whose trust is founde untrue" (1–4). His "cras'd" faith anticipates the "brittle crazie glasse" that is man in Herbert's "Windows." And when Southwell's sinner refers to himself as one "Whose hart the Alter is" (29), we recognize Herbert's famous shaped poem "The Altar" in which the speaker begins by declaring "A broken ALTAR Lord, thy servant reares, / Made of a heart and cemented with teares" (1–2).

Southwell's "Phansie" furnished a rhetorical model that is reflected in Herbert's Affliction poems, in which the speaker describes his movement from past happiness to present misery. The following stanzas from Southwell's poem suffice to demonstrate the progression from spiritual contentedness to spiritual despondency that characterizes each of Herbert's Affliction poems:

I sow'd the soyle of peace,
    My blisse was in the springe;
And day by day the fruite I eate
    That Vertues tree did bringe
To Nettles nowe my Corne
    My feild is turnd to flynte
Where I a heavie harvest reape
    Of cares that never stynt (49–56)

. . .

In was, stands my delighte,
    In is and shall my woe
My horrour fastned in the yea
    My hope hangd in the no (65–68)

. . .

Behould such is the ende
    That pleasure doth procure
Of nothing els but care and plaint,
    Can she the mynde assure
Forsaken firste by grace

    By pleasure now forgotten
Her payne I feele but graces wage
    Have others from me gotten (73–80)

These stanzas of poetry are as close as Southwell comes in his poetry to the kind of overt self-introspection that better characterizes the poetry of Herbert and Donne. And even in this lengthy complaint the speaker reaches a predictable resignation to the precepts of his faith: "Yet Gods must I remaine" (105). This is, with slight variation, the essential narrative pattern of Herbert's poems of spiritual complaint, which celebrate the "many joyes," "naturall delights" and "gracious benefits" that yield a "world of mirth" ("Affliction I") in the earliest stages of spiritual conversion, then descend towards despondency as in "I reade and sigh and wish I were a tree" (l. 57), and then finally reach faint resolution, "Let me not love thee if I love thee not" (l. 66).

While Robert Southwell authored some exceptional poems, no one would attempt to make a case that he is the superior poet to George Herbert who, besides being more prolific, exhibits a command of diction and a balance of poetic simplicity and complexity that has helped increase his reputation with time. Even so, I would argue that part of Herbert's poetic success came from heeding rather than ignoring Southwell's poetic example. We may ask ourselves, for instance, what would have happened if all of Herbert's poems had remained as void of imagery and didactic as "Redemption"? Infusing his verse with flames and knives and nails and wine gave Herbert's poems a life that they would not otherwise have had. That power was further increased when Herbert spoke with a voice more personal than Southwell would permit himself to do. This is what caused Louis Martz to observe over a half century ago that Southwell's poems lack the "quivering intensity" on display in the more personal laments of Donne and Herbert. In truth however, Southwell's poems do not lack personal intensity; it is just safely concealed within the device of prosopopoeia, as Southwell, following the prescription of Ignatius Loyola's *Spiritual Exercises*, speaks in the voice of the biblical figures of Peter, Magdalene, Joseph or David, examining his own and our own spiritual well-being through the circumstances of these biblical figures and their relationship to Christ. Much more seldom in Southwell is his use of "I" as in the above poem where the "I" examines his own spiritual predicament. By contrast, Herbert is, I would argue, more so than John Donne whose irrepressible wit counter-balances his sincerity, the first great Protestant voice in religious poetry. Exploring the inside of a Temple that serves as a metaphorical representation of his own self, the poet depicts more vividly than either Southwell or Donne the interior struggle of an individual trying to come to God. Southwell had prudently depicted such struggles in the characters of Peter or Magdalene, whose errors are legendary, whose redemption is established and whose tears are emblematic of all who would imitate them. The more personal "I" in Herbert's poetry is one with whom a reader can more readily identify without overcoming a barrier between themselves and a renowned saint. Thus there is more genuine suspense and doubt as to the spiritual outcome of any given poem like "the Collar" which begins with the speaker striking the board and declaring "No more. I will abroad." The narrative proceeds, like the "Affliction" poems, to recall the miseries of his life, which in contrast to the harrowing drama of Southwell's life, are but the boredom, disappointments and ill-health of a devout rural pastor who has forsaken the accoutrements of wealth and fame. One senses that, even if furnished paper and pen in his cell in the Tower in his later years, the tormented Southwell would have steered his writing away from the autobiographical and towards the communal; he likely would have regarded his own spiritual struggles with God, his "dark night of the soul" or "private ejaculations" as they would come to be called by Herbert, as being of no particular pastoral or literary value.[6]

The essential difference then between Southwell's and Herbert's verse, therefore is not just the innovativeness of Herbert's imagery, nor the fact that his piety is less formulaic and more subtle. Nor is it simply that Southwell's sacred parody of Elizabethan verse makes much of his poetry conventionally Petrarchan and sometimes cumbersomely baroque. Rather it is Herbert's embrace and articulation of what Shell calls a "Protestantised aesthetic" in which, spiritually speaking, "the fight [is] the thing" ("Catholicism, Controversy," 101). The speaker who discourses with God in Herbert's poems is more introspective than Southwell's and more sincere than Donne's. Seeking spiritual consolation, to discover the truth for himself, Southwell's speaker asks: "Fayre soule, how long shall / veyles thy graces shrou'd?" and "How long shall this exile withhold thy right? ("At Home In Heaven," 1–2). Herbert's speaker inquires much more emphatically: "Sweet Peace, where dost thou dwell? I humbly crave / Let me once know" ("Peace," 1–2). The contrition in Southwell's poem is born of the pain that the

6   Because of the compelling drama of his life, readers have predictably looked to Southwell's works with an autobiographical expectation. Until very recently his *Hundred Meditations on the Love Of God* were believed, as their nineteenth-century editor claimed in his Preface, to be the window into the soul of a martyr. Only in recent decades was it discovered that the prose meditations were actually a translation by Southwell of an Italian work, which was itself the translation of the original meditations composed by a Spanish Franciscan in the fifteenth century. See fuller explanation in Chapter 7.

speaker's sins cause Christ: "O lord my sinne doth overchardge thy breste, / The poyse thereof doth force thy knees to bowe ("Sinnes Heavy Load," 1–2). Herbert's speaker, by contrast, demands relief for himself: "Wherefore my faults and sinnes, / Lord, I acknowledge; take thy plagues away" ("Confession," 25–26).

George Herbert composed his poetry within what Shell describes as "a climate in which non-biblical religious poetry became increasingly acceptable" (58), a climate traceable to the publication in the 1590s of Southwell's works and his accompanying emphatic call to poets to create sacred verse. George Herbert heard and heeded this call, and despite the evident and sometimes precarious divide between the Church of England and that of Rome, and the resulting differences in the lives of these two men, they worked and wrote within the same poetic sphere. Had time and circumstances been altered some, they might well have been regarded as poetic peers. For what they shared in common was, particularly in retrospect, ultimately more substantial than the differences that distinguished them. Each man was a priest. And despite the very disparate exigencies of their daily existence, each attempted to live and instructed others to live in accordance with the ideals they delineated in their respective works *A Short Rule of Good Life* and *Country Parson*: "modesty, decency, affability, meekenes, civility, and curtesie, shew of compassion to others miseries, and of joy at their welfare, and of readiness to pleasure all, and unwillingnes to displease any" (excerpt of *Short Rule*, quoted by Martz in *Meditation*, 206). Each man was also a poet who dared in his verse to speak prophetically, and for each of them the compositions were intensely personal. Central to the poetry and life of each man was the Christian sacramental life, with its accompanying words and images, and an understanding and acceptance of human suffering within the context of the paschal mystery of suffering, death and resurrection. Southwell and Herbert both supplemented their priestly vocation with an early and sustained commitment to the writing of poetry "wherein it may be seene, how well verse and vertue sute together." And they both succeeded, creating poems that, only after their deaths, provided aesthetic enrichment and spiritual sustenance to a common audience of readers for centuries to come.

Chapter 5
A Meditation of Martyrdom:
Southwell and John Donne

John Donne knew Robert Southwell. This statement itself, while requiring some qualification and speculation in the pages ahead, is not one that can be made about any of the other poets in this study. In 1586 when Southwell arrived with Henry Garnet as the third wave of the Jesuit mission in England, Donne was a fourteen-year-old Oxford student, a devout and secret Catholic and the promising eldest son of one of England's more prominent recusant families. By the time Southwell was executed nine years later, an event that Donne may well have witnessed firsthand, Donne's disposition towards his Catholicism and religion in general had apparently begun to sour. Just when, during the years that followed, Donne would compose his various religious poems, remains as I have noted, an unresolved question. Eventually John Donne would become a professed Protestant with a publicly belligerent view towards Jesuits like Robert Southwell, a more private ambivalence towards Catholics like his mother and other living members of his family, and a view of religion generally that was, by any accounts, complicated.

The complications were not without cause. Consider that if, at the age of sixteen, the young John Donne had resolved like George Herbert to send to his mother the New Year's gift of a couple of original sonnets, the content might not have been altogether different from those that Herbert sent his mother some 22 years later. After all, Donne's mother was an intractable recusant Catholic who never forgot that she was the grandniece of the revered Sir Thomas More as well as the niece of Thomas Heywood, formerly a monk of St. Osyth's. She was also the sister of two Heywoods who were Jesuit priests,[1] and was

1   See R. C. Bald who observes that "each successive generation of Mores for two and a half centuries supplied the Roman Church with

certainly as devout in her faith as Magdalene Herbert and would have welcomed if not expected such religious verse. Her son, who with his brother had already conspired in a lie about their ages so that the two could avoid taking the oath required by the Act of Supremacy and thereby enroll as secret Catholics at Hart Hall Oxford,[2] had been brought up in a household where the Catholic religion was a pervasive, provocative and even adventurous part of his life. "There was around him a constant sense of watchfulness, of whispered conversation and innuendo, of disguises and secret comings and goings" (Bald, 41). The notorious Jesuits Campion and Persons likely visited the Donne household, bringing word of Donne's Jesuit uncle, Jasper Heywood, who himself arrived in England to take charge of the Jesuit mission when his nephew John was nine years old.[3] Bald suggests the clandestine

devout servants who suffered civil disabilities or exile for their religion, and at least eight—four men and four women—were members of Roman Catholic religious orders" (23). See additionally Dennis Flynn's *Donne and the Ancient Catholic Nobility*: "Donne's mother was not only, like his father, a Catholic, but a member of one of the most celebrated Catholic families in the land. She was the youngest daughter of the poet and playwright John Heywood; and Heywood's wife—Donne's grandmother—was Joan Rastell, the niece of Sir Thomas More. So on his mother's side Donne was descended from the More circle, the foremost group of intellectuals in early sixteenth-century England, internationally famous, and devout Catholics" (16).

2   Hart Hall was "a favourite resort of Catholics because it lacked a chapel and so made avoidance of public worship easier" (Carey, 7).

3   Jasper and Ellis Heywood were sons of Donne's grandfather who both became Jesuit priests rather than pursue professions in England that would have no doubt been lucrative. The elder brother Ellis (1530–1578), was educated at Oxford and then went to Italy where he served Cardinal Pole. He was received into the Jesuits in 1573 and was assigned to the Jesuit College in Antwerp. Jasper (1535–1598), actually served as a page in the Court of Queen Elizabeth before heading to Oxford like his brother. He joined the Jesuits in Rome in 1562, eleven years earlier than Ellis. He taught Theology at Dillingen until 1581. After being in charge of the Jesuit mission in England, Jasper was captured and imprisoned in the Tower for over a year. Shown

priest likely spoke with the Donne children and "made a deep impression on" them (40). Marius Bewley suggests that the impression left upon Donne by his "learned and (by all reports) arrogant uncle Jasper was as unfavorable as it was powerful" (21). Donne and his siblings would also have witnessed firsthand the comings and goings of secret priests with pseudonyms, costumed as courtiers, hiding in priest holes, operating underground presses and presiding at secret liturgies. "The children," says John Carey, "found themselves in the middle of a real-life adventure story," adding abruptly, "It was no game" (6).[4]

John Donne was eighteen and Robert Southwell was four years into his mission when Donne posed for a portrait that is the earliest surviving image of the young poet. In it he postures himself confidently as the kind of recusant hero his mother hoped for him to be. Accompanying the picture is the bold inscription in Spanish *Antes muerto que mudado*—"Sooner dead than changed." Donne's most recent biographer, John Stubbs, observes that the phrase "Like almost every other feature of the portrait . . . doesn't quite fit" (26). But freshly returned from Italy and Spain only a few years after the sinking of the Armada, sporting a decorative cross earring in one ear, and grasping with his hand the hilt of a sword, Donne may be seen in this picture to be affecting a look not unlike one of *"the pyrates of both temporall and spirituall treasure"* (PS-M, 133), that he would later accuse the Jesuits of being. Carey describes the image in the portrait as "a young blood recently returned from the Continental travels" and suggests that his ornaments and militant stance "may be a flamboyant assertion of his loyalty to the old religion" (9). The portrait marks the time in Donne's life when he became a new resident at the Inns of Court in London, where he would study law from 1591 to at least 1594. Here in this world he would find the kind of religious and political intrigue that had been part of his own household. As Wilfred Prest describes it, the Inns were a notorious hotbed of recusant activity: "Apart from

leniency by the Queen, he would eventually die in exile in Naples. The most colorful anecdote surrounding Donne's two Jesuit uncles is that they shared portions of a tooth of Thomas More's that had miraculously split in two so that each could carry this prize relic.

4   John Carey, *John Donne: Life, Mind, and Art* (New York: Oxford UP, 1981).

the alluring prospect of a flood of well-born converts, the Inns lay conveniently beyond the jurisdiction of the city and suburban justices, while the constant traffic of lawyers, clients, students and servants helped cloak a priest's movements, particularly if he happened to be a former student himself and knew the lie of the land" (176). Carey notes that "Lincoln Inn Fields were notorious as a haunt of priests who, it was said, would blow a special trumpet to summon the Inns of Court men to mass" (10).

Bald describes Donne in this world of Thavies Inn in 1591 as "not only a Catholic, influenced and guided by Catholic tutors, but also in contact with the most active Catholic proselytizers in England" (63). Bald is referring specifically here to Southwell and Garnet. As John Klause observes, "Southwell must have been most familiar to him, for the Jesuit missionary seems to have centered his underground activities in London during the 1590s in the Ward of Farringdon . . . precisely where Donne, still a young Catholic gentleman from a family with Jesuit connections, was living and studying" (203). In November of 1591 the government introduced stricter regulations designed to discover and eliminate priests and Jesuits, including the sort who might be harboring in and around the Inns. The crackdown would soon bring dire consequences to both Donne and Southwell. One seeming initial outcome, however, was to bring them together in the same place. Robert Southwell authored a response to the stiffening laws, "a humble supplication" to Her Majesty which would be considered and approved for publication at a clandestine meeting in the Tower of London that December (Bald 63). Bald's original speculation that this was the meeting that Donne was referring to years later when he wrote in *Pseudo-Martyr* "For so at a Consultation of *Jesuites* in the *Tower*, in the late Queenes time, I saw it resolved, that in Petition to bee exhibited to her, shee might not be stiled *Sacred*" (*Pseudo-Martyr*, 46), remains credible, and would account for at least one gathering at which Donne, "a brilliant young layman" and Southwell, the featured presenter, were together and where Donne, in Bald's words, would "have felt his [Southwell's] influence" (64).

Within two years the government's increased vigilance would have a devastating personal impact upon Donne and his family. In 1593 he turned 21 and coming of age he inherited his share of the wealth his father had left, the substantial sum of 750 pounds. In the words of

Stubbs, Donne's "personal horizons finally opened" and he "became his own man" (27). Stubbs's assertion that Donne's "spiritual superintendents disappeared" (27) is less certain, but within a few months an event would occur that would permanently affect his view of religion. That spring Topcliffe's priest hunters apprehended a secular priest, William Harrington, in the lodgings of Donne's younger brother Henry. Harrington, in execution proceedings that were dramatically macabre even by Elizabethan standards, was hanged, drawn and disemboweled. Henry Donne was jailed first in the Clink in Southwark and then, possibly in a scheme by authorities to bilk him of the inheritance he had coming,[5] transferred to the plague-infested and fatal confines of Newgate where he died within a month. One further complication in this episode was the growing conflict between the Jesuits and secular priests developing at this time and the suspicion that Harrington's circumstances were made worse by the Jesuits and that his discovery and thus Henry Donne's death might even be attributed in some manner to the Jesuits.[6] Whether or not this was the case or whether Henry's brother John suspected it, the shock and grief of the catastrophe took hold of his older brother.

Two years later John Donne's religious disposition had changed measurably, so that as he moved towards apostasy, he might easily

5   Stubbs speculates as others have that the transfer of Henry Donne to the plague-infested Newgate, essentially a death sentence, "seems to have been a calculated move on the part of the civic authorities . . . Henry, like his brother, was due to receive this portion [about 500 pounds] of his father's estate at the age 'of Twentie and one yeres' (Will of John Donne Sr.). The city had already just parted with John's endowment: The following year another payment had to be made." Quoting the Jesuit historian, John Morris, S.J., Stubbs writes: "There was a whiff of foul play: Henry's removal from the relative safety of the Clink to almost certain fatality in Newgate was 'in all likelihood contrived of purpose, to defeat him of his money'" (44). See John Morris, "The Martyrdom of William Harrington," *The Month*, 20 (1874), 417. This is the same Fr. Morris who was responsible for drawing the attention of Gerard Hopkins to the writing of Robert Southwell. See Chapter 6 of the present study.

6   See Bald 67 ff.

have been able to feign indifference as Robert Southwell was dragged on a hurdle from Newgate Prison past the Inns of Court. Just below the surface, however, he would have harbored a tumultuous mixture of feelings. And if he witnessed Southwell's subsequent execution at Tyburn—as we know by his own account that he had once "seene at some Executions of Trayterous Priests, some bystanders, leaving all old Saints, pray to him whose body lay there dead" (*Pseudo-Martyr*, 222)—the event would have made a lasting and unshakeable impression upon him. As we shall see, during decades as a poet, polemicist, and preacher, martyrdom was a topic, a source of imagery, and a trope from which Donne could never escape. His emergent ambivalence towards and break from the old religion and his eventual professed hostility towards the Jesuits notwithstanding, Donne would not be rid of Robert Southwell on that winter day in 1595. If the poetry of Southwell provoked the attention of Edmund Spenser and offered instruction to George Herbert, it may be most accurate to say that the writings of this poet priest whom he had once admired actually haunted the young John Donne, and continued to haunt him throughout his life as an aspiring statesman, an ostracized public servant, a private poet, and eventually as a prominent clergyman.

Only in its most literal sense may *haunting* be regarded as too strong a description of Donne's relationship with the old religion of his family and the likes of Robert Southwell in whose mission he and they were inextricably entangled. We may contemplate, for example, as John Stubbs recently has, that in his later years Dr. Donne shared the Anglican Deanery of St. Paul's not just with his aging and unflinchingly devout Roman Catholic mother, but something, well, *more*. Stubbs suggests the very real possibility that secure within the Deanery household with mother and son was the remarkable relic of none other than great-grand-uncle, Sir Thomas More's decapitated head. "The head was probably smuggled into the Deanery of St Paul's when Donne's mother came to stay. Hidden under a bed or in a cupboard somewhere, the Dean's Papist background was with him up to the very end" (471–72).[7] Another, and far less macabre instance of Donne's

7   Stubbs describes the declining fortunes of Donne's son, John, who "managed to survive into the Restoration as one of the shabby, contentious poetasters that hung around Bloomsbury and Covent Garden

inability to shake off his Catholic past is the controversy that has persisted during recent decades over the nature of his conversion, the dramatic or not so dramatic event of his apostasy, and the question of Donne and religion in general.[8]

One of the more judicious voices in the discourse about Donne's religion is that of John Klause who in his thoughtful essay "Hope's Gambit: The Jesuitical, Protestant, Skeptical Origins of Donne's Heroic Ideal" treats the complexity of Donne's maturation and his various models of heroism. As the title of the essay indicates, Donne in his various writings emerges as a man whose changes and choices were several and were often at odds with one another. No one portrait can contain the various internal and external selves that he fashioned, but Klause makes a persuasive case that whatever the location of Sir Thomas More's head, Donne's Papist past and his Jesuit ancestry were indeed with him up until the end:

> As a poet Donne did his best to sound original, to write as though he had no forbearers, but since no writer is a

Market, a threadbare gentleman of letters drifting through the coffee houses . . . During Cromwell's Commonwealth he was obliged to sell many of his possessions . . . but did hang on to one extraordinary family heirloom. In his will, he bequeathed to a friend the head of his ancestor Sir Thomas More" (471). Thus, Stubbs speculates, the head likely came into the Deanery with the younger's Catholic grandmother. Though he does allow for the possibility that "the bequest is a mere bluff, or a joke on a family myth," (471).

8   This question is taken up in the latter part of this chapter in my discussion of the *Holy Sonnets*. Flynn and Carey are the most prominent recent critics to focus attention upon Donne's Catholic ancestry and persistent Catholic connections. Carey, in particular, provoked controversy by emphasizing the dramatic nature of the decision that confronted the young Donne. Carey argues that it was nothing less than a question of salvation or damnation. From most contemporary perspectives it more often seen as a pragmatic or even political choice. It is worth noting that in the most recent biography of Donne by John Stubbs, Robert Southwell receives only two brief mentions, both times as a source for information about what happened to captured Jesuits.

phoenix, Donne's singularity could not have been achieved without a host of affiliations, which scholars have tormented poems and libraries to find. As an English Protestant he suggested to the world, without *exactly* saying so, that he had rid himself of his old Catholic masters, announcing that he had undertaken to "blot out certain impressions of the Romane religion" which his family and his tutors had instilled in him, that he had "wrestle[d]" against "the examples and against the reasons" by which Catholic teachers of "learning and good life" had formed and directed him. Recent scholarship, however, has begun to reveal how imperfectly Donne was able to suppress or obliterate all the effects of his early education (185).

The recent scholarship to which Klause refers is now nearly two decades old and in his own assessments of Donne's life and writings he was pointing the way towards a realistic understanding of Donne's conversion and how the poet's thoughts and actions evolved in time with all of the complexities that would accompany the mind of a person who departs from "truths" to which members of his family had yielded their property and their lives. "In turning away from his Catholic heroes," Klause notes, "Donne did not run frantically toward Protestant ones" (186). As an example of Donne's more complex and reticent evolution, Klause points out that while Donne's "first declaration that he was a Protestant came in a letter to his father-in-law in 1602" (212), the recent discovery of his copy of the Jesuit Bellarmine's *Disputationes de controversis Christianae Fidei, adversus huius temporis haereticos*, which Isaac Walton tells us Donne studied in coming to his decision to follow the new rather than the old faith, turns out to be the 1603 edition, not the earlier printings as Bald and others had assumed. This suggests, according to Klause that "even after his defection from Rome, Donne's desire to 'do something' in the world at large came into conflict with his need to hide the full length of his personal mystery" (212). Rather than a clean and absolute break from his Catholicism and the Jesuit heroes of his youth, therefore, Donne's disposition was likely more complicated and dynamic. Klause poses the psychologically realistic scenario that "Donne as a young man sent part of himself underground, and we cannot be sure that it ever fully reemerged" (213).

None of this is to suggest that the vehement hostility towards the Jesuits that Donne expresses so colorfully in both *Pseudo-Martyr* and *Ignatius and His Conclave* was not genuine. Clearly by 1610, and likely well before that time, Donne came to regard the Jesuits, including presumably his two exiled and deceased uncles as well as the executed Robert Southwell, as his enemies. Nonetheless, as Klause notes, "a man's enemies may tell a lot about him, especially if they were once among his heroes. We diminish Donne's mystery if we ignore or simplify the relationship he had with the Jesuits even after his 'apostasy'" (189). Donne could not, Klause says of the Jesuits who had been his earliest heroes, "merely shuffle them off. They are everywhere in his writings" (189). And like Donne, they were prolific in their prose treatises. Yet among them only one, Robert Southwell, was a poet, and a poet whose devotional verse continued to proliferate during Donne's lifetime. The poet Southwell also shared vividly— in his verse, in his life and in his death—the subject that preoccupied Donne's own life and writing, *martyrdom*. As Klause so aptly observes, "Donne's most anxious engagement with the Company of Jesus was not over topics like justification, grace, faith and works, the eucharist, purgatory, or papal authority—about none of which he had anything singular or momentous to say. His most passionate investment in controversy with the Jesuits concerned, rather, the issue of martyrdom" (196). Describing his own history, and indeed his own haunting, Donne states bluntly in *Pseudo-Martyr*, "as I am a Christian, I have beene ever kept awake in a meditation of Martyrdome, by being derived from such a stocke and race, as I believe, no family . . . hath endured and suffered more in their persons and fortunes, for obeying the Teachers of Romane Doctrine, than it hath done" (*Complete Works*, 310). Donne's self-described wakeful meditation— which may be understood to be either spiritual alertness or, more literally, sleeplessness—yielded more than just polemical arguments about the topic of martyrdom. "Across fifteen years of his sermonizing," Klause rightly notes, "the subject never vanishes, as the preacher continually tries to convince his auditory that they would do better to choose a 'white,' milky martyrdom, or martyrdom of water, which is the virtuous life, over the martyrdom of blood, which brings no greater glory in heaven and is too problematic to be sought after and embraced" (197).

Whether or not the execution of William Harrington or Robert Southwell became a part of the meditation of martyrdom that kept Donne awake, we must imagine that he did not walk away from such gruesome political, religious spectacles unaffected. Indeed, where religion is concerned he seems to have come away resolutely *disaffected*. Whether or not the young Jack Donne departing the Inns of Court in the mid-1590s anticipated one day writing religious polemics, we can be reasonably certain I think that anyone predicting that he would one day be preaching in a church of any denomination, would have received a rebuttal seasoned in Jack's severest sarcasm. A similar retort might be levied at the one who dared to call Donne a poet. As Stubbs puts it, "Writing was just something he *did*: something he took seriously, and something he knew he could do well. It wasn't going to be his profession" (28). Nor, despite how we regard him today, did poetry ever become John Donne's profession. In his self-authored epitaph he does not mention ever having authored a poem, including many that are among the most famous in the English language.

Since he was not intent upon publishing his poems, it remains difficult to say when many of them, including his religious sonnets, were written. It is therefore unwise to use his poems to try to formulate a cohesive narrative of Donne's life from prodigal to penitent to priest. Nonetheless, we are presented with startlingly contrasting dispositions towards life and love by the various speakers in Donne's poetry. In the brash, sexualized and rakish wit of his cavalier and in the macabre meditations of his more monogamous lover we hear two things relevant to this present study: first, a conscious determination *not* to be Robert Southwell, and second, an unsuccessful effort to leave behind his meditation on martyrdom.

When in the 1590s Robert Southwell called upon poets to cease using poetry as a pagan toy by doing homage to Venus instead of Christ, he was chastising those who were blithely following the examples put forth in *Tottel's Miscellany*; and when he optimistically called upon more skillful wits than himself to follow his example of turning verse to religious use, he expresses the optimistic hope that a new generation of poets would turn away from the wanton ways of Elizabethan verse. What he did not imagine was a poet whose verses would make Sidney's *Astrophil and Stella* and Shakespeare's *Venus and Adonis* seem tame by comparison; a poet who would not only steer as far as possible from the kind of piety Southwell prescribed, but would re-ject as well the lofty Neoplatonic sentiment of the poet as refiner of nature that Sidney had put forth in his *Defense*. Troubled by the idol-atrous strains of Petrarchanism, Southwell could not have foreseen a poet who would not only style Venus's rose, but teach her the full sex-ual pleasures of promiscuousness so that "Variety she swore." That the young John Donne he had known in recusant circles would ex-change piety for the persona of a brash young cavalier lover, for whom a keen wit was the greatest weapon and sexual conquest the greatest virtue, would have startled and saddened Southwell had he lived to see it. And yet, like the young executed priest, Jack Donne was not a rebel without a cause.

His first intent seems to have been to perform a sort of cultural vandalism upon all things Elizabethan, providing in his early poems a caustic affront to the delicate, subtle and metered lovemaking that poets had been putting in print ever since *Tottel's Miscellany*. Thus, the carefully wrought irony of Sidney's *Astrophil* becomes unrestrained sarcasm in the brash sexual braggart of early Donne lyrics like "Song," "The Flea," "The Baite" and "Elegy XIX." Rule one in Petrarchanism is a single object of devotion. This is the first rule to go in Donne's electrifying retorts that today can still awaken undergraduates who have slumbered through Spenser and missed most of Sidney's jokes. Out with singular devotion go such old-fashioned virtues as faithful-ness. Women are objects of play, but as with Shakespeare's Touchstone the sexual joke is but a means not an end, and the end game in both of their cases is a critique of poets and poetry and its nauseating pre-tense. Donne is effectively calling the Petrarchan bluff. Thus more un-gently than Shakespeare in his more famous critique of Petrarchanism in Sonnet 130,[9] Donne proclaims:

9   Shakespeare's Sonnets of course were not printed until 1609. That Donne would have been aware of Sonnet 130 when he wrote this poem is possible though unlikely, nor is my treatment of the two son-nets together in this paragraph meant to infer imitation. The critique of well-worn hyperboles that describe a woman's beauty are conven-tional by the 1590s. Thus in their critique of Petrarchan conventions Shakespeare and Donne are both conventional. Southwell's critique of those conventions has, of course, a higher purpose.

I never stoop'd so low, as they
Which on an eye, cheeke, lip, can prey,
    Seldome to them, which soare no higher
    Than vertue or the minde to'admire
For sense, and understanding may
    Know, what gives fuell to their fire:
My love, though silly, is more brave,
For may I misse, when ere I crave,
If I know yet, what I would have
    ("Negative Love," 50).

The first seven lines here remind us of Shakespeare's catalogued refutation of conventional hyperbole in "My Mistresses eyes are nothing like the sun." But the lines recall as well Southwell's declaiming against such idolatry. The difference is that Shakespeare would conclude his sonnet with a couplet that invokes the witness of heaven to proclaim his resolved singular devotion—"And yet by heaven I think my love more rare / Than any she belied with false compare" (13–14). Southwell of course rejects all such temporal devotion as misspent devotion. But Donne's only resolution is no resolution. He admits that his love may be as "silly" as that of his Petrarchan-styled predecessors, but boasts that it is more "brave" because it lacks any particular object. Since he does not know yet what he is aiming at he cannot miss. The lack of resolution is further complicated by the potential double meaning of "love" as beloved in which case "my love, though silly" echoes the syntactic sense of Shakespeare's "my love more rare."

    Whether it is his craving or the object of his craving or both that are deemed silly, the speaker's lack of resolve to pursue a singular beloved might well be interpreted as cowardly, but by calling himself brave Donne's speaker connotes here the courage of capriciousness. Like a determined young man entering a bar, his sexual craving is indiscriminate and therefore his conquest more likely. This broad sexual desire is the same which he suspects is the case for his poetic predecessors who in the name of moral and aesthetic decorum have concealed their cravings in Petrarchan tropes and fevered meditations upon eyes and lips and cheeks when what they actually desire lay concealed several latitudes south in the human anatomy, territory off limits from written language unless it be cloaked in tropological disguise.

Thus Astrophil's exasperated sexual Desire casts aside virtue and declares "Give me some food!" Whereas Donne's speaker forgoes even that not-very-subtle metaphor, undressing with a shocking literalness the object of his craving: "License my roving hands, and let them go / Before, between, behind, above, below" (Elegy XIX," 5–6); "As liberally, as to a Midwife, shew / Thy self" ("Elegy XIX," 44–46).

If this sexual cavalier was an affront to the delicacies of most Elizabethan verse, it was even more of an affront to the memory of Robert Southwell whose complaint that English poets were "busy[ing] themselves in expressing such passions, as onely serve for testimonies to how unwoorthy affections they have wedded their wils," had gained a substantial readership. It is almost certain that Donne would have read Southwell's well published prefatory epistle, but even if he had avoided it he would have at least been well acquainted with the rhetorical arguments for the sacred use of poetry, arguments originating with eminent Jesuits like Jacobus Pontanus, the German scholar who had argued that poetry, indeed all arts, should not be regarded as an end in itself, that it must not only "teach while it delights," but "teach more than it delights." Pontanus critiques those "removed from virtue . . . filling up whole books with amatory lewdness" (Roberts, 67). Antonius Possevinus, he argued, while he had endorsed the honey coating of the didactic pill, insisted that "the first purpose of the poet must be to make his reader better" (Roberts, 67).

If the young Jack Donne displayed annoyance with Elizabethan Petrarchanism, he reacted to the Jesuit literary catechism of Pontanus and Southwell with the anger of a parochial school boy turned vandal. But of course sexually explicit words and phrases scrawled upon the chalkboard or the wall are never really about sex at all. Just so, for all of their superficial sexual energy, Donne's "libertine" poems seduce no attentive women and ultimately have little to do with real sex. Marius Bewley astutely was among the first to point this out in his 1970 chapter, "The Mask of Donne," where he observed "the 'libertine' poems may have been written, not as a celebration of sexual experience, but as a subconscious strategy to assist Donne in prying himself free of Rome. It is the kind of thing that might occur subconsciously to any Jesuit-trained young man in Donne's position" (24).

In doing so he made known his intention in the title of a poem that can serve as well as any as the coda of the cavalier: "The Indifferent,"

a moniker that signals far more than mere carelessness. In his introduction to his *Spiritual Exercises*, under the heading First Principle and
Foundation, Ignatius Loyola writes:

> Therefore, we must make ourselves indifferent to all created
> things, as far as we are allowed free choice and are not
> under any prohibition. Consequently, as far as we are con-
> cerned, we should not prefer health to sickness, riches to
> poverty, honor to dishonor, a long life to a short life. The
> same holds for all other things. Our one desire and choice
> should be what is more conducive to the end for which we
> are created (*Spiritual Exercises*, 12).

This ideal of indifference to all created things, which is but a radical
articulation of the Gospel instruction to "prefer nothing to the kingdom
of God," is one that Donne would refer to years later in writing
Pseudo-Martyr in his "declaration of my selfe." As Klause describes it:

> He avowed that in weighing the claims of old and new
> faiths he had come to a decision through "the ordinary
> meanes, which is frequent praier, and equall and indifferent
> affections" (B3r). "Ordinary" here means, not "common"
> or "usual," but "ordinate, appropriate to achieving an
> end"; and the appropriateness of "prayer" and "indiffer-
> ence" to making a "choice of a way of life" was precisely
> what Ignatius had insisted on in the *Spiritual Exercises*.
> Donne wanted the ghost, and anyone else who required an
> accounting of him, to know that he had complied by the
> rules ("Hope's Gambit," 191).

In assigning the title "The Indifferent" to what amounts to a cal-
lous catalogue of female types and an argument for sexual variety, the
young Donne's last concern was compliance with Jesuit rules. He did,
however, in misusing this hallmark of Jesuit spiritual teaching in this
way, want to let his readers know that he knew the rules and was making a mockery of them. Saint Ignatius instructs that "we must make
ourselves indifferent to all created things, as far as we are allowed free
choice and are not under any prohibition."

"Okay," responds the brash rake of Donne's poem:

I can love both faire and browne,
Her whom abundance melts, and her whom want betrays,
Her who loves lonenesse best, and her who maskes and plaies,
Her whom the country form'd and whom the town,
Her who believes, and her who tries,
Her who still weeps with spungie eyes,
And her who is dry corke, and never cries;
I can love her, and her, and you and you,
I can love any, so she be not true
    ("The Indifferent," 1–9).

Ultimately, the speaker's indifference "to all created things" leads him
to declare to his apparent audience of one female: "Let mee, and doe
you, twenty know / Rob mee, but binde me not, and let me goe" (15–
16). Venus, hearing him "sigh this song," is persuaded and swears "variety" as her new ideal with which she accordingly begins to
proselytize. It would be a stretch I think to read "The Indifferent" as
a loose allegory of religious belief or unbelief, though it does offer as
emphatic an ode to faithlessness and promiscuity as has ever been written. That Donne gave it a Jesuit branding signals not just his own disaffection with his former heroes, but the sort of unlikely manner in
which his past would haunt him even as he sought to put dramatic
distance between himself and the young man he had been.

Religious language punctuates Donne's elegies where it adds to the
shock value of his speaker's boasts and pleas for promiscuity and variety. In his satires mention of religion is more as a deliberate target,
and in poems like *Satire III* the poet is an equal opportunity critic of
Puritanism, Catholicism and Anglicanism. In poems where Donne
foregoes the posture of rakish boasting, he boasts instead of a love
that is superior in kind to the pedestrian affections of other lovers. In
doing so he inhabits the convention of Petrarchan singular devotion,
but does so in conceits eccentric enough to attract their own eigh-
teenth-century descriptor as *metaphysical*. Several of these poems
might in fact be characterized as "meditations of Martyrdome" as they
ponder the temporal and eternal endurance of love by contemplating
the speaker's death, disentombment and dissection, and blend

conventional narrative frameworks of love devotion with imagery that is both startlingly macabre and unrelentingly Roman Catholic. This results in poetic meditations that convey an unprecedented contemplation of the intertwining of flesh and soul, poems that contain a curious baroque mixture of medieval and modern imagery that simultaneously elevates sexual love and debases religious artifacts and beliefs. Among other things, these poems demonstrate the inescapable Catholic habit of mind that Carey, Klause and others have noted. Bewley offers a perceptive speculation of motives of that mind: "The religious imagery, the Scholastic terminology and logic in which he regularly speaks of erotic experience, serves to build up imaginatively the incomplete actuality, to endow it with some of the emotional satisfaction which the lapsing Catholic in him stood in need of, and some of the spiritual substance, at least in appearance, which he missed" (25). More recently, Stubbs describes both the practical and personal exigencies for why "the old language was still needed [for Donne] to speak in the present time" and why "Donne continued to use the symbolic apparatus of his first faith in his writing" (384). Echoing Bewley's insight, Stubbs surmises that "purging himself of such symbols, as the Protestants in Europe had would have been an unacceptable act of psychological vandalism, a childishly destructive rejection of his own heritage" (384).

Donne deploys the old language liberally in the fashioning of poems that have an essentially Petrarchan preoccupation with the singular devotion of a man to a woman and the inevitable contemplation of the lover's own death. What results from this mixture are several poems that are as purposeful as they are peculiar. For, as with the misappropriation of the term "indifferent" to boast of a promiscuous sampling of all "created things," there is here in these poems a method to the madness. The combination of Petrarchan and religious imagery in poems like "The Relic" results in a kind of sacrilege that signals, I believe, the poet's deliberate attempt to counter the successful poetic blending of the sacred and profane in the works of Robert Southwell. As Southwell had woven the web of religious content upon the loom of Elizabethan Petrarchan conventions, just so, Donne constructs several poems in which he weaves the language of Catholic devotion (miracles, adoration, martyrdom, idolatry, sainthood, incorruptibility, priests and bishops, cloisters, relics, funerals and dismemberment) onto the very Petrarchan loom that Southwell had used. He does so not with the intent of elevating love, but of debasing the idolatrous customs of the Roman Catholic religion; and in this peculiar process he manages to reignite the smoldering coals of Petrarchan poetry. To illustrate the complicated weaving that I believe Donne is undertaking in his reconverted loom, we may consider besides "The Relic" three other poems whose narratives originate with the speaker's tropological death.

"The Funeral" opens with the speaker voicing part of a last will and testament by declaring in the elaborate opening sentence:

> Whoever comes to shroud me, do not harm
>   Nor question much
> That subtle wreath of hair, which crowns my arm;
> The mystery, the sign you must not touch,
>   For 'tis my outward soul,
> Viceroy to that, which then to heaven being gone,
>   Will leave this to control,
> And keep these limbs, her provinces, from dissolution (1–8).

To understand the radical affront that this stanza of poetry is to conventional Christian orthodoxy, we need only consider the dying wishes of a devout Christian, who might well desire to be buried with a rosary or other outward sign of his or her Sovereign, the Viceroy Christ, who alone can preserve the dying person's soul from damnation. In the above scene, the speaker wears "a subtle wreath" of hair about his arm that he not only calls his "outward soul," but his Viceroy. Christ's role as sovereign is displaced by the speaker's beloved, and her hair is not worn to protect the speaker from damnation, but to preserve his body from decay ("dissolution"). Incorruptibility is of course one of the most notable signs for Roman Catholic canonization for sainthood. Donne here twists this Roman Catholic custom to claim that his beloved Viceroy when "to heaven being gone" will, by way of her wreath of hair, keep "her provinces," his limbs, "from dissolution." Incorruptibility, which ought to serve as a sign of a dead person's sanctity, is here mocked by Donne, who has his beloved's wreath of hair serve as its cause. He further parodies the purpose for the flesh's preservation, not as an outward sign of holiness, but simply for the sovereign mistress to preserve her property, the speaker's dead limbs.

In the second stanza the speaker reasons quite peculiarly that if the "sinewy thread" (9) of his own hair holds his body together, then hairs which "upward grew . . . from a better brain, / Can better do it" (12–14). Immediately, however, within the very same line that he completes this odd physiological reasoning, he questions his beloved's intent in placing the wreath about his arm. "Except [unless] she meant that I / By this should know my pain, / As prisoners then are manacled, when they are condemned to die" (14–16). The pain of the condemned prisoner is presumably of the Petrarchan kind, and the image also hints ever so subtly at the fate of an accused Catholic traitor. Both of these thoughts are made explicit in the final stanza, which offers the conventional resolution of a scorned lover and a parody of Catholic martyrdom and idolatry.

The meaning of the subtle wreath of hair is left ambiguous: "Whate'er she meant by it, bury it with me" (17). For, he reasons, whether she intended it to preserve him or to torment him, "I am / Love's martyr" (19) and "If into others' hands these relics came" (20) they "might breed idolatry" (19). The gathering of relics at the scene of gruesome executions of priests like Southwell was familiar to Donne, and as noted, something that he witnessed first-hand, and with apparent disgust. Here he mocks the practice of what he regards as idolatry, making the relic a love token whose intention is at best ambiguous, and potentially sinister. He then retreats into the conventional complaint of a Petrarchan lover, acknowledging that it was an act of humility to "afford to it [the wreath of hair] all that a soul can do, / So," he concludes "'tis some bravery / that since you would save none of me, I bury some of you" (21–24). The speaker's beloved devolves in the course of the three stanzas from a Viceroy who sought to preserve him from dissolution with a sensual relic to an unappreciative lover who would not even save the speaker by reciprocating his love. His body and his soul are left to what comes after he is shrouded, and the wreath about his wrist is but a sign of his own misplaced affection, an "idolatry" to which he has become what Donne would assuredly call a pseudo-martyr.

Love martyrdom is displayed in an even more macabre fashion in "The Relic," a companion piece to "The Funeral," in which a lover speaks directly to his beloved about the wreath of her hair that others shall discover on the wrist of his corpse. The poems share not only this peculiar symbol, but a similar theme and intricate narrative argument by which Catholic customs are parodied.

The poem begins with the speaker forecasting his inevitable displacement by way of the common, grisly practice of graveyard double-stacking, the same conservation custom by which the bones of the jester Yorick were jostled in order to make room for Ophelia: "When my grave is broke up again," the speaker casually begins, "Some second guest to entertain" (1–2). Whereas "The Funeral" sustains a tone of high seriousness in its opening stanza, this poem strikes an immediate cynical tone, registering a conventional complaint against this unbecoming burial practice by placing its origins with unfaithful women: "(For graves have learned that woman-head / To be more than one a bed)" (3–4). We recall that coming upon such excavation in the churchyard, Hamlet is shocked not by the excavation of previously interred bones, but by the gravedigger's casual singing at such macabre work. Here in this poem, the sacredness of the graveyard is not just undermined by the unsightly necessity of grave-sharing, but by the speaker's sexual joke that mocks it. One other historical reason for disrupting a grave, besides a shortage of sacred real estate, of course, might be relic hunting, and in this instance the relic discovered is the familiar profane sacramental from "The Funeral": "A bracelet of bright hair about the bone" (6).

This bracelet of bright hair (presumably bright white by now), while assigned a specific meaning by the speaker, is in danger of being misinterpreted by those who would assign it their own sacred meaning. "Will he not let us alone?" the speaker pleas rhetorically, "And think that there a loving couple lies, / Who thought that this device might be some way / To make their souls, at the last busy day, / Meet at this grave, and make a little stay?" (7–11). The "us" which refers to the man's bones and the encircling bracelet also signals the couple whose planned rejoining on the day of judgment may be disrupted by the digging intruder. Even worse, the gravedigger might misinterpret the macabre love souvenir as a religious relic.

The speaker fears that if he and his wreath are disinterred "in a time, or land, / Where mis-devotion doth command, / Then he that digs us up, will bring / Us, to the Bishop, and the King, / To make us relics" (11–14). His mocking of Roman Catholic excess is punctuated when he cautions his beloved that the religious authorities will use her wreath of hair to make of her a mis-devotion, "a Mary Magdalene," the most popular counter-reformation saint, an important figure of devotion for English recusants, and of course the one whose tears and complaints as described by Robert Southwell had apparently caused more than one Catholic conversion. He surmises: "Thou shalt be a Mary Magdalene, and I / A something else thereby;" (18–19). The ambiguous humor of this latter line anticipates the comic punchline of the poem's final line. The man in possession of a wreath of hair from an iconic converted prostitute would certainly be "a something else" and he implies that the fanciful Bishops would concoct a narrative to invite the mis-devotion of the faithful.

Since we shall be adored in that future time by "all women . . . and some men" (19), the speaker resolves, inferring apparently that women are more given to the fancies of mis-devotion, "I would have that age by this paper taught / What miracles we harmless lovers wrought" (21–22). If we are prepared here for the worst possible parody of religious devotion by way of a description of sexual love, the single word "harmless" signals that the poem is not going to move explicitly in that profane direction. In fact, whereas the narrative progression of "The Funeral" is from the sacred to the profane (from mystery to scorn), "The Relic" would seem to progress from profane to sacred, from promiscuity to chastity, until its suggestive final couplet.

Whatever phantasms misguided Bishops might assign to these relics, the miracle of this couple, the speaker assures us, was simply to have "loved well and faithfully" (23). So pure was their love that "Difference of sex no more we knew, / Than our guardian angels do" (25–26). "Coming and going" they "Perchance might kiss, but not between those meals" (27–28); nor, he insists, did their hands touch "the seals / Which nature, injured by late law, sets free" (29–30). The implication here is that though it would have been natural to have sex, and that the laws that prohibit it are injuring nature, the couple nonetheless obeyed the law. "These miracles we did." This straightforward declaration of the couple's chaste love contrasts with the cynicism in which the poem began, such that the poet very nearly ends the poem with a kind of religious earnestness. That is, until the poem's final couplet in which the speaker declares slyly: "All measure, and all language, I should pass, / Should I tell what a miracle she was" (32–33). The suggestiveness of this final line—bolstered by the declaration early in the poem of women being "more than one a bed"—resides somewhere between the worshipful declaration of Shakespeare's final couplet in Sonnet 130, "And yet I believe my love more rare / Than any she belied with false compare" (13–14), and the more salacious outburst of Desire in Philip Sidney's Sonnet 73: "Give me some Food!"

We may therefore note the following progression in the argument of "The Relic." The first relic in the poem is the bright bracelet of hair about the bone of the speaker's corpse. He fears that an age of false devotion will make Roman Catholic relics (pseudo-martyrs) of the two of them. Then, in documenting the saintly qualities that could accompany their canonization, he deploys the most common of Petrarchan tropes, making an idol of his beloved whose qualities surpass words. The poem thus veers into religious subject matter long enough to mock Roman Catholic "mis-devotion," though its main narrative thread, if the bracelet of bright hair is correctly understood, brings us to the conventional profession of Petrarchan idolatry against which Southwell had complained years before. As final punctuation to this narrative, the speaker deploys his wit to suggest the ambiguous nature of his own mis-devotion. Namely that the miraculous qualities of his beloved were something other than the miracle of chastity.

A third Donne poem that begins with the speaker's death features not a shrouding or disinterment, but an autopsy. "The Damp," a title connoting a pestilent vapor as well as the speaker's eventual death stupor,[10] presents an extreme version of Petrarchan complaint, wherein the speaker tells his lady:

> When I am dead and Doctors know not why,
>   And my friends curiosity
> Will have me cut up to survey each part,

10 The O.E.D. offers "1. An exhalation, a vapour or gas, of a noxious kind . . ." and "2. visible vapour: fog, mist" with the examples here being mostly from Shakespeare, and "4. A dazed or stupefied condition; loss of consciousness" with examples from 1442 through Milton and Adison.

When they shall find your Picture in my heart,
    You think a sudden damp of love
    Will through their senses move,
And work on them as me, and so prefer
Your murder to the name of Massacre (1–8)

The performing of a primitive autopsy by friends, while it would be-come vogue among scientists in the later eighteenth century,[11] would have been regarded as an eccentric sacrilege in Donne's time, no matter the age of the deceased. What was not uncommon, of course, and what Donne had himself witnessed, was the public spectacle of dis-emboweling bodies not yet dead and dismembering them afterwards, the formulaic torture and execution reserved for the likes of Harring-ton, Southwell and all other Catholics convicted as traitors. Whether Donne had ever witnessed a heart being removed during such proceed-ings cannot be known, though at Southwell's trial an exasperated at-torney general, Sir Edward Coke, defending the tortures performed by Richard Topcliffe, declared, "We will tear your hearts out of a hundred of your bodies" (Brownlow, *Robert Southwell*, 19).[12]

The aortal relic unceremoniously removed from the "Damp's" speaker in his grim prophecy parodies the popular Catholic icon of the Sacred Heart that originated among mystics in the middle ages; the Sacred Heart is seen only in images of Christ or Mary and is rep-resented as within the center of their chest, or sometimes held in the hand; it is encircled by a crown of thorns, bleeding from wounds and often accompanied by a cross and/or a flame. In the apparently love-wounded heart of Donne's speaker his friends will behold an image of his object of devotion, "your Picture in my heart." As with those

11 See for example the description of the scientists of the French Acad-emy in the eighteenth and nineteenth centuries in Russell Shorto's *Descartes' Bones*.

12 In her book *The Trail of Martyrdom*, Sarah Covington cites Foxe's description of Protestants seizing relics of one John Hullier: "His flesh being consumed, his bones stood upright even as if they had been alive . . . Of the people, some took what they could get of him, as pieces of bones. One had his heart, the which was distributed so far as it would go" (Covington 178).

beholding the sacred heart, the audience here will be awed and recognizing the power of her face to "work on them as me" will prefer to murder her—destroy the heart as well as the woman presumably—lest she be allowed to massacre them. Murder and massacre might both be avoided, he tells her, if she would kill "th'enromous *Gyant*, your *Disdaine*" (11) and "let th'enchantress Honor, next be slain" (12). If she is unwilling to kill her own disdain and honor, he prefers, he says, that she "Kill me as a Woman, let me die / As a mere man" (21–22), for "Naked you have odds enough of any man" (24). The common sexual double entendre of "let me die" and the final bawdy joke upon naked odds combine with the maudlin allusion to the plague in the poem's title and the astounding hyperbole of the entire lyric to make this one of Donne's most curious poems. Its Petrarchan-style scorn is matched only by "The Apparition," where the speaker declares "When by thy scorn, O murderess, I am dead," and goes on to prophesy his ghost's future visit to her bed where she is with her new man. He could spare her the fate from which she will be suffering then (apparently venereal disease contracted from her new lover) if he were to tell her now what he will wait and tell her then.

These poems demonstrate, if not an ongoing "meditation of martyrdome," Donne's steadfast preoccupation with death displayed in what could even be taken as a mockery of the resurrection as they move from preparation for burial to the discourtesy of disentombment, to the extracting of body parts by friends, to the return of the speaker's ghost to haunt the living. The poems were apparently written while Donne was in the service of Lord Egerton, a man who, as Stubbs puts it, was more

> than a prosecuting counsel or judge in the campaign of terror against leading Roman Catholics in the 1590s. Appointed Attorney General in 1592, Egerton became the operational head of the police system that ensnared, captured and tortured these enemies of the crown—many of whom [like Harrington and Southwell] were known to Donne personally (90).

This campaign of capture and torture had subsided by the time Donne came to work for Egerton (Stubbs, 91), but the young secretary might find himself copying out missives from his boss such as the bill that declared of recusant Catholics that they were "natural vipers, ready to eat out the belly of your mother" (Stubbs, 91). Fortunately for Donne his own mother was—belly intact—living in exile in Antwerp when he entered the service of Egerton. His brother and his Jesuit uncles were all dead, so he had no explaining to do to any but himself.

Stubbs suggests that if Donne were to leave behind Catholic language altogether he would have been "unable to articulate some of his deepest spiritual concerns" (384). However, when Donne takes to the spheres and leaves behind the trappings of both the religious language and the Petrarchan narrative that haunted him, I would argue that he actually achieves his purest and most original verse in signature poems like "A Valediction Forbidding Mourning," "Air and Angels," and "The Ecstasy." Consider, for example, the contrast between the martyr-haunted poems examined above and Donne's "Dissolution." The word, which he uses in "The Funeral" to mean physical decay, is deployed here to describe instead the dissolving of the speaker's sorrow, not by way of conventional religious consolation, but by way of a metaphysical meditation. Absent from this poem are casual descriptions of the dead body, satiric joking about relics and any remnant of Petrarchan complaint. Instead, this poem offers a meditation on the oneness of the lovers' elements—flesh and spirit. "Dissolution" describes not decay, but the metaphysical transformation wrought by death in two who are joined as one flesh and soul. "She is dead," the poem begins starkly, and then begins a complex metaphysical syllogism: "and all which die / To their first elements resolve; / And we were mutual elements to us, / And made of one another. / My body then doth hers involve" (1–5). The logic of grief is that being "mutual elements" the two will endure the same fate. He will decay emotionally and physically just as she decays. Instead, through an argument and syntax equally complex, the speaker resolves that his "sighs of air / Water of tears, and earthly sad despair" (9–10) are materials of his that she "doth by her death repair" (13). He might live long thus, except that the more she replenishes the more he spends in grief because "This death, hath with my store / My use increased" (20–21). He concludes his meditation with the peculiar conceit of bullets being fired from a gun. His soul, he declares, has been "more earnestly released" than his beloved's and "Will outstrip hers; / as bullets flown before / A latter bullet may o'ertake, the powder being more" (22–24).

Donne's Neoplatonic masterpieces that focus attention upon the dexterity and everlastingness of the individual soul and the purity of joined souls put him clearly on the "winding stair" side of the question of how to ascend towards the divine in poetry. By 1608, with his apostasy and dramatic secret marriage well behind him and resulting professional and financial uncertainty still before him, Donne was far from imagining a career in the church, and his deployment of religious language for a wide variety of poetic purposes notwithstanding, the writing of the devout poems for which he is best known was something that still lay in front of him.

What prompted him to fashion these poems is difficult to know, but Frank Brownlow, among others, recognizes Robert Southwell's handprints in Donne's first attempt at writing conventional religious verse, and suggests that his motivations for turning to religious poetry at this time were, like his authorship of *Pseudomartyr*, as much external as internal. Noting that "there is always an element of social performance, even of display" in Donne's presentation of a theme ("Sonnets," 6–7), Brownlow observes:

> As for the religious poems that he was writing about the same time, they reflect, besides his own interests, those of the courtly circles in which he was moving, which included male friends like Henry Goodere, Sir Henry Wotton, and the earl of Dorset as well as those fashionable and devout ladies, the countess of Bedford and Mrs. Herbert. Those interests were social and cultural as well as religious; Donne was writing stylized love poems to Mrs. Herbert and the countess at the same time that he was writing them equally stylish religious poems ("John Donne," 4–5).

That his religious poems were stylish does not of course preclude Donne's expression of sincere religious devotion. There is no more difficult thing to accurately detect and assess in a work than the sincerity of an artist, whose words can move deftly on the springs of ironic tension even while resting upon underpinnings of emotional earnestness.

Several elements of Donne's' earliest religious sonnets, "La

Corona," reflect the lingering influence of Robert Southwell. First and most obvious is the subject matter of the seven linked sonnets that narrate events in the lives of Mary and Jesus. Donne offers an introductory prayer and then treats the Annunciation, the Nativity, the Temple, the Crucifixion, the Resurrection and the Ascension. Years earlier Southwell had fashioned a similar sequence of fourteen poems, meditative narratives that begin with Mary's Conception and end with her Assumption. Louis Martz suspected that both poets' sequences referenced a version of the Rosary called "the Corona of our Lady," but as no such form of the Rosary has ever been found, it is generally agreed that the connections between the sequences and the Rosary are only the broad similarities the mysteries treated. Though Southwell's sequence is more Roman Catholic in subject matter, with Mary being the central subject of each poem as well as the thematic energy of the sequence, Donne's shorter sequence actually behaves more like a Rosary. To form his crown he uses the device of anadiplosis, wherein the last clause of one sonnet serves as the first of the next, and ultimately the seven poems are "clasped" into a circle when the first line of the first sonnet is used as the last line of the seventh sonnet. Another trait of Donne's "La Corona" that reflects possible influence from Southwell is the relatively impersonal tone upon which many critics have remarked. In comparison to the rest of his poetry, these seven poems are unusually calm and elegant. Only two of the poems have no first person pronoun, but the intrusions of the "my" into the others seem genuinely and unobtrusively pious. The dramatic, insistent, energetic and unpredictable "I" of Donne's other poems, including his other religious sonnets, is kept at bay by the earnest petitions of "my hands" and "my soul." The uninterrupted piety in these sonnets does not by itself indicate the influence of Southwell's relentlessly earnest religious poems, but Southwell certainly would have been delighted to see what Donne, with his "skillfuller wit," had achieved in this crown of seven prayers. Brownlow notes that the poems of Southwell's Sequence on the Virgin Mary and Christ were "popular and well known" and "easily accessible to him [Donne] in the manuscripts which circulated throughout the seventeenth century" (7). He suggests that at the very least "Donne's approach" to "La Corona" "was based on Southwell's" (7).

The approach that the two poets share in common is traceable to their common Ignatian origins, and specifically the application of *The*

Spiritual Exercises. Over a half century ago Louis Martz identified Southwell as the first English poet to bring to the writing of poetry "the elaborately detailed explanation of the Jesuit's 'application of the senses' to the art of meditation."[13] Martz summarized it thus:

> Everyday life must come to play its part, for the meditative man must feel that the presence of God is here, now, on his own hearth, in his own stable, and in the deep center of the mind: thus [in St. Ignatius's words] "we may help ourselves much to the framing of spiritual conceits, if we apply unto our matter familiar similitudes, drawne from our ordinary actions, and this as well in historicall, as spirituall meditations" (introduction, *English Seventeenth Century Verse,* V 1).

For Southwell of course such instructions were an integral part of his daily life, the spiritual discipline that sustained him. For Donne they were part of a past that he had forsaken, but as becomes apparent in reading his "Holy Sonnets," they offered an artistic approach that he found useful, if not irresistible. In fact, the unusually staid tone of Donne's "La Corona" may have resulted from a combination of his general apprehension in approaching religious subject matter and his misapplication or even mis-remembering of one of the initial instructions in *The Exercises* that directs the participant:

> In all the Spiritual Exercises which follow, we make use of the acts of the intellect in reasoning, and of the acts of the will in manifesting our love. However, we must observe that when in acts of the will we address God our Lord or His saints either vocally or mentally, greater reverence is required on our part than when we use the intellect in reasoning (2).

13 Martz first drew readers' attention to Ignatian influence in seventeenth-century poetry in his 1947 ELH article, "John Donne in Meditation: The Anniversaries." He developed his case for Ignatian influence significantly for his first major book, *The Poetry of Meditation,* in 1954.

In fashioning "La Corona" Donne seems to have taken to heart the "acts of intellect in reasoning" necessary to fashion religious poetry and to have forgotten or deliberately shied away from Ignatius's instructions that require the participant's intellect and will to be engaged through concentrated attention to the sensory elements of the Gospel stories, where Christ is the central figure.

Southwell, on the other hand, understood all too well the intent and method of these exercises. Practicing them daily, he knew better than most that in the deep center of the mind the presence of God is here, now, on this hearth, in this stable, or perhaps down in this priest hole. As Martz first pointed out, Southwell the poet did not hesitate to translate *The Exercises'* intended spiritual outcomes to artistic ones. In fact, one need not go searching for a lost version of the rosary to find the origins of Southwell's Sequence as well as the subjects of each of the poems in Donne's crown of poems. The verses of each are traceable to the instructions for the first day of the second week of *The Spiritual Exercises*:

103. SECOND PRELUDE. This is a mental representation of the place. It will be here to see the great extent of the surface of the earth, inhabited by so many different peoples, and especially to see the house and room of our Lady in the city of Nazareth in the province of Galilee (49).

112. SECOND PRELUDE. This is a mental representation of the place. It will consist here in seeing in imagination the way from Nazareth to Bethlehem. Consider its length, its breadth; whether level, or through valleys and over hills. Observe also the place or cave where Christ is born; whether big or little; whether high or low; and how it is arranged (52).

114. FIRST POINT. This will consist in seeing the persons, namely, our Lady, St. Joseph, the maid, and the Child Jesus after His birth. I will make myself a poor little unworthy slave, and as though present, look upon them, contemplate them, and serve them in their needs with all possible homage and reverence. Then I will reflect on myself that I may reap some fruit (52).

116. THIRD POINT. This will be to see and consider

what they are doing, for example, making the journey and laboring that our Lord might be born in extreme poverty, and that after many labors, after hunger, thirst, heat, and cold, after insults and outrages, He might die on the cross, and all this for me (53).

FIRST POINT. This consists in seeing in imagination the persons, and in contemplating and meditating in detail the circumstances in which they are, and then in drawing some fruit from what has been seen (54–55).

SECOND POINT. This is to hear what they are saying, or what they might say, and then by reflecting on oneself to draw some profit from what has been heard (55).

THIRD POINT. This is to smell the infinite fragrance, and taste the infinite sweetness of the divinity. Likewise to apply these senses to the soul and its virtues, and to all according to the person we are contemplating, and to draw fruit from this (55).

FOURTH POINT. This is to apply the sense of touch, for example, by embracing and kissing the place where the persons stand or are seated, always taking care to draw some fruit from this (55).

On the second day of this week of *Exercises*, meditations move from the nativity proper to the Presentation in the Temple, the Flight into exile in Egypt (57). On the third day contemplations include the Obedience of the Child Jesus to His parents and Finding of the Child Jesus in the Temple. Exercises may be lengthened to include the Visitation of Mary to Elizabeth, the Shepherds, the Circumcision of the Child Jesus, the Three Kings, and also others (67–68).

One need not agree entirely with Scott Pilarz that Southwell's "writings should be understood as an exercise in pious utilitarianism" ("To Help Souls," 42) to recognize from the very titles of Southwell's *The Sequence on the Virgin Mary and Christ*, that he fashioned its first twelve poems from the Spiritual meditations above. This is why *The Sequence* begins with meditations upon Mary in Nazareth, including "The Virgine Maries conception," "Her Nativity," "Her Spousals," and "The Virgins salutation." These are followed by "The Visitation," "The Nativitie of Christ," "His circumcision," "The Epiphanie," "The

Presentation," "The Flight into Egypt," "Christs returne out of Egypt" and "Christs Childhoode." The manner of contemplation that encourages the participant to use his senses to contemplate "in detail the circumstances" which the biblical characters are in, thereby "drawing some fruit from what has been seen" yields some provocative images such as Mary traveling by foot to see her cousin Elizabeth, performing acts of charity as she goes: "With Pilgrim foote, up trying hils she trod / And heavenly stile with handmaids toile acquaints, / Her youth to age, her health to sicke she lends, / Her heart to God, to neighbor hand she bends" (3-6). Southwell calls Mary a prince who a "mightier prince doth beare." His meditation upon the young, pregnant woman's journey through the rough landscape leads him to consider the awful possibility that she might fall; hence "heavenly Quires attendant were, / Her child from harme her selfe from fall to save," (10).

Donne's "La Corona" is virtually absent of such provocative details as these. If it is the Ignatian act of intellect and reasoning that prompted him in these verses, he seems not to have had any interest in the accompanying Romish act of "smell[ing] the infinite fragrance, and tast[ing] the infinite sweetness of the divinity" or the even more idolatrous act of "apply[ing] the sense of touch, for example, by embracing and kissing the place where the persons stand or are seated, always taking care to draw some fruit from this." Nonetheless, the opening sonnet in Donne's sequence contains two echoes which indicate that Southwell may have offered Donne both a rationale for and a way forward in composing religious verse. Both of these echoes, however, come, not from Southwell's Sequence, but from his chastising of English poets. Up until his writing of "La Corona" Donne's poetry had mostly ranged from the shockingly scandalous to the slightly impious. Whether "La Corona" was primarily to please a devout patroness or whether it arose, as the poet claims, out of his own "devout melancholy," it represents a sharp departure from the poetry that preceded it. It is interesting, therefore, that of all the verbs that Donne might have used to describe this departure and the writing of these, his first religious poems, he chose as his central action of composition Southwell's signature metaphor for reforming poetry: weaving. "Because the best course to let them see the error of their works is to weave a newe Webb in theire owne loome," Southwell had proselytized in his well-known epistle. More perhaps in a long delayed resignation than in tribute, Donne begins "La Corona" with this prayer: *"Deign at my hands this crown of prayer and praise,* / Weav'd in my low, devout melancholy" (l. 1–2).

A few lines later we may again recognize shades of Southwell's influence as Donne describes the central symbol of his sequence, the crown:

> But do not, with a vile crown of frail bays,
> Reward my muse's white sincerity.
> But what thy thorny crown gain'd, that give me,
> A crown of glory, which doth flower always (l. 5–8).

Donne could not be any sharper in his departure from the kind of poetry that Southwell called "paynim toyes" than to reject as "vile" the poet's laurel crown of "frail bays." He petitions that the white sincerity of his muse be rewarded not with Christ's crown of suffering, but the fruit that it gained, "a crown of glory" with everlasting flowers. In the background of this imagery we may recognize the Jesuit poet from whom Donne had turned long ago. Southwell, in his prefatory verse to *Saint Peter's Complaint*, contrasted the crown worn by Christ with the frail flowers worn by English poets:

> "Christ's Thorne is sharp, no head his Garland weares:
> Still finest wits are stilling Venus Rose
> In paynim toyes the sweetest vaines are spent:
> To Christian workes, few have their talents lent" (l. 15–18).

Southwell here identifies the poet's laurel crown as a vain and comfortable "Garland" in contrast to the crown of suffering worn by Christ. By perceiving the implicit shame in sporting the iconic laurel wreath even in light of Christ's own bloody crowning, we better understand Donne's choice of the words "vile" to describe this "crown of frail bays." Interestingly, though, Donne avoids here any "meditation of martyrdome." Unlike his executed predecessor, Donne seeks no share in Christ's suffering, only what "thy thorny crown gain'd," namely an eternal garland.

Other possible echoes of Southwell in Donne's "Corona" may well be simply a matter of overlapping subject matter or common Ignatian method, as when Donne describes Christ's conception using the clothing metaphor: "and though he there / Can take no sin, nor thou give, yet he'll wear, / Taken from thence, flesh, which deaths force may try" ("Annunciation," 6–8). Southwell had similarly described Mary's own conception, "Our second Eve putts on her mortall shrowde" ("The Conception of our Ladie" 1). In the same sonnet Donne dwells on the paradoxes of Christ's conception: "Whom thou conceiv'st, conceiv'd; yea thou art now / Thy Maker's maker, and thy Father's mother" (l. 11–12). In his Sequence Southwell had declared with less elegance, but more dramatic succinctness : "Behold the father is his daughters sonne" ("The Nativity of Christ," 1).

Brownlow's assessment of "La Corona" as more of a triumph of wit than devotion, reaching its conclusions more by verbal play than logic, is certainly fair, as are his observations that Donne's syntax is more complex, and all would agree that his "sonnets are technically more accomplished than Southwell's" (8). That "Southwell's sequence makes the stronger effect because the poems are focused entirely upon their materials" (8) is a judgment with which I happen to concur, but others might find the intrusion of the speaker's own self and his own spiritual concerns, no matter how unresolved, precisely what makes the sonnets more interesting than Southwell's Sequence.

In fact, in "Crucifying" when the speaker prays, "Now thou art lifted up, draw me to thee" (12), the poet may be heeding Ignatius's instruction to consider how "after insults and outrages, He might die on the cross, and all this for me" (116. THIRD POINT, 53). In any case, it seems that Donne conceived of his sequence with an eye to Southwell's, as well as to their shared prescriptions in *The Spiritual Exercises*, albeit with a determination to fashion something different from pious Jesuit devotions. Thus, while Southwell's poems engage our senses, "La Corona" is more like a reformed style church. Its piety is cold and bloodless. Neither the meditation upon the crown of thorns, nor Donne's sonnet on the crucifixion yield more than "one drop of thy blood" to moist "my dry soul" ("Crucifying" 14). By contrast Southwell offers readers a descriptive poem on Christ's circumcision, with the startling first line, "The head is launc't to worke the bodies cure" (1). Before we contemplate the paradox, we first wince at the act. Nor does the poet relent. The second stanza begins, "The veyne of life distilleth droppes of grace / Our rock gives yssue to an heavenly springe / Teares from his eyes blood runnes from the wounded place" (l. 7–9). Such baroque imagery is the very kind that Donne seems intent on avoiding.

Interestingly, the other element of "La Corona" that causes them, in Brownlow's opinion, to fail as liturgical devotion, is an element which, as seen above in "Crucifying," may actually be Ignatian; namely the fact that from the first line to its repetition at the end, Donne's "Corona" is about the speaker's own spiritual circumstance. When Southwell translates the imaginative meditations resulting from *The Spiritual Exercises* into verse, he does so, not for his own benefit, but for the spiritual edification of his readers.[14] His *Sequence* is no exception. Implicit in each of the poems as well as the cohesive narrative is the matter of *our* salvation, which is understood as general, rather than individualized. One cannot conceive of Southwell declaring, as Donne does in the final poem of "La Corona": "O strong ram, which has batter'd heaven for me" (l. 9). The action of battering as well as this individualized act of salvation[15] forecast the poet's more bold and famous religious sonnets which, though few in number, offer a combination of recognizable Ignatian construct, Petrarchan-style wizardry, spiritual ambiguity and seeming personal angst. Consequently they

14 Referencing Anthony Raspa's 1983 study, *The Emotive Image: Jesuit Poetics in the English Renaissance* (Fort Worth: Texas Christian University Press), Helen Brooks reminds readers in her recent essay of the distinction between "an unresolved conflict in the Ignatian model between the Protestant-like emphasis on a private, inward spirituality and the Roman Catholic emphasis on a communal, or church- mediated spirituality" (103), as well as the difference between the deployment of meditation like the Exercises for aesthetic rather than ascetic purposes (103). See Helen B. Brooks, "When I would not change in vowes, and in devotione": Donne's 'Vexations' and the Ignatian Meditative Model, *John Donne Journal* 19 (2000), 101–137.

15 The "I" of Ignatian self-examination blurs with "a particular application to the self, analogous to the 'application' so prominent in Protestant sermons of the period" (148), by which Barbara Lewalski reads Donne's verse as part of the Protestant poetic (see *Protestant Poetic* in fn 16).

have attracted as much critical commentary as anything Donne wrote. As Gary Kuchar states succinctly, "Donne's *Holy Sonnets* testify to the ambivalence that a self-assertive and intelligent person might experience in the process of repentance" ("Petrarchanism and Repentance" 551).

Robert Southwell and Ignatius Loyola both seem to be part of that ambivalence, for even while Donne employs the technique of the *Exercises* to imagine dramatic spiritual circumstances for his soul, he abandons altogether the tone of relative piety heard in "La Corona" and returns to the first person shock and awe of his earlier poems. In his *Holy Sonnets* Donne seems more determined than ever, even while constructing ostensibly "holy" sonnets, to spin finally out of reach of Southwell's sphere, landing after remarkable phantasms of wit, intricate rhetorical arguments and dramatic hypotheticals, in a space of spiritual as well as theological irresolution.

Having long ago rejected the old faith of his Heywood uncles and Robert Southwell, not to mention his own father and mother,[16] John Donne was still left with the inescapable problem of death and the accompanying predicament of damnation or salvation. It is no surprise, therefore, that he returns to these subjects in his poetry, but the impious manner in which he treats these subjects and the irresolution of his religion are still capable of surprising some readers. The very elements of these Holy Sonnets that would have startled or even appalled orthodox Protestant and Catholic readers of his day are of course what have made the poems so appealing to twentieth- and twenty-first- century readers. The self-fashioned Augustinian

---

16 Though this statement reflects the belief of most Donne biographers, Anthony Low holds open the possibility that "Donne as a young man may have been a Church Papist, especially during the years when he worked for Sir Thomas Egerton in a semi-governmental capacity. That would have involved his attending an Anglican church on Sundays, something that need not have troubled a believing Catholic so long as he inconspicuously refrained from receiving communion" (102). He further speculates, in light of Flynn's recent research, that during Donne's thirteen years of quasi-unemployment, "Donne was continuing in some way his earlier connections with patrons belonging to the ancient Catholic nobility" (108).

narrative that would have us see these sonnets as the work of a formerly loose-living young man now in the act of a religious conversion that would lead eventually to his being vested as the pious Dr. John Donne is one that, the scholarship of recent decades notwithstanding, some are not quite willing to relinquish, and the full complexity of which we are only just beginning to comprehend. "For," as Anthony Low recently reminded us:

> it was not just a case of the profligate Jack Donne, that "great visitor of ladies," becoming Reverend Dr. Donne, Dean of St. Paul's. There was also the more problematic conversion of John Donne, faithful Catholic, into John Donne, conforming Anglican, once fearful of visiting the court lest he be betrayed and now the King's obedient servant and the loyal client of the Duke of Buckingham ("Absence," 101).

Somewhere between these two well-cultivated personas, comes an ambitious Englishman still mired in his family's meditation of martyrdom, the self-assertive and intelligent author of the *Holy Sonnets*, which are literary monuments not only to his own religious complexity, but the complexity of the age. As Catherine Gimelli Martin observes, "the aesthetic instability of Donne's *Holy Sonnets* and *Anniversaries* reflects the reckless competition for psychic and social assurance prevalent throughout a 'culture of anxiety'" (193).[17]

So, while the ambivalence to which Kuchar refers above arises out of a culture of anxiety, the *Sonnets'* aesthetic as well as theological instability have led many critics to try to understand or at least summarize their author's theology. Not long after Martz had drawn attention

---

17 See Catherine Gimelli Martin, "Unmeete Contraryes: the Reformed Subject and the Triangulation of Religious Desire in Donne's Anniversaries and holy Sonnets," in *John Donne and the Protestant Reformation; new perspectives*, 2003. Martin argues that, "in making insecurity its own ostentatiously insufficient answer to his constant 'crisis' of faith, Donne also supplementally stabilizes his spiritual turmoil through a dramatic triangulation of religious desire" (194).

to Donne's reliance on the techniques of Ignatian meditation,[18] Douglas L. Peterson's "John Donne's *Holy Sonnets* and the Anglican Doctrine of Contrition" attempted to settle Donne more comfortably into the theological camp to which he eventually vowed public allegiance. A decade later Patrick Grant alternatively offered an Augustinian understanding of the *Sonnets*. Soon after Barbara Lewalski was enrolling Donne's poetry among the aesthetic of Protestant poetics. Noting that they had been "studied relentlessly" for their religious contexts, Stephanie Yearwood long ago suggested that rather than "aim to correlate the poems with religious movements, patterns of thought, dogma, and traditions, prevalent in Donne's time," we consider instead "Donne's own theology . . . his own understanding of conversion" (208), the emotional and doctrinal aspects of which, she suggested, Donne "was forming, or formed when he wrote the Holy Sonnets" (209). The *Holy Sonnets*, read properly, in other words, presumably yield their own cohesive theology of conversion. Richard Strier's "John Donne Awry and Squint: The *Holy Sonnets*," attempted through the different looks his title suggests to reconcile the theological ambivalences that he acknowledged in the sonnets. More recently, Paul Cefalu has resurrected John Stachniewski's suggestion that Donne's anguish in the sonnets is akin to "Calvinist despairers" (Stachniewski, 699), who view "godly fear as a virtue that is put to use by the moral agent" (Cefalu, 86).[19]

18 While Martz argued that all of the Holy Sonnets were in some way a product of Ignatian meditation, he identified four poems in particular whose narratives were fully developed Ignatian meditations, including 4 ("At the round earth's imagined corners . . ."), 5 ("If poisonous minerals . . . "), 7 ("Spit in my face . . ."), and 15 ("I am a little world . . ."). See the *Poetry of Meditation*, 48–53. Some fifty years later, Anthony Low affirmed, "Indeed, none of the poems Martz discusses, by Donne and by other seventeenth-century devotional poets, including the Anniversaries, so thoroughly answers to the Ignatian method as the Holy Sonnets" ("Absence," 97).

19 See Douglas L. Peterson's "John Donne's *Holy Sonnets* and the Anglican Doctrine of Contrition," *Studies in Philology* 65 (1959): 504–18; Patrick Grant's "Augustinian Spirituality and the Holy Sonnets of John Donne," *ELH* 38 (1971), 542-61; Barbara K. Lewalski,

And so the discussion continues. According to a recent essay by David Anonby "Donne's complex theological identity as apostate Catholic, Arminian doubter, and Calvinist self-critic find expression" and "cohere" in the *Holy Sonnets'* "theme of repentance" (88),[20] although, like Yearwood long before him, he does not manage to show exactly how. In fact, as Kuchar makes disappointingly clear to readers who seek cohesion in Donne's *Holy Sonnets*, ambivalence seems to prevail over any particular or combined theology:

> We still come up against a basic ambivalence at the heart of the poems: the speaker wants to express full contrition for his sins (either as a way to participate in or to be assured of salvation) at the same time as he experiences terror over the narcissistically traumatic insight that such contrition entails. In this respect, the fundamental drama of the *Holy Sonnets* is characterized by the speaker's terrifying recognition that repentance requires him to experience his lack of autonomy—to undergo a psychically violent process in which he comes to realize, existentially as well as cognitively, that in himself he is nothing ("Petrarchanism and Repentance," 537).

For contemporary readers, this drama can even turn to a kind of black comedy, when Donne's speaker avoids conventional contrition

Protestant Poetics and the Seventeenth-Century Religious Lyric (Princeton: Princeton University Press, 1979), pp. 264–72; Stephanie Yearwood's "Donne's Holy Sonnets: The Theology of Conversion," *Texas Studies in Literature and Language* 24 (1982), 208–21; Richard Strier's "John Donne Awry and Squint: The *Holy Sonnets*," *Modern Philology* 86 (1989), 357–84; John Stachniewski's "The Despair of the "Holy Sonnets," *ELH* 48 (1981); Paul Cefalu's "Godly Fear, Sanctification, and Calvinist Theology in the Sermons and 'Holy Sonnets' of John Donne," *Studies in Philology* 100 (2003), 71–86.

20 See David Anonby's "The Sacred Pain of Penitence; The Theology of John Donne's *Holy Sonnets*" in Nelson, Holly Faith (ed. and intro); Szabo, Lynn R. (ed.); Zimmerman, Jens (ed.) *Through a Glass Darkly: Suffering, the Sacred, and the Sublime in Literature and Theory* (Waterloo, ON: Wilfrid Laurier University Press), 2010.

altogether, when his soul is "more shifty than defiant" (Brownlow, 16).

If Kuchar's assessment of these poems seems sobering, it at least still credits the poet with genuine theological ambivalence and recognizes real terror and psychic violence in his verse. Among the above congregation of critics attending to the religious elements in these sonnets, Frank Brownlow's more stark assessment that the *Holy Sonnets* are "examples of witty, inventive poetic art written for an aggressively competitive male readership by a man uncommitted to a church or theological position" (14) comes as a splash of cold unblessed water. Brownlow sees even Donne's theological ambivalence as disingenuous, or arising in any case more from aesthetic than ascetic concerns. He cautions "unchurched scholars who exhaust the resources of learning attempting to enroll Donne in an ecclesiastical party" that they "should consider that at such moments" as the final couplet of Sonnet 3 when the poet declares, "Impute me righteous, thus purg'd of evil, / For thus I leave the world, the flesh, and devil" (13–14), that "the poet's aim is not to declare an allegiance, but by hook or crook to find a quiet place for a frightened soul in the theological pandemonium" (18).

One very churched Donne scholar, Anthony Low,[21] shares Brownlow's concern that "nothing at all happens"[22] in these sonnets: "There is none of the spiritual progress that properly belongs to Ignatian or related styles of Catholic meditation," Low complains, "either within any individual sonnet or within the sequence as a whole. We find no journey from hell to heaven, from sinfulness to grace, from fear to hope, from sickness to salvation" (96). Unlike Brownlow, Low offers a plausible, and somewhat sympathetic theological explanation for the poet's penitential paralysis. Low suggests that Donne in effect is

21 Like Brownlow, Anthony Low is a former British High Anglican turned Roman Catholic. He reports in his essay on Donne, "I attended Kent which in those days was fairly High-Church . . . I went on to Harvard, where I discovered on Riverside Drive in Cambridge an even higher Anglican church run by a religious order known as the Cowley Fathers . . . A few years later at Harvard I became a Catholic" (105).

22 See Brownlow, *Sonnets* 16.

trapped between a very specific hook and crook within theological pandemonium, and he offers an assessment of Donne's predicament that helps us to appreciate where his journey has taken him since his departure from the likes of Southwell. The *Holy Sonnets*, Low insists, "are pervasively Catholic in method, yet at the same time . . . they are deeply influenced by Calvinism in their doubts and anxieties" (96). This paradox would seem to offer the penitent poet the worst of two theological worlds. "Why," Low asks rhetorically

> does Donne sound like an apprentice Jesuit following all the traditional methods of the Ignatian exercises at the same time that he sounds like a guilt-ridden Scottish Presbyterian closeted in his private room, examining his inward conscience for signs of election, yet fearful that he will prove to be among the reprobate, for whom there is no hope? At this time in his life he seems to be neither Jesuit nor Presbyterian, but lost somewhere in between the two (97).

Low's assessment of Donne's spiritual disorientation is in fact matched by Donne's own long-time friend Sir Toby Matthew, who spoke with him during the time just before the *Sonnets* were written. Upon returning to England as a newly converted Roman Catholic in 1607, Matthew was imprisoned by authorities. Donne was among his friends who came to visit him in prison and Matthew was appreciative that "Donne and Martin were very full of kindness to me at that time, though it continued not to be hearty afterward" (Bald 188). Clearly resolved in his new old faith, Matthew observes of his two friends: "I found that they were mere libertines in themselves; and that the thing for which they could not long endure me was because they thought me too saucy, for presuming to show them the right way, in which they liked not then to go, and wherein they would disdain to follow any other" (Bald 188). To dismiss Matthew as an intolerant convert or his words as simply the hurt of a man stinging from the rejection of his fair-weather friends is to miss some valuable information about the author of the *Holy Sonnets*. As Brownlow notes, Matthew is not here accusing Martin and Donne of moral looseness or of atheism. The topic which turned them off of their old friend was religion, and Mathew's use of the word libertine is to describe "a religious stance"

(Brownlow, "Sonnets" 14). What Matthew was observing in Donne and his friend, Brownlow suggests, was their disposition as free-thinkers who wanted no particular truck with "any ecclesiastical commitment" ("Sonnets" 14).

Brownlow's suspicions of Donne's religious insincerity in the *Sonnets* are further fueled by the sonnet to the E[arl] of D[orset] that apparently accompanied the first six of the poems. In the poem Donne boasts "Seaven to be borne at once"[23] signaling more a spirit of artistic competition than spiritual repentance. The benefit of joining Brownlow in viewing these poems within the context of his sonnet to the Earl and in light of Toby Matthew's observations is that we are freed from trying to bend the poems to fit conventional, orthodox, theological narratives of repentance. We may recognize them as the remarkable poems they are, and the work of the same John Donne we have always known, wherein we see without surprise their "ambiguous theology, neither whole-heartedly Catholic or Protestant; their readiness to shock with outrageous or even comical imagery; their recurrent tone of histrionic, masculine bravado, and their witty ingenuity—these were the marks of Donne's poetic style from the beginning, and he has not changed in order to write upon religious themes" ("Sonnets," 14). Death and salvation are serious subjects to be sure, but if we insist that Donne be steadfastly serious about them, we are placing

23 **TO THE E OF D : WITH SIX HOLY SONNETS.**
> SEE, sir, how, as the sun's hot masculine flame
> Begets strange creatures on Nile's dirty slime,
> In me your fatherly yet lusty rhyme
> —For these songs are their fruits—have wrought the same.
> But though th' engend'ring force from which they came
> Be strong enough, and Nature doth admit
> Seven to be born at once; I send as yet
> But six; they say the seventh hath still some maim.
> I choose your judgment, which the same degree
> Doth with her sister, your invention, hold,
> As fire these drossy rhymes to purify,
> Or as elixir, to change them to gold.
> You are that alchemist, which always had
> Wit, whose one spark could make good things of bad.

expectations upon his poetry which he is bound to disappoint. The octave of his first Holy Sonnet is, with only one parenthetical admission of self-betrayal, a pious declaration of devotion. When he begins the sestet with the question, "Why doth the devil then usurp me" (9), we are immediately in a more interesting and less theologically certain poem that ends not with professed resolve to repent or to serve, but in a lover's triangle as hot and provocative and as clever as any of Shakespeare's latter sonnets: "Oh I shall soon despair, when I do see / That thou lov'st mankind well, yet wilt not choose me, / And Satan hates me, yet is loath to lose me" (12–14).

In the hypothetical predicament of Sonnet 2 the speaker's soul is summoned by sickness and compared to a pilgrim banished for treason who "dar'st not turn to whence he's fled" (4) or a thief "deliver'd from prison, / but damn'd and haled to execution (6–7). The sestet proposes grace as a solution and repentance as the means, "But who shall give thee that grace to begin?" (10). The solution is to wear holy black and become red with blushing since Christ's blood, being red, dyes red souls to white. As Brownlow puts it, "a condition [spiritual peril] that begins with metaphor is cured with metaphor, while the unfortunate felons of the simile continue on their way to execution" ("Sonnets," 17). The action the soul is exhorted to take is more tropological than penitential, and the sort of despair, angst and seeking for grace that we read in Southwell's *Saint Peter's Complaint* is utterly absent.

If we try to imagine Donne as other than how Matthew describes him, what do we make of the poet in Sonnet 5 asking, "If lecherous goats, if serpants envious / Cannot be damn'd, alas why should I be?" (3–4). His Job-like question at the start of the sestet, "But who am I that dare dispute with thee / O God?" (9–10) may offer consolation, but his final couplet would be aptly accompanied by a familiar wink: "That thou remember them, some claim as debt; / I think it mercy if thou wilt forget (13–14). In the famous affront to death in Sonnet 6 are we not to smile at the allusion to post-mortem bloating when the speaker asks, "Why swell'st thou then?" When the speaker dialogues with his soul and meditates upon its dwelling in an image of the crucified Christ in his heart in Sonnet 9, is the seriousness of his argument not undermined when he recalls in the sestet the arguments that he used to make to seduce his "profane mistresses" and compares the beauty of Christ's corpus to their form?

One need only consider the most famous Sonnet 10, the anthropomorphized God[24] and the accompanying desire for divine rape rather than marriage to realize how much more tropological than penitential these poems actually are, how much more prevalent their dramatic vehicles are than their frequently ambiguous tenors. It is difficult to refute Brownlow's claim that "Donne's readiness to shock and surprise, and to flirt with the impermissible, continually sets problems of tone for the reader of the *Holy Sonnets*" (17). Nor is he the first to offer such an assessment. Long ago, in his sobering assessment of the sexual violence of Sonnet 10, William Kerrigan remarked: "It is one thing to run circles of wit about the straight-line orthodoxy of Petrarchan love poets, quite another to bend the cherished corners of dogma."[25] For many of today's readers of course the bending is all one and the same and the tonal problem of which Brownlow complains is actually one of the chief pleasures in the poems. Donne's own contemporaries, however, were not post-modernists. Salvation and damnation were not abstractions and death and torment were not mere tropes to the likes of Henry Donne, Robert Southwell or Toby Matthew; nor, for all of the wit, pyrotechnics and spiritual ambiguity of his verse, were these matters unimportant to John Donne, though in his poems they remain frustratingly unresolved.

Understanding the lack of spiritual progress in the *Holy Sonnets* is the key to understanding just how far Donne had moved from Southwell's Catholic and Ignatian poetic sphere and to what effect. In his assessment of the problematic Sonnet 5—"What if this present was the world's last night?"—Kuchar observes that while "the speaker initiates an Ignatian meditation upon the Passion that is framed within

24 See William Kerrigan's "The Fearful Accommodations of John Donne," *English Literary Renaissance* 4, no. 3 (Autumn 1974). Kerrigan observes: "What has disturbed critics of 'Batter my heart,' is Donne's eagerness to display the most anthropomorphic consequences of anthropomorphism—in short, to imagine with some detail the sexuality of God. Approving the theological tenor, we suspect the anthropomorphic vehicle" (quoted from Bloom, 39). And again, "Donne has opened a suggestiveness near to crude anthropomorphism. And crude anthropomorphism is another name for outright blasphemy" (Bloom, 43).

25 Quoted in Bloom, 37.

the hypothetical setting of the judgment day," he is soon rationalizing rather than repenting. "The speaker veers away from the image of Christ's suffering in order to persuade himself of the heterodox idea that Christ is incapable of damning souls as such" ("Petrarchanism and Repentance," 559). Kuchar reiterates Richard Strier's observations that the poem fails because it cannot seem to render "divine love apart from images of force" ("Petrarchanism and Repentance," 559). What Strier and Kuchar are elucidating is the poet's predicament between the hook of Calvinism and the crook of Ignatian Catholicism, such that, despite his seeming penitential intentions in the opening lines, "the poem fails . . .

> because the speaker's recourse to an analogy between Christ's appearance and his merciful judgment exposes the contradictions between Ignatian meditation and Protestant thought. Just as 'Batter My Heart' expresses confusion over Catholic and Calvinist views on reason . . . so 'What if this present' exposes the tensions between the Ignatian dependence on sense experience and the Protestant disavowal of such experience. In other words, Donne's meditation fails because it oscillates between Catholic meditative tradition that is predicated on an Aristotelian epistemology and a Protestant tradition based on an Augustinian epistemology" ("Petrarchanism and Repentance," 560).

What the poet lacks in this meditation, as well as in the other sonnets and the entire cycle, is more than merely epistemological. It is experiential. For the ultimate sense experience, the direction towards which Catholic meditation necessarily moves is the sacraments. As Low astutely observes after five decades of reading and teaching these poems, "Donne's *Holy Sonnets* not only fail to achieve resolutions of amendment or similar acts of the will. They also fail to evoke the Sacraments as the proper goal—or at least, for a Catholic, as essential stages along the way toward the goal—of such meditative exercises." Low's chief concern is that given the speaker's expressed terror of death and damnation, none of the sonnets moves towards the most obvious sacrament of all, confession. "There are no signs that the speaker in Donne's Holy Sonnets ever considers such a sacramental outcome from his meditative sequence . . . although confession is the obvious way for a Catholic to cleanse himself of his sins and receive grace in order to reunite himself with God" (107).

The ambivalence in Donne's *Holy Sonnets* may arise from the uncertainty of that troubled age in England, from his own indifference or disaffection with religion, or even from his failure to resist the aesthetic triumph over the ascetic choice. However, that his speakers posture themselves for repentance in such dramatic Ignatian fashion and then fail to accomplish anything meaningful makes Low's suggestion as probable as any of these. Namely that Donne's "peculiar mixture of Catholic method and Calvinist despair" (112), arising "from necessity, inward discouragement, or gradually changing religious views" (108) meant that he could not "find God's grace and presence in the sacraments" where Ignatian meditation would naturally lead, and so had to seek that grace "by some other, less certain means" (108–09).[26] Whatever this less certain means is, it seems for the conflicted cradle Catholic authoring these poems, and for his attentive readers, to be inadequate. The poet may realize, in Kuchar's words, that "existentially as well as cognitively, that in himself he is nothing," but seems unwilling or incapable of taking the next step from this spiritual emptying. In fact, he is enthralled, bound, captive, enslaved.[27] "He has no shred of free will that will allow him to repent or change" (Low 112).

To all of this enticing but fruitless drama there could be no more

26 John Klause points out that "even in Donne's Catholic days there are reasons why he would not look to confession as an 'obvious' recourse. According to Catholic theology, true repentance was necessary for absolution. 'Contrition' might be perfect (based on the love of God) or imperfect (i.e., 'attrition'), based on a fear of damnation. Without confession, perfect contrition was necessary for the forgiveness of sins. With confession, attrition was sufficient. The problem for Catholics in Donne's time was of course that there were so few priests, one could never count on access to confession. This would lead to an emphasis among the Catholic devout on achieving perfect contrition; and even a Catholic (not just a Calvinist) might question the 'perfection' of his repentance, and hence fear damnation" (electronic correspondence, quoted with permission).

27 The verbs belong to Sonnet 10, but are representative of the cycle.

stark contrast than the poetry of Robert Southwell with which Donne was well acquainted. Whatever its baroque excesses and sixteenth-century aesthetic limitations might be, no poem in English better puts the methodology of *The Spiritual Exercises* to the service of poetry than the popular and oft re-printed *Saint Peter's Complaint.* "Launch foorth my Soule into a maine of teares" the poet boldly begins and he does not cease for 792 lines of unqualified repentance and weeping.[28] Select any stanza and we find them all "full fraught with griefe":

If love , if losse, if fault, if spotted fame.
If daunger, death, if wrath or wrecke or weale,
Entitle eyes true heires to earned blame,
That due remorse in such events conceale;
Then want of teares might well enroll my name,
As cheefest Saint in Calender of shame (493–98).

* * *

Come shame, the livery of offending minde.
The ougly shroud, that overshadoweth blame:
The mulct, at which fowle faults are justly fynde,
The dampe of sinne, the common sluce of fame,
By which impostum'd tongues, their humors purge.
Light same on me. I best deserve the scourge (517–22)

* * *

My eye, reads mourneful lessons to my hart,
My hart, doth to my thought the griefes expound,
My thought, the same doth to my tongue impart,
My tongue, the message in the eares doth sound;
My eares, back to my hart their sorrowes send,
Thus circkling griefes runne round without an end (673–78).

28 A friend I know made a version of an Ignatian retreat many years ago. A rugged war veteran with thick skin and astute intellect, he reported "I spent nearly the entire weekend in tears."

Unlike Donne, the circling griefs so extravagantly expressed by Peter do not run around without an end. After 132 stanzas of confession the penitent's tears may be exhausted, and he has arrived unambiguously, un-ambivalently and resolutely in a state of readiness for grace. Having confessed, he concludes in the final two stanzas first by begging forgiveness,

> With mildenesse, Jesu, measure my offence:
> Let true remorse thy due revenge abate:
> Let teares appease when trespasse doth incense:
> Let pittie temper thy deserved hate.
> Let grace forgive, let love forget my fall:
> With feare I crave, with hope I humbly call (781–86)

> Redeeme my lapse with raunsome of thy love,
> Traverse th'inditement, rigors doome suspend:
> Let frailtie favour, sorrow succor move:
> Be thou thy selfe, though changling I offend.
> Tender my suite, clense this defiled denne,
> Cancell my debtes, sweete Jesu, say Amen (78792).

The purpose of such a meditation as this is not for the sake of the poet, of course, but as an example for readers. This was, from uncertain start to bloody finish, Southwell's mission. It was not John Donne's. "Donne's spiritual perplexities," Low resolves, "produced a sonnet sequence not very useful for those looking for devotional exercises to improve their souls" (114). Herbert's poems, he notes rightly, could be and were used for such a purpose by Vaughan and Wesley and others. And Southwell's poems had of course been put to use as spiritual exercises by devout Catholics and Anglicans alike. His example is one that Donne, having perhaps tested it in "La Corona," decided to reject.

To whatever causes one assigns the various poetic tensions in Donne's *Holy Sonnets*, the drama is undeniable and the poems' appeal to critics and students will likely not only endure, but increase. One of the effects of this is that some of Donne's less dramatic works may suffer neglect by comparison. Such works include the 28 nine-line stanzas of *The Litanie* composed around the same time as the *Holy*

Sonnets. Elegant and straightforward by comparison to the *Sonnets*, they may be said to succeed liturgically and are as good an example of religious poetry as Donne composed. If his *Sonnets* demonstrate the conflict between his Protestant and Catholic selves, *The Litanie* demonstrates a deliberate steerage between extremes. The *Sonnets* seem calculated to shock, *The Litanie* determined not to offend. Donne wrote to his friend Henry Goodere about the poem: "Neither the Roman church need call it [*The Litanie*] defective because it abhors not the particular mention of the Blessed Triumphers in heaven; nor the Reformed can discreetly accuse it of attributing more than a rectified devotion ought to doe."[29] Within one of the stanzas of the poem, Donne even asks God to deliver him from the temptation towards impious cleverness which he had deployed (or would deploy) in *The Holy Sonnets*: "When wee are mov'd to seeme religious / Only to vent wit, Lord deliver us" (XXI, 8-9).

The Litanie's meditations begin effectively with the sign of the cross, with a stanza devoted to The Father, The Son and The Holy Ghost, and each of the subsequent hymn-like stanzas is directed to the Trinitarian God or specifically to one of the three persons of the Trinity. The meditations move forward in salvation history from The Trinity, The Virgin Mary, The Angels, The Patriarchs, The Prophets, The Apostles and The Martyrs. The stanza devoted to the martyrs therefore refers to the earliest Christian martyrs, not those subsequently martyred through the ages and certainly not the recent "pseudo-martyrs" of Donne's own country and acquaintance. Nonetheless, as it is Donne's only actual meditation on martyrdom, it is worthy of our attention:

> And since thou so desirously
> Did'st long to die, that long before thou could'st,
> And long since thou no more couldst dye,
> Thou in thy scatter'd mystique body wouldst
> In and ever since
> In thine; let their blood come
> To begge for us, a discreet patience

29 *The Poems of John Donne*, ed. Herbert J. C. Grierson (Oxford, 1912), II, 239.

Of death, or of worse life: for Oh, to some
Not to be Martyrs is a martyrdome (82–90).

This prayer to Christ honors him as the exemplar for all martyrs, whose longing to die is traceable even to his tropological presence in the murdered Abel, and ever since in his own mystic body that can no longer die.

It is the final three lines of this prayer that are of interest in light of what we have come to know about the complex religious trajectory of Donne's life, from a family of martyrs to a stalwart of the official state religion. The poet begs for patience to suffer death "or of worse life," stating in effect that worse than a martyr's brief and violent suffering is a life of prolonged suffering where death does not come to the rescue: "for Oh, to some / Not to be Martyrs is a martyrdome." It is, considered within the context of Donne's life, one of the more suggestive things he ever wrote. The emphatic "Oh" we presume is not there to round out the meter, but signals an emotional pining that suggests that the poet might well number himself among the "some" for whom not being a martyr is its own martyrdom. At the very least there is, I think, a tinge of regret or nostalgia for the heroic youth of his first painted image who had declared *Antes muerto que mudado*. The bold motto fit the actions and final deeds of many to whom Donne was related and others whom he knew. It was the very sort of brashness that led to his own brother's death. That he himself was sooner changed than dead does not bespeak cowardice, but rather disaffection with the cause his family served. And here in these lines he acknowledges the suffering, the slow, prolonged martyrdom that comes in not being a martyr. His disaffection with the cause notwithstanding, pseudo-martyrs like Robert Southwell and his Heywood relatives still haunted him with the heroism of their lives and deaths. As Klause describes it,

> Because Donne could not escape the Jesuits cleanly, his hero was a martyr—but a surviving 'witness' to the authentic value of personal necessities that were smaller yet no less important than truth. Finally, his hero was a temporizer, like himself, who on the verge of taking orders in the English Church found that it provided a worship 'convenient' (or fitting) and 'advantageous,' rather than true (*Essayes*,

51), but who rejoiced that its tolerance, sufficient for him, allowed his hope time for a sea-change" (Klause, 215).

This revised, more level-headed version of heroism nonetheless contains some nostalgia for the certainty of those who went before him. Catherine Martin observes that even in Donne's *Holy Sonnets* "irony is tinged with envy at the 'faithfull soules' now 'alike glorifi'd in heaven while their sons have been left behind, struggling and perhaps failing to find 'signes' of salvation 'that be / Apparent not in us immediately (HS 8)" (194). Carey recognized a similar regret at loss of certitude in Donne's earlier Satire III where Donne "is busily shuffling off his Faith, the conviction that there is one 'right' church which alone certifies salvation" that was "part of his Catholic upbringing" (14). The place and prestige that Donne would find in the Anglican Church notwithstanding, Carey seems quite right in noting that "no church would ever mean so much to him again, and consequently when he abandoned Catholicism he lost an irreplaceable absolute" (14).

Robert Southwell was part of that irreplaceable absolute, which Donne seems determinedly, though not altogether successfully, to have left behind. Carey imagines the possibility that "in trying to startle a congregation towards the end of a sermon, Dr. Donne echoed the words of Robert Southwell. Reminding his congregation of "the endless pain of the cursed soul and of the instant of decision that led to it," Donne tells them, "Upon this minute dependeth that eternity" (25). Nearly three decades earlier in a document that Donne himself may have heard presented and discussed in the Tower, Southwell had described in his *Humble Supplication* the choice that England's Catholics faced of whether to remain a Catholic or become an apostate. This choice, Southwell wrote, was that "dreadful moment whereupon dependeth a whole eternity." The words, Carey surmises, "seem to have stuck in Donne's mind." This well may be so, or the similar language may be only an ecclesiastical coincidence across the decades. What seems far more certain is that Donne lived and wrote and preached within Southwell's sphere, that Southwell's coarse threads of verse and prose manuscripts reverberated in him even as he strove to distance himself from them and their author.

Robert Southwell's heroic Roman Catholic life and dramatic English mission intersected with John Donne at a time when the drama of

Donne's own life was taking an irreversible turn. The executed priest seems to have left an indelible impression upon Donne's memory, and his literary work seems to have had a lasting effect upon the range and kind of verse the younger and more talented poet would write. Begging "discreet patience of death, or worse life," the life and words and death of Robert Southwell remained a part of Donne's lifelong "meditation of martyrdom."

Chapter 6

The Sphere's Last Tears:
Southwell and Richard Crashaw

When Richard Crashaw's poems were printed for the first time in London in 1646, Robert Southwell had been dead for half a century. Crashaw himself was living in Paris "in reduced circumstances,"[1] as an exiled Catholic convert. He was assisted in his exiled state by, among others, his friend and fellow Cambridge poet and Royalist sympathizer, Abraham Cowley, who was serving as Secretary to Queen Henrietta Maria. It is not clear whether Crashaw had authorized the printing of his verse, nor do we know the identity of the friend who took the initiative to do so. *Delights of the Muses* and *Steps to the Temple* contain between them the complete poetical works of Crashaw, save for several additional poems that Crashaw apparently sent to his friend before the works were printed in a second edition in 1648 (*Complete Poems*, Introduction, xxi). The *Delights* contain poems in Latin and English written during Crashaw's days at Cambridge. Mostly academic and occasional poems, they contribute little to his reputation as a poet. *Steps to the Temple*, as the title suggests, announces Crashaw's place in the tradition of English sacred poetry, with one of the poems and the title of the volume making explicit tribute to George Herbert. As Crashaw editor George Walton Williams observes, the poems also reflect inspiration not just from sacred scripture and Anglican thought and practice, but from the poems of John Donne and Robert Southwell (xxi).

---

1   xix *Complete Poems*. This and other biographical descriptions, as well as all quotations from Crashaw's poems are taken from *The Complete Poetry of Richard Crashaw*, Edited with and Introduction and Notes by George Walton Williams, New York University Press, 1972.

Through the influence of Queen Henrietta, Crashaw finally attained a reputable position in the Catholic Church as a follower of Cardinal Palotto. He was made a canon at the Santa Casa at Loreto where, just a year after his poems were published in London in their second edition, he died of a fever in the summer of 1649 (xx). Unlike Southwell's death, which fifty years earlier was a significant public event in London with various reverberations, Richard Crashaw's passing from earth in exile would have been regarded in England only by his royalist friends.[2] Yet in retrospect, particularly for the tradition of English sacred verse to which he contributed, his passing acquires particular significance.

Remarking upon Crashaw's death in his introduction to *The Paradise Within: Studies in Vaughan, Traherne and Milton*, Louis Martz made a rather stark claim, the implications of which are still being explored some fifty years later. Noting that Crashaw's death in Loreto in 1649 came a mere six months after England's King Charles was executed at Whitehall, Martz asserts that these two deaths mark the end of an era "for English political and religious institutions, and also for English religious poetry" (3). For "with Crashaw's death," he explains:

> the power of liturgical and eucharistic symbols died away in English poetry of the seventeenth century: the symbols earlier celebrated by Southwell, Alabaster, Donne, and Herbert. These poets had their doctrinal differences, and I do not wish to minimize those differences; but they had something more in common: a devotion to the mysteries of the Passion and to a liturgy that served to celebrate those mysteries. All five of these poets entered into holy orders; all five would have agreed with George Herbert's vision of "The Agonie":

Who knows not Love, let him assay
And taste that juice, which on the crosse a pike

2   "The Author's friend" who prepared Crashaw's poems for publication in 1646 referred to Crashaw in the Preface as "this Learned young Gentleman (now dead to us)." Since Crashaw was very much alive at the time it is unclear to what sort of death he is referring, "geographically or theologically? Or both?" asks Williams (xx).

Did set again abroach; then let him say
If ever he did taste the like.
Love is that liquor sweet and most divine,
Which my God feels as bloud; but I, as wine (3).

Such sacramental imagery, Martz claims, disappears from English poetry along with the priests who created it. The publication of Vaughan's *Silex Scintillans* as well as John Milton's miscellaneous *Poems* in 1645, Martz says, "marks the emergence of the layman as a central force in religious poetry of the period" (4).

If, keeping in mind the caution from Story and Gardner that "the continuity of devotional literature in England is easy to over-emphasize" (xxiii), we nonetheless take seriously Martz's version of literary history, we must recognize that when we speak of the religious poetry of the seventeenth century we are speaking of a kind of poetry, inaugurated by Robert Southwell,[3] and fashioned by priests, both Anglican and Roman;[4] a poetry whose central symbols are the liturgical and sacramental ingredients of the Mass, and which has at its very center, at the height of its steps to the Temple, the altar, upon which resides the Eucharist, God made flesh and blood in the consecrated bread and wine. This consecration was and is the essential work of the Roman priest, and to a slightly lesser extent the Anglican. If we heed what Martz says as well as the example of Herbert's poetry he presents, we understand

3 As I acknowledge below, Anthony Raspa traces the origins of this poetic aesthetic in England to John Donne's uncle and Southwell's Jesuit predecessor, Jasper Heywood. Heywood may have written poems (most of his work has been lost) that prefigured Southwell's own and Southwell may even have been influenced by his work, but it is Southwell, not Heywood, who called for and effected a reformation in the kind of poetry that poets wrote.

4 Of the five poets Martz names, Herbert was the only life-long Anglican and Southwell the only life-long Roman Catholic. Donne's switch to the Church of England may have come in his twenties, but his ordination was much later. Crashaw's conversion from high Anglicanism to Roman Catholicism likewise came in his maturity and Alabaster's back-and-forth life between the two religions is well known.

that the sacred work of these priests was, to a greater or lesser extent in each case, inextricable from the work that each of them would have regarded as their secondary vocation, writing verse and prose.

The determination to fashion poetry that served as a spiritual salve or inspiration to those who would follow Christ vanishes in seventeenth-century England only insofar as its origins remain invisible. In fact, one reading of Martz's observation is that the death of Crashaw marks the end of the age of Southwell, Crashaw's work being, as it were, the outer extension of Southwell's sphere. The young Jesuit's poetic influence and call for the reformation of poetry extended, we see, into the 1640s. Southwell had returned to England from the continent to minister to Roman Catholics. Forty-eight years after his execution, the Laudian Crashaw fled from England to the continent in the wake of the Puritans' occupation of Cambridge in 1643. Four years before his death in exile Crashaw converted to Roman Catholicism, though by then the majority of his poetry had already been written.

Where the emergent Protestant aesthetic was concerned Crashaw had always been the wrong kind of religious lyricist. Preoccupied as he was with the sacramental, the saints, tearful conversions and mystical visions, his verse was more explicitly Catholic than either Donne's or Herbert's. Their religious poetry can confront the Divine argumentatively and their dialectic verse engages readers' intellects so that appreciative literary critical conversation has taken place across the decades between readers of a religious disposition and their more agnostic colleagues who have come to far outnumber them. Richard Crashaw, though, with his unabashed devotion, baroque sensuality and floods of tears, is more like Alabaster, an eccentric relative with whom family members and friends associate uneasily. He is, as Williams says "the most un-English of all the English poets" (*Crashaw*, xv). Crashaw's poetic voice, Williams observes:

> is a small voice, and among discriminating critics, few are sympathetic to it. It is the voice of the ecstatic vision, the sensuous transcended and made sublime, the suavity of pain, the long-sought joy of mystical death. It is a voice of confident and unquestioning faith. This voice is a small voice, yet no other English poet has ever sung it so well" (*Crashaw*, xxii).

Crashaw's small voice is unique in its intonations and its baroque hyperbole, but its origins are not purely continental. He belongs to the tradition of English sacred poetry that originated with Southwell and most of the descriptors that Williams offers here may be applied as well to the writings of Southwell. It is pointless to ask which poet's small voice sang better since this is a question of taste and since they share an interdependence in their struggle to avoid canonical exile. As Shell aptly puts it, "the invisibility of Southwell and the deracination of Crashaw within English literary history are not separate phenomena, but symbiotic; where one is under-emphasized, the other looks alien" (97). Still they are each substantial English poets, and in order to preserve their reputations as such, Shell, as we saw in the previous chapter, traces what she calls "a fluent indigenous tradition of tears-literature in England" (97), in the hope that "the English baroque, with all its attendant Catholic implications, becomes as unproblematic a term for literary critics as it is for architectural historians" (103). This hope remains unfulfilled, likely because of the unwillingness on the part of many critics to read appreciatively not only Alabaster's sonnets but the abundant tearful verse of the many minor poets whom Shell catalogues. To see Crashaw as the outer edge of a span of devotional verse in Early Modern England that originated with Southwell's mission, however, demands only that we recognize the common scriptural, liturgical and sacramental threads in the poets I have treated in this study; that we recognize the similarities and the differences between Magdalene's first English tears and her last.

Thirty years ago, partially in response to the emergent emphasis on Protestant poetics,[5] Anthony Raspa published *The Emotive Image*, an important redirection of aesthetic understanding in which he

5   Published four years after Barbara Lewalski's hugely influential *Protestant Poetics and the Seventeenth-Century Religious Lyric*, Raspa located himself critically on a clear line of demarcation that he identified between those like himself who "supported the position that has become identified with Martz and were giving "renewed attention to Ignatian meditation" (Van Laan, Webber, Mitchell, Ramsay, Brown, Roberts) and those like Lewalski who "minimized or denied Ignatian influence" (Gardner, Bald, Lewalski, Halewood, Mueller). See p. 2 of *The Emotive Image*.

"argues that Jesuit poetics were constituted of three main elements—
'image,' 'affections,' and 'love'—and that they influenced English poets
for diverse historical and literary reasons" (1). As Shell would later
identify Crashaw's work as the culmination of baroque tears in English
poetry, Raspa in his studied examination of the Jesuit poetic aesthetic
focused primarily upon Crashaw, recognizing his work "as the flowering of Ignatian tradition" (4). He notes at the outset that the issues
he treats in his study "are at once wide and particular" and that par-
ticularity is evident not just in his careful attention to Jesuit aesthetic
treatises, but to his treatment of Jasper Heywood and Eldred Revett
as the first and the last of the five English poets he identifies who,
"touched by the debate over the presence of Ignatian structures in English verse," represent to us the "flowering, and disappearance in England of the Counter Reformation Jesuit poetic movement" (2). The
other three poets he treats as part of this movement are Southwell, Alabaster and Donne, and since his study runs more in parallel than in
contradiction to this present work and is generous in its recognition
of Southwell's influence upon Crashaw and the other poets, I am more
anxious to acknowledge my debt to than departure from his work.

Nonetheless, we can well understand how a study that requires
critics to recognize Jasper Heywood as a significant poetic influence
and recognize at the other end the one volume of poems in 1657 of
Eldred Revett (about whom we know practically nothing) as the outer
edge of the Jesuit Counter Reformation in England was not a significant enough bulwark to stem the critical tide of Protestant poetics that
has swept across the past several decades. Just so, Raspa's voice and
others were early harbingers of the revolution in thinking about
Catholicism that has characterized the most recent decade. Clinging
as it does to the thin thread of the Jesuit Counter Reformation in England, Raspa's study tends to collapse time such that Southwell, Alabaster and Crashaw become part of a poetic school of sorts. While
Southwell and Alabaster wrote in the same world, Crashaw wrote at
a distance of four eventful decades and in speaking of Southwell's influence upon his work here, I readily acknowledge that distance and
acknowledge once more how easy it is to overstate the continuity of
the literary devotional tradition in England. So, we may see Richard
Crashaw as the last in "a fluent indigenous tradition of tears- literature
in England," as Shell does, or as the culmination of the Jesuit aesthetic

as Raspa does, or we may simply acknowledge the truth that Martz spoke when he began this conversation over six decades ago by calling Crashaw the last poet to rely upon "the power of liturgical and eucharistic symbols." What all three of these descriptors share in common is that Robert Southwell is the first significant practitioner of each, so that we can describe Richard Crashaw as the outer edge of Southwell's sphere without straining credibility.

Where similarities in poetic style are concerned, Crashaw's verse shares a closer resemblance to the work of Alabaster than that of Southwell, something recognized by Raspa as he focuses upon their depiction of the understanding: "In Crashaw's and Alabaster's verse, the understanding played a creative role similar to that in Southwell's poems. There, however, its manifestations were more aesthetic. Crashaw's and Alabaster's imagery reflected the work of the understanding more poetically than Southwell's" (69). What Raspa recognizes as "more poetic" in Alabaster and Crashaw is what most readers experience in their poems when they have their attention drawn to the elaborate and sometimes shocking conceits, such that the tenor of the poems is often overtaken by the vehicle. For example, in "The Teare" Crashaw writes in his second stanza,

> O 'tis a not Teare,
> 'Tis a starre about to drop
> From thine eye its spheare;
> The Sunne will stoope and take it up.
> Proud will his sister be to weare
> This thine eyes Jewell in her Eare (2–7).

The sorrow of Mary Magdalene that the tear represents might actually become secondary or even forgotten altogether in the metaphorical layering and unfolding of the images themselves. Southwell, while he indulges in some poetic extravagance of this kind, seems always to recall the aim of his primary mission, to teach, console and inspire the oppressed Catholics in his mission, to pull others back to the faith. Poetry was a way of doing this, but should its imagery become too luxurious or demanding the attention of readers would be upon the loom or the web, rather than the intended spiritual instruction, and his purpose would be defeated. Crashaw bore no such responsibility, so was free to compose an epigram like "Upon the Infant Martyrs" where the meditation is more upon the conceits than the injustice of the murdered babies:

> To see both blended in one flood
> The Mothers Milke, the Childrens blood,
> Makes me doubt if Heaven will gather,
> Roses hence, or *Lillies* rather

The reader of this poem is more likely to notice the cleverness than to experience spiritual instruction or edification. By contrast, Southwell's "The flight into Egypt," a poem upon this same topic which also deploys the comparison of the slaughtered infants to flowers, speaks to Catholics in their immediate circumstances where a "Herod" may be seen to be making martyrs among them:

> O blessed babes, first flowers of Christian springe
> Who though untimely cropt fayre garlandes frame
> With open throats and silent mouthes you singe
> His praise whome age permits you not to name
> Your tunes are teares your instruments are swords
> Your ditye death and bloode in lieu of words (13–18).

Southwell's verse is necessarily more politically charged by the atmosphere of "death and blood" in which he writes, and while his artful description of the "cropt fayre garlandes . . . With open throats and silent mouthes" is artful, his tropological comparisons do not distract by drawing attention to themselves.

Another clear contrast between the poets is evident between Southwell's "The Assumption of our Lady" and Crashaw's "Hymn in the Assumption." Here we see one poet compelled to explain in syllogistic terms the theological justifications for Mary's Assumption and another poet free to simply sing of the glory of the blessed event. The first four lines of each demonstrate the contrast. First Southwell, "If sinne be captive grace must finde release / From curse of synne the innocence is free / Tombe prison is for sinners that decease / No tombe but throne to guiltless doth agree" (1–4); now Crashaw: "Hark! she is call'd, the parting houre is come. / Take thy Farewell, poor world!

heaven must goe home. / A piece of heav'nly earth; Purer and brighter / Then the chast stares, whose choise lamps come to light her" (1–4). Crashaw in this case fashions a far superior poem.

Despite their differences in emphasis, poetic style and intent, Crashaw and Southwell also of course share in common a determination to use verse as a vehicle to proclaim the faith and there are many instances of resemblance as well as places where Southwell's influence seems evident. For example, Southwell wrote "Man to the wound in Christs side," a reflection in quatrains in which Christ's wounds are likened in a hyperbolic manner to a harbor in which the weary speaker may seek rest. In his "On our crucified Lord Naked, and bloody" Crashaw referred to the wound as "the purple wardrobe of thy side" (4), and then composed a poem called "On the wounds of our crucified Lord," where in the identical stanza form and meter as Southwell's poem he compares Christ's wounds to mouths and eyes. Addressing the wound in Christ's side, Southwell in his poem writes "Heere is the spring of trickling teares" (21). Crashaw, far surpassing Southwell in Baroque extravagance, describes the wound in one of Christ's feet as a mouth with lips that could "pay the sweet summe of thy kisses" (14), in the other foot "To pay the Teares, an Eye that weeps / In stead of Teares such Gems as this is" (15–16). In another poem, "On the bleeding wounds of our crucified Lord," Crashaw again deploys the same stanza form and rhyme pattern as Southwell's poem to meditate upon the wound in Christ's side:

> But o thy side! thy deepe dig'd side
>   That hath a double Nilus going,
> Nor ever was the Pharian tide
>   Halfe so fruitfull, halfe so flowing (13–16).

Southwell's imprint upon Crashaw's work is more apparent in each poet's treatment of the nativity. In "The Nativity of Christe" Southwell proclaims in his opening lines, "Behould the father is his daughters sonne / The bird that built the nest, is hatched therein" (1–2). In Crashaw's "Hymn in the Holy Nativity," written in the same six line stanza form as Southwell's poem, Crashaw formulates this refrain for his shepherds: "We saw thee in thy Balmy nest." Southwell's second stanza describes light coming into the world with these imperative sentences:

O dying soules behould your living springe
O dazzled eyes behould your sunne of grace
Dull eares attend what world this word doth bringe
Up heavy hartes with joye your joy embrace
From death from darke from deaphnesse from despayres
This life this light the word this joy repaires (7–12).

Crashaw, perhaps borrowing some of this imagery and maybe even alluding to "The Burning Babe," brings the light into the world through the babe's own face:

Gloomy Night embrac't the place
   Where the noble infant lay:
The Babe lookt up, and shew'd his face,
   In spight of Darknesse it was Day.
It was the Day, Sweet, and did rise,
Not from the East, but from thy eyes (16–21)

In "New Prince, new pompe," Southwell describes "a sely tender babe / In fressing Winter nighte / In homely manger trembling lyes / Alas a piteous sighte" (1–4). Crashaw's adoring shepherd Thyrsis is more clownish in offering forth his depiction of the same scene:

I saw the curl'd drops, soft and slow,
   Come hovering o're the place's head;
Offring their whitest sheets of snow
   To furnish the fair INFANT'S bed
Forbear, said I; be not too bold.
Your fleece is white But t'is too cold (51–56)

To appreciate how the extravagance of Crashaw's verse represents the outer edge of a genre which Southwell had inaugurated, I offer one final contrast. In one of many remarkable prose passages from *Mary Magdalen's Funeral Tears* Southwell describes the desolate state of the grieving Magdalen:

And though tears were apter to nourish than diminish her grief, yet now being plunged into the depth of pain, she

yielded herself captive to all discomfort, carrying an overthrown mind in a more enfeebled body; and still busy in de-
vising, but ever doubtful in defining, what she might best
do: for what could a silly woman do but weep, that, floating in a sea of cares, found neither ear to hear her, nor
tongue to direct her, nor hand to help her, nor heart to pity
her in her desolate case (14–15).

The emotion contained here is far distant when Crashaw in "The
Weeper" describes Magdalen as weeping "Upwards" so that "Heavn's
bosome drinks the gentle stream / Where th' milky rivers creep," (IV),
so that "Every morn from hence / A brisk Cherub something sippes /
Whose sacred influence / Addes sweetnes" (V). This stanza offers the
hint of similarity and clear contrast as well as any:

> Yet let the poore drops weep
> (Weeping is the ease of woe)
> Softly let them creep,
> Sad that they are vanquish't so.
> They, though to others no reliefe,
> Balsom maybe, for their own greife (X).

The tears that flowed from "the depth of pain" of an "overthrown
mind in a more enfeebled body" in the early 1590s become a half century later not necessarily those of the crocodile, but ones so personified
that they have a grief of their own, an anatomy and life at least as
complex as the weeper herself. Gary Kuchar notes how the style of
"The Weeper" contrasts, not just with Southwell's *Funeral Tears,* but
with *Saint Peter's Complaint,* the "key difference" being "that the female penitent [in Crashaw's "Weeper"] is more idealized and thus
more other worldly" (*Religious Sorrow* 78).

Kuchar reads "The Weeper" as "a kind of Counter-Reformation
response" to the Calvinist poetics of Herbert's "Grief" where the
speaker begs rhetorically:

> O WHO will give me tears? Come, all ye springs,
> Dwell in my head and eyes; come, clouds
>   and rain;

My grief hath need of all the watery things
That nature hath produced: let every vein
Suck up a river to supply mine eyes,
My weary weeping eyes, too dry for me,
Unless they get new conduits, new supplies,
To bear them out, and with my state agree (1–9)

The speaker's dry and weary eyes get no assistance from "Verses" of poets that he rejects as fit for lovers, and ultimately the poem declares the very futility in the act of weeping: "What are two shallow fords," the speaker asks? " two little spouts" (10–11). Those two little spouts had, Herbert knew, been pouring forth public penitence from the time Southwell's Magdalene first spoke in 1591. Now Crashaw, reclaiming their significance, brings Magdalene's tears to life again. According to Kuchar he translates Herbert's poem "from the private , meditative context of solitary prayer and into the public, liturgical space of Eucharistic worship" (*Religious Sorrow* 77). In doing so, Kuchar argues, Crashaw:

> not only expresses but seeks to convey the Eucharistic mystery of Real Presence—a conjoining of sign and signed, of what is said and the position of enunciation from which it is said. The overall result of this deepening of the animating force of prosopopoeia is a poem that asks us to perceive Magdalene's tears from every conceivable angle until finally we, as readers, are called into the text itself—until we are constituted by it as a face that we not only look at but whose imperceptible look returns our gaze (*Religious Sorrow* 79).

The incarnational pull of the poem upon the reader through the extravagant deployment of prosopopoeia reaches its climax in the final two stanzas when the tears themselves speak in response to the speaker who addresses his "watery brothers," and "simpering sons of those fair eyes," imploring of them: "Whither away so fast?" (l. 168). The "poor drops" tell him:

> We go not to seek
> The darlings of Aurora's bed,

> The rose's modest cheek,
> Nor the violet's humble head.
> Though the field's eyes, too, weepers be,
> Because they want such tears as we.
>
> Much less mean we to trace
> The fortune of inferior gems,
> Preferr'd to some proud face,
> Or perch'd upon fear'd diadems.
> Crowned heads are toys. We go to meet
> A worthy object, our Lord's feet.

The stanzas, which Kuchar admits "push to the breaking point the distinction between apostrophe and invocation" (*Religious Sorrow* 77), may collapse the distance between reader and text as the words become elaborate prayers of praise that reject the appealing things of nature in favor of Christ's feet. However, for the reader resistant to the baroque extravagance of Crashaw's other-worldly idealization, the speaking tears may be seen as the climactic hyperbole of a poem that is ultimately a parody of itself, if not the entire genre of tears poetry. "The Weeper" may be seen to respond successfully to the private grief of Herbert's weary eyes with a public "conjoining of sign and signed." But it may also be seen as taking Southwell's initial outpourings to an artistic extreme where vehicle dominates tenor in a fashion that causes readers to forget not just the poet's original intention, but the authentic emotion, spiritual power and cultural impact of his original sixteenth-century model.

However one regards the talking tears of Crashaw's "Weeper" and the other eccentricities of his religious devotional verse, it must be conceded that he did not have any successful English imitators. The thin and knotted thread of English devotional tradition gives way, as Martz long ago observed, to "the emergence of the layman as the central force in religious poetry" (4). When we speak broadly of the meditative or metaphysical poetry of this century we include Vaughan, Traherne[6] and Marvell. In the first two we find a poetry that is more

6   Thomas Traherne (1636?–1674), was, of course, no layman, having been ordained an Anglican priest in 1661, a fact which disrupts some-

spiritually exotic than conventionally devotional. Their poetry is unmistakably Christian, and uses ingredients from both Old and New Testament scriptures, but it contains far fewer of the liturgical and Eucharistic symbols to which Martz refers. Vaughan, who wrote his poems at about the same time as Crashaw, looked not to Southwell or Alabaster, but to Herbert. He claims in fact to have set aside all "idle books" after reading Herbert's *Temple*. Then in his own writing he took meditative verse to a place where it had not yet been, and to a place that Herbert might scarcely have recognized, specifically the hills and fens of the Welsh landscape. In "Christ's Nativity" he proclaims: "I would I were a stone, or tree, / Or flower by pedigree" and "I would I were some *Bird*, or Star, / flutt'ring in woods, or lifted far/ Above the *Inne* / and rode of sin!" As the last of the "metaphysical" poets and a harbinger of the far-off Romantic movement, Vaughan recollects, not original sin, but original innocence: "Happy those early dayes! When I/ Shin'd in my Angell-infancy" ("Retreat"). Resembling Blake and Wordsworth more than Herbert or any of the poets who came before him, he substantiates Martz's assertion that sacramental symbol and energy had been displaced by a more generic emphasis upon the Self, Nature and Scripture. Vaughan writes of "Holy Communion" in verse, but not like his predecessors who had practically come near to performing the sacrament in their poems. Traherne's meditations are so thematically similar to Vaughan's that when his work was rediscovered in the early twentieth century it was mistaken as missing work of Vaughan's. As for Marvell, we find nothing of the sacramental in his poetry and even his intricate meditations on the nature of the soul reference Plato more so than scriptures.

Meanwhile, pious Catholics and Anglicans would continue to read Southwell, Herbert, Crashaw and even Alabaster. Donne of course

what Martz's theory of the emergence of the layman poet. Traherne lived without fame and died "utterly out of the minds and memories of men" until his poetry was discovered in a London book-stall by Professor Bertram Dobell at the beginning of the twentieth century. Dobell's first labor was to prove that his discovery was not the work Henry Vaughan, for in his provocative prose meditations on paradise and childhood wonder Traherne very much resembles Vaughan, though there is no instance of direct influence.

would be identified later in the century by Dryden as having fashioned images that were "meta" rather than truly physical. Neither pyrotechnics nor tears were in vogue by the time the eighteenth century arrived. The restoration of the monarchy did not precipitate a restoration of religious poetry, and, though preoccupied with moral decorum, the rational tide of neoclassicism more or less swept away religious devotion in poetry along with excessive emotion. The post-royalist suspicion of the ornate led to the emergence of the plain style, and the growing prominence of prose began to counter the popularity of poetry even as the sermon and dialectic became the dominant forms of religious expression in the eighteenth century.[7] This century saw a flourishing of Christian hymn writers, and while there were re-printings of Catholic and Anglican devotional texts during the century, the composition of devotional poems seems to have diminished. A notable exception is the recent rediscovery of religious verses written by workingclass women like Susannah Harrison, author of *Songs in the Night* (1780).[8]

When the popularity of lyric poetry returned in the nineteenth century, it did so with renewed earnestness, but in an increasingly vague spiritual landscape. Biblical, liturgical and sacramental ingredients had largely evaporated into a mist somewhere above the ruins of Tintern Abbey. Nature and the Self now took their place as the central meditative ingredients of English poetry, and in this vague, pantheistic spiritualism of the Romantic era the reforms of Robert Southwell were as forgotten as the original purpose of "the bare ruined choirs where late the sweet birds sang," which had by now become only emblems in a sublime landscape.

Yet before this century was over and nearly three centuries after Southwell's mission in England, another English Jesuit priest, living in

7   The religious lyric is but one of several early modern literary genres to vanish during the age of reason and satire. Besides the religious lyric, one could count on the endangered literary species list in the eighteenth century the love lyric generally, the sonnet cycle, pastoral poetry, epic, romance comedy and tragedy.

8   See Bridget Keegan's "Mysticisms and Mystifications: The Demands of Laboring-Class Religious Poetry" in *Criticism*, Volume 47, Number 4, Fall 2005, pp. 471–91.

his own peculiar exile, would pick up the thread from that aged South-wellian loom. Gerard Hopkins, fashioning religious poetry as a Roman Catholic priest in the later nineteenth century was, of course, not just out of place, but out of time. That his predecessors were re-mote rather than immediate seems not to have bothered this professor of classical languages, for whom the lapse of a mere three centuries on the literary timeline meant little. In applying his own powerful and peculiar poetic vision to the fashioning of religious lyrics, Hopkins was not seeking necessarily to pick up a literary thread or to resurrect a literary genre. He was simply doing what his most prominent English Jesuit literary predecessor[9] had done centuries before: demanding that his second vocation proceed from his first. The result was a body of poetry, modest in quantity and bold in innovation, that when finally recognized long after the poet's death would actually resurrect in Eng-land "the dust of dead supplies" that Southwell had long before in-spired.

9   Gerard Hopkins may have been aware of the other Jesuits preceding him who wrote religious verse. In her 1939 collection of selected works of *Recusant Poets* Louise Imogen Guiney includes poems by John Donne's uncle, Jasper Heywood, S.J. (1535–1598); Thomas Pounde, S.J. (1539–1614); Henry Fitzsimon, S.J. (1566-1643), and Henry Walpole, S.J. (1558–1595). In an 1881 letter to R. W. Dixon, Hopkins notes that "there have been very few Jesuit poets." He sin-gles out Southwell as a minor poet and praises Campion (presumably for his prose writings), but he does not mention any of the Jesuits listed here by name.

Chapter 7
The Dust of Dead Supplies:
Southwell and Gerard Manley Hopkins

"The vanity of men," wrote Robert Southwell in his famous prefatory epistle, "cannot Counterpease the authority of god" (1). His use of the old French term *counterpoise*, while somewhat unusual, was not unique. William Shakespeare and Edmund Spenser both used the term,[1] which, like our present-day equivalent, counterbalance, seems to have served equally well as a verb ("to balance by a weight on the opposite side") or a noun ("a weight which balances another weight"). More unusual, though not entirely anachronistic, is Gerard Hopkins's use of this very word in 1881 to describe the poetic career of Robert Southwell. In a letter to his friend R. W. Dixon he observed that Southwell "wrote amidst terrible persecution and died a martyr, with circumstances of horrible barbarity: this is the counterpoise of his career" (*Correspondence*, ii, 94).

We need not infer just what Hopkins means by the term counterpoise since he makes it clear as he goes on to consider the disappointingly small number of poets cultivated in the Society of Jesus throughout history:

1   The OED offers an example from Book V of Spenser's *Faerie Queene*: "That all the world he would weigh equallie, / If ought he had the same to counterpoyseth." In Shakespeare's plays the word is used seven times, four of which describe a marriage dowry as when Claudio asks Don Pedro sarcastically "And what have I to give you back whose worth / May counterpoise this rich and precious gift?" (IV, I, 25–26) and three times in relationship to power, as when Hotspur is cautioned by a letter, "Your whole plot is too light for the counterpoise of so great an opposition" (1HIV II, iii, 12–13).

We have had for three centuries often the flower of the youth of a country in numbers enter our body: among these how many poets, how many artists of all sorts, there must have been! But there have been very few Jesuit poets and, where they have been, I believe it would be found on examination that there was something exceptional in their circumstances or, so to say, counterbalancing in their career (*Correspondence*, ii, 93).

Hopkins then mentions "Fr. Beschi who in Southern Hindustan composed an epic which has become one of the Tamul classics and is spoken of with unbounded admiration by those who can read it," and "In England we had Fr. Southwell a poet, a minor poet but still a poet" concluding, as I noted above, that Southwell's persecution was "the counterpoise of his career." Hopkins then devotes considerable praise to Edmund Campion, calling him a genius and asking rhetorically "Was not he a poet? Perhaps a great one, if he had chosen" (*Correspondence*, 94). But as Campion did not choose to write any verse in English, the answer to Hopkins's question is, of course, no; Campion, the pioneer English Jesuit of the recusant era, eloquent prose author, preacher and martyr, was, for all that, not an English poet.

Hopkins is left in his brief litany with one minor poet as his sole English Jesuit predecessor.[2] And of this minor poet's career he has, it seems,

2   Besides sharing the distinction as the only two Jesuits in the canon of English literature, Hopkins and Southwell are among the few Roman Catholic priests in the English canon. Others include the Anglican convert, Fr. R. H. Benson, (1871–1914) whose works of historical fiction like *By What Authority* and *Come Rack! Come Rope!* dramatize the plight of Catholics in the English Recusancy. Then there is Fr. Ronald Knox (1888–1957), who, besides his numerous books, essays and novels undertook in 1936, at the direction of his religious superiors, a successful translation of the *Latin Vulgate Bible* into English, using Hebrew and Greek sources. Knox delivered the homily at the funeral Mass of the English writer, G. K. Chesterton whose influence had helped inspire his own conversion to Catholicism. Then of course there is most prominently Cardinal John Henry Newman (1801–1890), who besides his great ecclesiastical achievements was

but a partial understanding, expressing belief still popular at that time that Southwell wrote his poems in prison.[3] We now know that ink and paper were part of the deprivations suffered by Southwell from the time of his arrest until his execution nearly three years later. True, of course, there was, as Hopkins says, something "exceptional" in Southwell's "circumstances," living first as a young exile from his native country and then clandestinely during his six years in England preceding his capture, torture, prolonged imprisonment and execution. Considered in contrast to these harrowing enterprises, Hopkins's rather mundane and often dreary life as a nineteenth-century English Jesuit priest might seem to offer no counterpoise at all. However, considered more thoughtfully, with attention to the beliefs that inspired and formed these two men, we find in their lives, I believe, a common weight that counterbalanced their poetry. Each man, in addition to being a poet, was a Jesuit Roman Catholic priest, and each as a result was estranged from his native country and his family.

In Jerome Bump's essay "Hopkins, Metalepsis, and the Metaphysicals," he observes that Hopkins's short lyric "Heaven Haven"[4] recalls

an author whose writings were admired by, among others, James Joyce. Newman was the one who received Hopkins as well as other members of the Oxford Movement into the Catholic Church.

3   This is a popular misunderstanding that still persists. On a web-site *Litany of Jesuit Saints* by Louis J. McCabe, S.J., and Philip Steele, S.J., Southwell is invoked as "Robert Southwell, prisoner-poet of comfort and strength," Campion as "fearless orator and source of courage to the persecuted," and the un-canonized Hopkins as "catcher of fire and crafter of words."

4   "Heaven-Haven"
(a nun takes the veil)
I have desired to go
Where springs not fail,
To fields where flies no sharp and sided hail
And a few lilies blow.

And I have asked to be
Where no storms come,
Where the green swell is in the havens dumb,
And out of the swing of the sea.

the verses of Herbert and Vaughan, as well perhaps as the following
lines from Robert Southwell's "Seeke flowers of heaven":[5]

Graze not on worldly withered weede
    It fitteth not thy taste,
The flowres of everlastinge springe
    Doe growe for thy repaste

(. . .)

Whose soveraigne sent surpassing sense
    So ravisheth the Mynde
That worldly weedes needes must be loath,
    That can these flowres finde (stanzas 2 and 6).[6]

Bump concludes that the echoes between these poets can be traced to
"the common source . . . *the Psalms*, especially Psalm 107" (311).
While this may well be the case in this particular instance as well as
elsewhere, within the lives of Southwell and Hopkins a daily reading
of the *Psalms* was but one important aspect of their common spiritual
disciplines, the practice of Ignatian meditation as a prayerful form of
apprehending scripture being a more specific and significant influence
upon both of their lives and poetic endeavors. In fact, if there is a single

5   *John Donne Journal*, 4:2, (1985). In his article Bump gives attention
    to Hopkins's reliance upon seventeenth-century religious verse. While
    he acknowledges one or two echoes of Southwell in Hopkins's verse,
    he advances the conventional case that Herbert (1593–1633) was the
    most significant English influence upon Hopkins prior to Christina
    Rossetti.

6   While, as elsewhere, this passage is from Davidson and Sweeney's edi-
    tion of Southwell's *Collected Poems*. Bump's own citation of these
    lines from Southwell are confusing at best. "Seeke flowers of heaven"
    is typed with a colon at the beginning of the rest of the lines, but he
    tells the reader in a footnote that the lines are from "Christs returne
    out of Egypt" from *The Sequences on The Virgin Mary and Christ*.
    This is surely not the case. Bump also misquotes line two of this cita-
    tion, transcribing "Graze" as "Gaze," a rather substantial difference.

counterbalance that yields a poetic and human equilibrium for these two poets, it is their shared discipline of practicing the regenerative meditative prayers of *The Spiritual Exercises*.

These *Exercises* "became the rule and guide of his whole being," David Downes says of Gerard Hopkins. The same may be said of Southwell, and if we allow for the fact that Southwell lived a shorter life than Hopkins,[7] and that he never attempted a written commentary upon the *Exercises*, nearly every word in the following description by John Pick concerning the significance of the *Exercises* upon Hopkins could be said as well of Southwell:

> For twenty-one years Hopkins dedicated himself to the Society of Jesus; for twenty-one years he studied, meditated, and practiced the *Spiritual Exercises*. They became part of his life and attitude. They gave direction to all he experienced, thought, and wrote. They influenced his most exuberant and joyous poems; they were part of his suffering and desolation. He delivered sermons suggested by them, started to write a commentary on them; he gave them to others. They fashioned his reaction to nature and beauty. Their echo is found in his consciousness of imperfection, in his abnegation and in the integrity with which he faced hardship and disappointment. His attitude towards poetry and fame was shaped by them. They moulded his native temperament and sensibility to an ideal of perfection. Without knowing something of them we can hardly know the priest-poet (25–26).

At the very least readers of Hopkins and Southwell must appreciate the prescribed engagement of the exercitant's senses and imagination in responding to specific passages of scripture, their engagement and development of what Anthony Raspa calls "the emotive image."

It was only a few years after Pick had offered this description of the significance of the *Spiritual Exercises* in understanding Hopkins

7   In his letter to William Cecil Southwell states: "Of this Order I have been fourteen years—I would to God I could say these four and twenty years" (*Two Letters*, 80).

that Martz began to make his case that these same *Exercises* were behind the seventeenth-century poetry that modern readers had come to know as "metaphysical."[8] Martz, we recall, called this poetry instead "the poetry of meditation" and claimed that it originated "not in John Donne, but in Robert Southwell" (*Meditation* 3). Southwell, he observed was the first English poet to fashion poetry that was the product of "the common practice of certain methods of religious meditation" (3); namely, the Ignatian "application of the senses," which was a form of prayer as well as an excellent method for writing poetry. For Southwell and Hopkins it was, by vow and vocation, both of these things.

In 1959 David Downes presented a thorough treatment of the role that the *Spiritual Exercises* played in the fashioning of Hopkins's poetry in his book *Gerard Manley Hopkins: A Study of His Ignatian Spirit*. When a second edition of Downes's landmark book was issued four decades later upon the centenary of poet's death,[9] Hopkins's literary reputation had increased dramatically and spread internationally. Neither post-modernism, nor a proliferation of accompanying new literary theories has slowed the steadily increasing popularity and literary reputation of Hopkins. Though not yet with comprehensive specificity, treatment of the Ignatian ingredients in Southwell's poetry has also been significant, especially by Janelle, Martz, Roberts, Raspa, and most recently Scott Pilarz. The term Jesuit is such a politically charged one in the history of sixteenth-century England, that Southwell's dramatic life as a priest in the Elizabethan era can easily overshadow his more fundamental disposition as a disciplined practitioner of Ignatius's prescribed *Exercises*. Nonetheless, as the aforementioned critics have demonstrated in their analysis, what Downes says of

8   Pick's book was published in 1942. Martz first drew readers' attention to Ignatian influence in seventeenth-century poetry in his 1947 ELH article, "John Donne in Meditation: The Anniversaries." He developed his case for Ignatian influence significantly for his first major book, *The Poetry of Meditation*, in 1954.
9   The 1990 edition of Downes's book is entitled *The Ignatian Personality of Gerard Manley Hopkins*. Downes's understanding of Hopkins's Ignatian personality is informed and shared by several early stalwarts of Hopkins criticism, including Walter Ong, Alfred Thomas, James Cotter and Robert Boyle.

Hopkins's mature poetry is every bit as applicable to Southwell's: "the nature of the Ignatian influence is shown in general to be that of providing the poet with an ordered and intelligible Christian world view, with an applied spiritual approach to Nature, man, and God, and lastly with emotional and mental internalizations convertible to poetic techniques" (3). Describing the earliest applications of Ignatius's *Exercises* to the writing of poetry, Raspa details the similarities succinctly:

> Although the poem was on a page and the exercitant's image was in his imagination, their roles were largely similar. Because of their common recourse to the senses, they differed only in the ascetic and the aesthetic character of their appeals. Springing from the ancient Aristotelian principle that nothing was in the mind which was not first in the senses, they sought a common meditative effect. Their respective appeals were outwardly psychologically different, but they shared identical sensory and visionary values in the framework of one psychology (37).

Southwell and Hopkins, and at times Donne, achieved this common meditative effect. However, Hopkins's application of the *Exercises* in his poetry is on the whole more subtle than Southwell's insofar as he does not convert scriptural meditations into meditative narratives that imagine what particular characters might have spoken.[10] He fashions no sequence of poems on the Nativity or the Passion. Neither, however, does his poetry ignore these topics, and critics like Downes contend that Hopkins scarcely fashions a poem that is not in some way affected by the meditative demands of *The Exercises* that he practiced himself and recommended to others. To best understand the difference between the influence of the *Exercises* upon Southwell and upon Hopkins, one need only consider what came between their

10 The one poem in which Hopkins has a biblical character speak in internal monologue well preceded his experience of Ignatius's *Spiritual Exercises* or reading Southwell. His fragments of *Pilate*, an incomplete dramatic monologue, ("Then I seek out the shadow and stones / And to those stones become akin" 8–9), reflect, as Catherine Phillips points out, more the influence of Tennyson.

respective careers, or rather who, namely: Herbert, Donne, Crashaw and Vaughan; Coleridge, Wordsworth, Shelley and Keats. The distance between Southwell's and Hopkins's poetry is the distance between the sixteenth and nineteenth century which, poetically, became the distance between the third and the first person, or between the framed narrative and the personal confession. In Ignatian terms it is the distance between "seeing the persons" and "reflecting on oneself."

Anthony Low suggests that the most difficult aspect of John Donne's priesthood in the Anglican Church was not preaching, but presiding "over the celebration of the Lord's Supper" because "he would have to believe not only that the Anglican Church was the one true Church, but that its sacraments were valid" (114). Hopkins's conversion was of course the reverse of Donne's and it was precisely the real presence in the Eucharist that moved him from Anglican to Roman Catholic. Beyond the fact that Southwell's and Hopkins's poems contain numerous liturgical and sacramental elements, therefore, a more precise and substantive question is what, for these two Roman Catholic priests, was the connection between the sacraments they performed and the poetry that they wrote? Did they recognize a relationship between the words they spoke to effect a change in physical matter, and the words they wrote to effect a change in readers? What we discover as we consider such questions, I believe, is that at the very essence of Southwell's and Hopkins's sacramental and literary work was the central Christian event of the Incarnation. The word had been made flesh and it was their vocation as priests as well as poets to keep it so.

If we consider the shared metaphorical and linguistic nature of Catholic sacrament and poetry, we discover a connection between priest and poet that is more fundamental, substantial and intimate than has been understood and expressed by many critics of both poets. Both Southwell and Hopkins would have recognized that the Catholic sacraments and poetry each rely upon the spoken word to give them shape, so that, in Margaret Ellsberg's words, "poetic words shared the responsibility and power of sacramental words" (57). The common responsibility and power of sacrament and poetry, for these two poets, resided in the shared metaphorical capacity of each to signify as well as effect. Thomas Aquinas, as he applies the Aristotelian categories of form and matter to the seven sacraments, elucidates the shaping function of word in sacrament. For example, in the sacrament of Baptism the matter of the sacrament is water, while the form of the sacrament is the spoken baptismal formula, "I baptize you in the name of the Father, Son and Holy Spirit." The matter of each sacrament may vary, but each waits upon the spoken word to give it form. Bread, wine, water, oil, or human penitents may be present, but without the spoken word, no sacrament occurs. Poetry is similarly dependent upon the spoken word to give it shape. The poet may have at his disposal any variety of images, ideas or abstractions that, without words to give them shape, remain but fragmented thoughts and scattered images.[11]

These similarities notwithstanding, the act of writing religious poetry, like the act of preaching, was accompanied for these men by a certain paradox. The Word had become flesh, and the work of the preacher and devotional poet was to turn that flesh back into words. Hence, George Herbert's question: "Lord, how can man preach thy eternal word?/ He is a brittle crazie glasse" ("Windows," 1–2) is not merely rhetorical. This very question—concerned as it is with preaching and with man's impurity—hints of a slightly more Protestant disposition than that of Southwell or Hopkins. So too does Herbert's resolution, for as he extends his comparison of the preacher to refracting stained glass windows, he resolves that "Doctrine and life . . . /

11 Northrop Frye describes this dual attribute of the word in poetry in the following manner: "In symbolism the word does not echo the thing but other words, and hence the immediate impact symbolism makes on the reader is that of *incantation* [emphasis mine], a harmony of sounds and the sense of a growing richness of meaning unlimited by denotation" (Anatomy, 1). So, on the one hand, as a denoter of a specific image or idea, the word, in both sacrament and poetry is exact in its meaning. As a sound image, on the other hand— echoing not the thing but other words—the word is, as Frye says, unlimited, infinite, in the sensual, emotive responses it might provoke within the listener. In the case of sacrament, much more so than in poetry, the chosen image, whatever infinite emotive and sensual images it evokes, is neither incidental nor decorative, but prescribed and sacred. The sacred sign (bread, oil, penitent sinner) shaped by the word becomes the sacrament. Just so, albeit with less specificity, the selected images of the poet shaped by words become the poem.

When they combine and mingle, bring / A strong regard and aw: / but speech alone / Doth vanish like a flaring thing / And in the eare, not conscience ring" (11–14). Like the combination of color and light in the window, the preacher must, Herbert concludes, match the life he lives with the words he preaches in order to make the eternal Word flesh. Is it any wonder that many of Herbert's other poems are filled with so much disappointment and discouragement? Both the emphasis on preaching and the demands that he places upon the preacher reflect, I believe, an anxiety born of Calvinist influence, angst that Southwell and Hopkins would not have shared in the same portion. For, while they too would have striven to imitate Christ, to suit their actions to the words they preached, they would have recognized more keenly that the post-lapserian reality of being "brittle crazie glasse" did not prevent or excuse them from their priestly duties.[12]

Their own human brittleness, as we saw in the previous chapter, was reinforced in these two men by their practice of Ignatius's *Spiritual Exercises*, exercises that originate with and hearken the exercitant back to the singular fact of the Incarnation. "Christ lived and breathed and moved in a true and not a phantom human body," Hopkins reminded his congregation in a sermon at Bedford Leigh in 1879 (*Works*, 277). In what, unbeknownst to him, would be the last year of his life, Hopkins wrote in his retreat journal:

And my life is determined by the Incarnation down to most of the details of the day. Now this being so that I cannot even stop it, why should I not make the cause that determines my life, both as a whole and in much detail, determine it in greater detail still and of the greater efficiency of what I in any case should do, and to my greater happiness in doing it? It is for this that St. Ignatius speaks of the angel *discharging his mission,* it being a question of action leading

12 Both Southwell and Hopkins in their training for the Catholic priesthood would have been made to understand Augustine's famous argument against the Donatists in which he makes the case that the validity of one's baptism, as well as the other sacraments, cannot be dependent upon the particular virtues of an individual priest. That is, sacraments work *ex opera operato,* not *ex opera operantis.*

up to, as now my action leads from, the Incarnation. The Incarnation was for my salvation and that of the world: the work goes on in a great system and machinery which even drags me on with the collar round my neck though I could and do neglect my duty in it. But I say to myself that I am only too willing to do God's work and help on the knowledge of the Incarnation (*Works*, 304).

Still there is the brittleness. For Hopkins immediately follows this reluctant resolution with the admission "But this is not really true: I am not willing enough for the piece of work assigned me" (304). The piece of work assigned to him that he performs unwillingly is the teaching of Greek and the laborious grading of qualifying exams at the fledgling University College on Stephens Green in Dublin, a fate that he compares to the census issued by Caesar Augustus that sent Joseph and his pregnant wife wandering into Judea. This recollection of the circumstances of Christ's own incarnation is Hopkins's only consolation: "but the journey to Bethlehem was inconvenient and painful; and then I am bound in justice, and paid. I hope to bear this in mind" (304).

We have, unfortunately, no such private reflections from Robert Southwell. It is clear, however, that just as *The Spiritual Exercises* brought Hopkins back to the significance and difficulty of Christ's incarnation, so too, they did the same for Southwell. The inconvenience and pain, not just of the journey to Bethlehem, but nearly every part of Christ's improbable coming into the world (from conception to circumcision) are treated by Robert Southwell in his poetry. Sixteen of his poems (over a fourth), including eleven from his Sequence on the Virgin Mary and Christ, as well as his most famous poem, "The Burning Babe," have as their subject some aspect of the Incarnation.

Hopkins and Southwell's preoccupation with the Incarnation would lead them always back to the essential work of their priesthood. For the Word could not be made flesh by matching their inadequate and sinful lives with their preaching; nor could this be accomplished by writing poetry, no matter how devout. Ultimately the Incarnation occurred in their sacramental work as priests, and nowhere more significantly than the changing of bread and wine into the corporeal presence of Jesus in the Eucharist. In 1864 Hopkins wrote to E. H. Coleridge that "the great aid to belief and object of belief is the doctrine of the Real Presence in the Blessed Sacrament of the Altar. Religion without it," he declares, "is somber, dangerous, illogical," but "with that it is—not to speak of its grand consistency and certainty—*loveable*. Hold that and you will gain all Catholic truth" (Letters, III, 173–72). Justifying his conversion to Roman Catholicism, Hopkins wrote to his father in 1866:

> I shall hold as a Catholic what I have long held as an Anglican, that literal truth of our Lord's words by which I learn that the least fragment of the consecrated elements in the Blessed Sacrament of the Altar is the whole Body of Christ born of the Blessed Virgin, before which the whole of the host of saints and angels as it lies on the altar trembles with adoration. This belief once got is the life of the soul and when I doubted it I shd. become an atheist the next day (*Letters*, 92).

It is perhaps mere coincidence or theological convention that in both of the above declarations of faith Hopkins uses the very words of the title of a Robert Southwell poem, "Of the Blessed sacrament of the Aulter." In any case, his belief, and the fervency with which he proclaimed it, would have been shared by Southwell who, during his years in England, never once celebrated the Eucharist without risk to his life. Thus when we regard the sacramental symbols in the works of these two priests, we need to recognize that we are speaking not merely of religious imagery, but of symbols that represent for them, "even in the least fragment" or the briefest mention, "the whole Body of Christ born of the Blessed Virgin." In doing so we see the deliberateness with which these sacramental symbols were incorporated into poetry and the seriousness of intention that accompanied their work for the benefit of those who would "make a gain." It would have been their hopeful expectation that the use of liturgical and Eucharistic symbols and language in their verse would alert, inspire and catechize and remind their readers. In the case of Southwell's underground audience, his poetry might even serve as a kind of remote, inadequate substitute for the sacraments themselves.

In considering the common exile that these two poets experienced as a result of their religious beliefs, we should acknowledge that neither of them was ever formally exiled from England. However, both, by virtue of being Roman Catholics and Jesuit priests, were estranged from their families and their country, for which they expressed great affection and loyalty. Where actual political disaffection is concerned, Southwell's is a clear case. Born on the grounds of the ruined Benedictine abbey of St. Faith, Norfolk from which the last monks had departed a quarter century before his birth,[13] he would be sent abroad to Europe when he was fourteen. It seems that it was his mother's determination that landed young Robert in a Jesuit school in Belgium in 1576. His biographers surmise that he spent a good portion of his early adolescence in and around the household of his mother's brother, Thomas Copley, who presided over one of the most prominent Catholic households in all of England before entering exile in 1572. Robert and his siblings may then have resided at Warblington, the estate of his mother's cousin, George Cotton. The household's oldest son, John Cotton, was Southwell's companion on the secret voyage to Belgium. When he and Cotton boarded the boat to cross the Channel they had to be mindful that they might never again set foot on English soil.

When Southwell did return, after ten years of education in Jesuit schools and seminaries in northern Europe, France and Rome, he did

---

13 Southwell's grandfather had acquired the ruined abbey in return for his loyal service to King Henry VIII, service that included, among other things, serving as the chief accuser at the trial of his kinsman and boyhood companion, courtier poet, Henry Howard, Earl of Surrey. Christopher Devlin describes Sir Richard's career as one "whose watchword had been to serve the king and save his own skin at whatever moral hazard," noting how he "slipped adroitly from one party to the other like a cormorant riding the waves" (Devlin, 4–5). Southwell's father, through ill fortune and poor business decisions, ultimately lost the substantial wealth of the Southwell household. The world into which Robert was born, however, was one "entrenched in that most privileged of all classes . . . the Tudor-made oligarchy founded on Church spoils" (Devlin, 5). Kindred with two of England's most prominent families, the Cecils and the Copleys, all may have been considered well in the Southwell household, save for an occasional encounter with one of the aging, pension-stripped vagabond ex-monks who roamed the countryside.

so in his words, "as a foreigner" (*Letters*, 4). He was an ordained Catholic priest known in Rome as Father Southwello, who, now in England, assumed the inconspicuous pseudonym of "Mr. Cotton." It is an irony worthy of reflection that the strange land in which Robert Southwell would fulfill his romantic young dreams of being a missionary and martyr was his native England. He would be discouraged from embarking upon the English mission by those in Rome who were putting his talents as a writer, teacher and administrator to excellent use, but the desire to return to England and the powerful example of Edmund Campion were far more persuasive than the cautions of his superiors.

Southwell's return as "a foreigner" meant, among other things that he would remain estranged from his family since these households would have been under the watchful eyes of the pursuivants who sought to capture the elusive priest. Later, during his prolonged imprisonment in the tower, Southwell reported to Robert Cecil that he had returned to England to serve as a pastor to his family (*Letters*, 81). Insofar as this claim implies that his mission was merely of a private nature, it would seem, especially in light of the ambitious printing enterprise, to be an equivocating understatement at best. Even so it does express a sincere desire in which Southwell was disappointed.

In "An Epistle of Robert Southwell to his Father" dated 1589, the young priest addresses his father in a lengthy letter in which a private remonstrance is embedded within a highly stylized rhetorical presentation. The letter concerns itself with the failings of his father who he says has "long sowed in a field of flint which could bring [him] nothing forth but a crop of cares" (*Two Letters*, 8). The epistle is private only in the same sense that Southwell came to England *only* to be a pastor to his family. The author's concerns may be private and familial, but the printed letter, like his ministry, is for a broader audience of readers. The epistle begins by describing the author's necessary estrangement from his family:

> Yet, because I might very easily perceive by apparent conjectures that many were more willing to hear of me than from me, and readier to praise than to use my endeavors, I have hitherto bridled my desire to see them with the care and jealousy of their safety, and banishing myself from the

scene[14] of my cradle, in my own country I have lived like a foreigner, finding among strangers that which in my nearest blood I presumed not to seek" (4).

The domestic exile of the self-bridled and self-banished priest moves readers to sympathize with the writer, but such sympathies might fade as the reader perceives his apparent lack of sympathy for his father. The elder Southwell's teasing nickname for his young son has now come back at him with a certain ironic vengeance: "from my infancy you were wont in merriment to call me 'Father Robert,' which is the customary style now allotted to my present state" (7). "I am at once both the kind of Father who may assist you now spiritually," the younger Southwell explains, "as well, of course, your dutiful son."

Southwell's familial separation and his remonstrance of his own father help us to understand the very similar counterpoise in the poetic career of Gerard Hopkins, though their circumstances were dramatically different. Hopkins's life lacked the dangerous adventure of Southwell's imperiled and secretive existence. The intellectually gifted, eldest son of a successful English merchant and a very High Anglican mother, Hopkins was raised in the suburbs of Victorian London, afforded a proper education that would gain him entry to Oxford where his devout nature and orthodox High Anglicanism would inspire an attraction to Roman Catholicism. His disaffection with the liberal Anglicanism of Balliol College, his attraction to the charism and writings of Henry Newman, and a particular zeal for the doctrine of the real presence of Christ in the Eucharist all combined to confirm his conversion to the Roman Church. In this, the most significant decision of his life, we see in Gerard Hopkins a paradoxical combination of orthodoxy and eccentricity that would characterize his actions and words, and keep him in a kind of estrangement from others for his entire life.

14 The actual text from which I have taken this quote is edited by Nancy Pollard Brown for the Folger Shakespeare Library and reads "*scent of my cradle.*" While there is no more respected editor of Southwell's work than Professor Brown, others using her edited text have, like myself, opted here for what seems to be the more sensible reading "*scene of my cradle.*"

All of this is on display in an exchange of letters between father and son (which thankfully were not printed as an epistle), in which the young Gerard Hopkins let his father know that his determination to become a Roman Catholic was necessary and irreversible and that no counsel from his parents or mentors could dissuade him:

> You ask me to suspend my judgment for a long time, or at the very least more than half a year, in other words to stand still for a time. Now to stand still is not possible, thus: I must either obey the Church or disobey. If I disobey, I am not suspending judgment but deciding, namely to take backward steps fr. the grounds I have already come to. To stand still if it were possible might be justifiable, but to go back nothing can justify. I must therefore obey the Church by ceasing to attend any service of the Church of England.

As to the estrangement that his determination has created between himself and his family, Hopkins tells his father that he has contemplated it for months. The solution at which he has arrived matches precisely Southwell's own prescription for his father. In brief, Hopkins declares, his parents must convert to Roman Catholicism. If they do not, it is they who are responsible for the estrangement, not he. While his logic is cold, his declaration is anything but brief. His call to his parents to surrender themselves to the intercession of the Holy Family is elaborate and dramatic. As with Southwell's epistle, the overall effect is that of a sermon, rather than a young man addressing his parents:

> Our Lord's last care on the cross was to commend His mother in the person of St. John. If even now you wd. put yourselves into that position wh. Christ so unmistakeably gives us and ask the Mother of sorrows to remember her three hours' compassion at the cross, the piercing of the sword prophecied by Simeon, and her seven dolours, and her spouse Joseph, the lily of chastity, to remember the flight into Egypt, the searching for his Foster-Son at twelve years old, and his last ecstasy with Christ at his death-bed, the prayers of this Holy Family wd. In a few days put an

end to estrangements for ever. If you shrink fr. doing this, though, the Gospels cry aloud to you to do it, at least for once if you like, only once approach Christ in a new way in which you will at all events feel you are exactly in unison with me, that is not vaguely, but casting yourselves into His sacred broken heart and His five adorable Wounds. Those who do not pray to Him in His Passion pray to God but scarcely to Christ. I have the right to propose this, for I have tried both ways, and if you will not give one trial to this way you will see you are prolonging the estrangement and not I (*Letters*, III, 94–95).

Having issued this improbable and condescending invitation; having, in effect, tossed down the holy gauntlet to his father and mother, and laid the blame for their estrangement from him upon their own unwillingness to convert to Roman Catholicism, the resolute young Oxford scholar concludes, "after saying this I feel light-hearted" (95). Needless to say, the effect upon his parents was quite the opposite. Replying to Gerard's letter, his father concedes at the outset that the things he might say will likely not be regarded by his son: "At least the tone of your letter is so hard & cold, it gives me little encouragement" (*Letters*, III, 96). As for the challenge to convert, Manley Hopkins is appropriately succinct and equally dramatic: "You answer by saying that as we might be Romanists if we pleased the estrangement is not of your doing. O Gerard my darling boy are you indeed gone from me?" (97).

Fortunately, as this was the nineteenth and not the sixteenth century in England, Gerard was not literally gone from his father or his family. He would return home that Christmas and again for extended visits at holidays, and he sustained a regular and affectionate correspondence with his mother for years to come. His decision to become a Jesuit priest two years later would be met more with resignation than melodrama. The estrangement that his conversion had prompted, it seems, was countered by familial loyalty, respect and affection, and any lingering hurt feelings were suppressed in the name of Victorian manners and getting on with one's life. Nonetheless, when his life with the Jesuits became one of "fortune's football" in which he was moved from place to place with disruptive frequency, and then ultimately made an actual foreigner by being assigned to University College Dublin, Hopkins's exile was complete. The combination of dank living conditions, arduous teaching responsibilities and his irrepressible Englishness among the Irish population made him every bit the stranger that his hunted Jesuit poet predecessor had been. One of the most stark and honest poems he wrote there, but for the reference to Ireland, could have been spoken by and would have consoled Southwell at any moment in his mission. In fact, the estrangement expressed in this sonnet could have been voiced by any one of the poets treated in this study:

> To seem the stranger lies my lot, my life
> Among strangers. Father and mother dear,
> Brothers and sisters are in Christ not near
> And in my peace/my parting, sword and strife.
>
> England, whose honour O all my heart woos, wife
> To my creating thought, would neither hear
> Me, were I pleading, plead nor do I:
> I weary of idle a being but by where wars are rife.
>
> I am in Ireland now; now I am at a third
> Remove. Not but in all removes I can
> Kind love both give and get. Only what word
>
> Wisest my heart breeds dark heaven's baffling ban
> Bars or hell's spell thwarts. This to hoard unheard,
> Heard unheeded, leaves me a lonely began (*Works*)

As we have seen, Gerard Hopkins's only specific written mention of Robert Southwell is in a letter to R. W. Dixon written in 1881. The letter was written, Hopkins notes, "the very day 300 years ago of Father Campion's martyrdom" (*Correspondence*, 92). Southwell himself, following almost directly in Campion's recusant footsteps, would be martyred to the same cause fourteen years later. Campion would emerge very early as the more famous Jesuit; Southwell, eventually, the more important literary figure. The dates of both men's martyrdoms would likely have been remembered in the Jesuit houses. That

Hopkins has no more to say elsewhere, either in his journals or correspondence, about Robert Southwell has apparently been enough to
discourage any serious consideration of these two poets' commonality.
Hopkins's neglect, however, is general; that is, he never again takes up
the subject of his scant Jesuit literary heritage. Campion himself is
mentioned only a few other times in Hopkins's writings, and that not
in a literary context. What he does say of Southwell indicates a familiarity with the details of the young Jesuit's persecuted life, and his assertion that Southwell was "a minor poet but still a poet," could only
responsibly have come from a first-hand knowledge of Southwell's
works.

Making a case for Crashaw's influence on Hopkins in his book
The Revival of Metaphysical Poetry, Joseph Duncan argues that it is
"difficult to believe that so staunch an Englishman and so ardent a
Catholic as Hopkins did not know at least a little about the work of
the foremost English Catholic devotional poet of the past" (100).
While I do not wish to challenge Duncan's assertion or debate who
was the foremost English Catholic devotional poet in Hopkins's past,[15]
I would borrow Duncan's logic and echo his insistence in asserting
that it is even more difficult to imagine that Hopkins would not know
the works of the most prominent English Jesuit poet to precede him.
Hopkins's acquaintance with the life and works of Southwell did not
come, I think, all at once, but instead accompanied, and likely
strengthened his progression from High Anglicanism to Roman
Catholicism, and then increased with his subsequent vocations as Jesuit priest and poet.

Hopkins did of course own a copy of George Herbert's *The Temple* as well as Henry Vaughan's *Private Ejaculations*, and a deliberate
search through the family library's twenty-one volumes of Chalmers'
Works of the English Poets, Chaucer to Cowper (1810) would have
yielded him a generous selection of John Donne as well as a sampling

---

15 Duncan's case for Crashaw's influence on Hopkins is even more difficult than my present one for Southwell, as Hopkins never so much
as mentions either Donne or Crashaw anywhere in his writings. Their
presence in Chalmers' *Works* (see note 14), offers some support to
the case that Duncan makes for the two poets' influence upon Hopkins.

of Richard Crashaw, but no Southwell.[16] It seems unlikely that the young Hopkins would have heard of Robert Southwell except by some peculiar, unrecorded chance. His first acquaintance with Southwell's martyrdom, and perhaps his poetry, may have occurred during his years at Oxford as he began to move more and more in the Roman Catholic circle.

Hopkins's interest in what he termed "Herbert and his school," which may have brought him into contact with the poetry of Southwell, would have been part of the general renewed interest on the part of High Anglicans and Catholics, at Oxford and elsewhere, in this previously neglected poetry. "The metaphysical revival and the Catholic revival," Duncan observes, "cross-fertilized each other" (89), noting that "it was natural that English Catholicism should turn to metaphysical poetry, with its frequent dependence on incarnational and sacramental symbolism" (90). Duncan quotes Hopkins's contemporary, Francis Thompson's defense of metaphysical conceits, colloquial language and "the very foolishness and madness of devotion" (90). Thompson, Duncan notes, "began his early essay on Shelley by calling upon the church to take poetry back into the fold" (90). How reassuring it must have been to Hopkins later on to find at the very origins of this newly popular devotional verse of the seventeenth century a Jesuit predecessor railing against the misuse of poetry and calling upon poets to turn their devotions to divine subjects. Editions of Southwell to which Hopkins had access would have contained at the beginning his famous epistle urging poets to take poetry back into the church's fold instead of busying "themselves in expressing such passions, as only serve for testimonies to how unworthy affections they have wedded their wils" (*Poems*, 1).

A more substantive acquaintance with Robert Southwell's life and works probably occurred for Hopkins during his early years as a Jesuit. This subsequent exposure to Southwell's prose and poetry coincides, I believe, with his own most fruitful years as a poet. It is quite possible that during his novitiate at Roehampton Hopkins heard or read a narrative of Southwell's inspiring martyrdom. During his

16 See "Books belonging to Hopkins and his family" in *The Hopkins Research Bulletin*, No.5 (1974), as well as the supplement "Books Hopkins had access to" in *HRB*, No. 6 (1975).

subsequent years at Stonyhurst (1870–73) and St. Beuno's (1874–77), Hopkins would have both increasing motivation as well as ample opportunity to read Southwell's poetry. At Stonyhurst there were as many as five editions of Southwell's poems in the Library: two editions published at the English College Press at St. Omer's, 1616 and 1620 (the library held two copies of the 1620 edition); an edition of *Saint Peter's Complaint with Other Poems* by the Rev. Robert Southwell, edited by W. Jos. Walter, published by Keating, Brown and Co. London, 1817, and *The Complete Poems of Robert Southwell*, edited by Rev. Alexander Grosart, Printed for Private Circulation in 1872.[17] Also at Stonyhurst Hopkins would perhaps have seen the only known picture of Robert Southwell, a crayon drawing made from a now missing oil portrait, and the only extant image we have of him.

No case of influence better illustrates Hopkins's familiarity with Southwell's writings made during these years than that which resulted under the influence of his instructor and Southwell editor, Father John Morris, S.J. When we consider the rather improbable connections of four priests—Fathers Diego de Estella, Robert Southwell, John Morris, Gerard Hopkins—made across two continents and three centuries, we discover between our two Jesuit poets a remarkable case of influence in the flight and descent of a familiar regal hawk.

A half century ago Mother Mary Eleanor, S.H.C.J., published a short article entitled "Hopkins's 'Windhover' and Southwell's Hawk" (*Renascence*, v. 15) in which she called "attention to a curiously parallel image in a little known book of meditations by Robert Southwell [1561–1595] on the Love of God" (21). Mother Eleanor's modest claim was that the image of Christ as a hawk in flight from "Meditation 56" of Southwell's *A Hundred Meditations on the Love of God* "may or may not provide a clue to the source of Hopkins's image; but it at least reinforces one's sense of the appropriateness of such an image, since it has occurred to another poet, formed in the same school of spirituality and arrested by the same fact of Christ's redeeming

17 This latter edition would have been available to Hopkins only when he returned to Stonyhurst to teach classics in 1882. For all of the information regarding the Stonyhurst holdings I am gratefully indebted to the late Father Frederick J. Turner, S.J., longtime Librarian at Stonyhurst College.

action" (21). This provocative discovery of Mother Eleanor's, a peculiar Renaissance needle in the vast haystack of literary influence, went largely unheeded, scholarly readings of "The Windhover" having proceeded for the past fifty years as though her suggestion had never been made. This may be in part due to the considerable modesty with which she presented her case, but is attributable as well, no doubt, to the fact that she offered no external evidence to suggest how or why Hopkins, as a young nineteenth-century Jesuit, might have come to read, let alone borrow from, these little known meditations of his martyred sixteenth-century Jesuit predecessor. How, in other words, did Hopkins stumble upon this same "needle" and who exactly put it in the haystack?

The answer to these questions resides in a coincidence which connects the nineteenth-century publication of *A Hundred Meditations on the Love of God* with Gerard Hopkins, and demonstrates the likelihood that Hopkins not only read at least some of the *Meditations*, but may have been guided in his reading by its editor, Father John Morris, S.J., who, as it turns out, would soon be one of Hopkins's professors, as well as one of the few Jesuits to encourage Hopkins in his own efforts as a poet. After we have first examined this connection between Hopkins and the *Meditations* editor, we can then turn to the "curiously parallel image" between "The Windhover" and Southwell's "Meditation 56," which Mother Eleanor observed all those years ago. When we do so, I think, we will recognize that Hopkins's indebtedness to Southwell extends beyond just the central image.

We must begin with the peculiar history of *A Hundred Meditations Upon the Love of God* itself. Recall that by 1636 *Saint Peter's Complaint With Other Poems*, accompanied by a now famous dedicatory epistle, had been printed in London no fewer than eleven times. Nonetheless, *A Hundred Meditations Upon the Love of God*, which in its published form comprises some 538 pages of prose, survived unpublished and presumably unread in one single transcribed copy at Stonyhurst College until 1873. The text, which must have been regarded as something of a literary, if not religious relic, might have remained in utter obscurity if not for Father John Morris, S.J., Lecturer of Ecclesiastical History at St. Bueno's Seminary in Wales. Morris, trusting in the "Transcriber's Dedication," believed incorrectly that he was bringing to light an extraordinary work of original recusant prose.[18] In fact, however, it turns out that the *Hundred Meditations* are not Southwell's original work, but an English translation which he made from an Italian version of a Spanish work, *Meditaciónes devotíssimas del amor de Dios* written by a Franciscan Friar, Fray Diego de Estella and published in Salamanca in 1576.[19]

It is likely that during his enforced leisure in London Southwell translated an Italian version of Diego's work, an ambitious undertaking which would have several purposes, the first being to help the young priest diminish his estrangement by helping him hone his competence in the English language after a decade on the continent. Whether Southwell knew that his Italian version of these meditations was a translation of Diego's Spanish work we will never know, but one can appreciate his attraction to these meditations, as they suit perfectly his other purpose of preaching the Gospels with no other public pulpit than his covert printing press. Each meditation is comprised of several pages of prose that consider in layered thought and imagery

18 Morris cannot be blamed for trusting himself to the claims of a transcriber who was him/herself but making an honest mistake. The Dedication reads as follows: TO THE RIGHT HONOURABLE AND VIRTUOUS LADY, THE LADY BEAUCHAMP. Noble Lady, —Having long had in my custody the original of these ensuing discourses, written with Mr. Robert Southwell's own hand (a gentleman for his holy life and happy death of eternal memory), and knowing certainly that he especially wrote and meant to have printed them for your holy mother's devotion, singularly by him honored and affected, I have, in an eminent esteem which I profess myself to have of your virtuous and noble worth, moved also thereunto by one of your noblest and nearest kinswomen, presumed to make your honour partaker of such a treasury of devout discourses . . . " (*A Hundred Meditations Upon the Love of God*, xix).

19 Fray Diego de Estella, whose worldly name was Diego Ballesteros y Cruzas, lived from 1524–1578. He is known, though not admired, for his authorship of *Meditaciones devotissimas amor Dios*. The work is regarded as an example of the sort of popular mystical works which were common at this time, primarily doctrinal rather than apologetic. His *Meditaciones* are filled with the abundant nature revelry characteristic of Franciscan spirituality.

the nature of God's love, especially as revealed in the life, passion, death and resurrection of Christ. Southwell's printer apparently did not share his enthusiasm for producing such a massive volume, so his completed translation, if it circulated at all, circulated in private hands, becoming an obscure recusant manuscript until Father Morris took up Southwell's ambitions some two hundred and eighty years later.

Of importance to our present argument is not that Southwell's work was original, but that Father Morris believed that it was, and described it to his readers with a zeal appropriate to that belief. He wrote in his Preface:

> The interest of these Meditations is greatly enhanced by the recollection that it is a Martyr, at whose intercourse with God we are present. It is a revelation to us of the interior union with God of a brave heart that aspired to and attained martyrdom . . . In these Meditations, then, we see into a Martyr's heart, or rather . . . see the thoughts by which the heart was made heroic and apt for the great sacrifice of martyrdom. It was filled with the love of God. Everything spoke to it of the Love of God. It drew the love of God to itself from all around, and in its meditation all creatures, instead of weakening, helped to strengthen its love of God. (*A Hundred Meditations*, vii–viii).

One of Morris's motivations for publishing *A Hundred Meditations*, in fact, was to help "hasten the day when the Martyrs to whom we owe our inheritance shall receive their honors from the Church to which they were loyal unto death" (x). Southwell, along with the other English martyrs of the sixteenth-century recusant movement to whom Fr. Morris refers, would eventually be canonized, but not for another century.[20]

As for Morris's edition of *A Hundred Meditations*, it remains the only one to have ever been published, and while regarded until fairly

20 Robert Southwell was canonized a saint by Pope Paul VI in 1970. He was canonized together with a group known as "The Forty Martyrs of England and Wales," men and women regarded by the Catholic Church as martyrs because they were put to death during the English Reformation for their Catholic beliefs. These were all recusants and

recently as Southwell's original work, its audience has been comprised of, shall we say, a devout few. Extant copies of the text remain only in private collections, selected religious houses and in fewer than two dozen libraries world-wide.[21] In fact, the greatest impact of Morris's labor may have been the unintentional spawning of Hopkins's extraordinary sonnet, "The Windhover," which the poet himself regarded as one of his finest poems. Just what do we know then about Fr. Morris and his eccentric pupil, Gerard Hopkins.

At the time at which Morris's edition of *A Hundred Meditations on the Love of God* was published, and during the previous three years while Morris was presumably working with the original manuscript at Stonyhurst, Gerard Hopkins was studying in the Jesuit Philosophate at St. Mary's Hall, Stonyhurst (1870–1873). That the two men would have met and conversed in some manner during this time seems quite possible as there were only thirty-five residents at St. Mary's Hall, including the three priests. That Morris may have brought to the young poet's attention his work upon what he believed were Robert Southwell's *A Hundred Meditations* is likewise possible since Morris admired Southwell's poetry, and, with Hopkins's composition of "Ad Mariam" at Stonyhurst, his own talent as a poet, or at the very least his interest in poetry, was known among his fellow Jesuits there. In any case, even if Morris and Hopkins completely escaped one another's notice at this time, they would meet three years later in Wales when Morris was now Hopkins's professor for both Canon Law as well as Ecclesiastical History at St.Beuno's.[22]

other resisters executed between the years 1535 and 1679. Like Southwell, the other 39 were all convicted by the English realm of treason-related offences.

21 I retained my own copy of *A Hundred Meditations* from the library at the College of the Holy Cross. It arrived in such a scandalously poor condition, held together with string, that it was clear to me that the library had no knowledge of what a relatively rare volume they possessed. I returned it with a letter describing its origins and scarcity and trust it has since been given proper repair and preservation.

22 See Catalogus Provinciae Angliae Societatis Jesu (Roehampton: Typographia Sancti Joseph, 1875), p. 10: "P. Joannes Morris, Lect. hist. eccl. . . ." and Catalogus Provinciae Angliae Societatis Jesu (Roe-

When he was sent to St. Beuno's in Wales, Hopkins would not have left behind his access to or acquaintance with Southwell's works. At St. Beuno's he would have had access to at least two volumes of Southwell's works, both prose and poetry, including two copies of the 1872 Grosart just mentioned.[23] Besides the presence of Father Morris whose interest in Southwell was likely well known, and most assuredly at least one copy of his new edition of the *Meditations*, there was the presence of St. Winefride's Well which came to be Hopkins's favorite spot. "During Elizabeth's reign the chapel had been secretly placed in the care of Campion's and Southwell's contemporaries" (White, 243).[24] One need not believe with Norman White that Hopkins found "a sensuous pleasure about martyrdom" (252) in order to surmise Hopkins's increased appreciation of the "circumstances of horrible barbarity" in which Southwell lived and his consequent interest in the poetry of this, his only English Jesuit literary predecessor.

By this time, biographer Norman White suggests, "Hopkins must have been known to his colleagues as a poet. This reputation probably [having] followed him from Stonyhurst where he had written the Marian poems, and 'The Wreck of the Deutschland' would of course be known to the Rector" (262). What White does not mention is just what a very peculiar reputation "poet" would have been for Hopkins to have acquired among his fellow Jesuits. The order, as we see from the brief litany in Hopkins's letter to Dixon above, was not exactly overcrowded with would-be laureates. One other person who would be keenly aware that the English Jesuits had but one poet to speak of would, of course, have been Fr. Morris who refers in his Preface to

hampton: Typographia Sancti Joseph, 1876), p. 10: "P. Joannes Morris, Lect. jur. can. et hist. eccl. . . ." I am grateful to Father Joseph Feeney, S.J., for securing this data on my behalf. Though we have no description of Fr. Morris as a lecturer, we are told of his reading of his Italian colleague, Fr Perini's lectures in English in the evenings (Alfred Thomas, S.J., Hopkins the Jesuit: The Years of Training, 1969).

23 The volumes are now located in the Heythrop Library collection. I am grateful to Mr. Michael Walsh, the Librarian at Heythrop, for furnishing me with this information.

24 "The hounded itinerant Society of Jesus and its well," observes White, "had become an important center of Catholic resistance" (243).

"Mr. Grosart's admirable edition of Father Southwell's Poetical Works" (*A Hundred Meditations*, v).[25] that was published in 1872, the year before his own edition of the *Hundred Meditations*. What Morris thought about Hopkins's poetry is suggested by an incident in 1876. For fittingly, this champion of Southwell's works was also responsible for the first and only printing of a Hopkins poem during Hopkins's own lifetime, "The Silver Jubilee."[26] In 1876 Fr. Morris had preached a special sermon on the occasion of Bishop James Brown's Jubilee visit to St. Beuno's that year. The sermon, the Bishop's address, and the poem Hopkins composed for the occasion were subsequently published together in a pamphlet at the Bishop's request. When "Hopkins had protested against his poem being included . . . Fr. Morris had gracefully persuaded him that he needed its publication in order to entitle the sermon 'The Silver Jubilee'" (White, 262). Morris's motives may have been as simple and pragmatic as they sound; however, his tactful persuasion suggests at least the possibility of a sympathetic mentoring of the young poet away from feigned modesty and towards publication. It is, in any case, the small sum of what we know for certain about the relationship between Morris and Gerard Hopkins.

The next year, 1877, was a seminal year for Hopkins as a poet. Along with ten of his best poems,[27] he would write the extraordinary sonnet, "The Windhover." Before turning to the resemblance of this poem to "Meditation 56," we should note that from the 538 pages which comprise *A Hundred Meditations*, Fr. Morris offers a sampling of only five brief passages in his short Preface to the work. The longest

25 The edition to which Morris refers is Alexander Grosart's *The Complete Poems of Robert Southwell* (1872) which was the first collected edition of Southwell's poetry.

26 Says Norman White: "It was the first work he had published since entering the Society of Jesus, and it was also the only serious complete English poem written after he became a Jesuit which he would ever see in print" (White, 262).

27 According to Norman White's biography, Hopkins wrote the following poems in 1877: "God's Grandeur," "the Starlight Night," "As Kingfishers Catch Fire," "Spring," "The Sea and the Skylark," "In the Valley of Elway," "The Windhover," "Pied Beauty," "The Caged Skylark," "The Lantern Out of Doors," and "Hurrahing in Harvest."

of these by far, and the one to which he gives the most attention, is the passage of the regal hawk in flight compared to Christ from "Meditation 56." Hence, Hopkins would not have had to read beyond Morris's Preface to discover this unusual metaphor. Although circumstantial, this evidence indicates that Hopkins may very well have had his attention drawn to these meditations by Fr. Morris.

As to Hopkins's famous poem, it is easy to see why "The Windhover" was his favorite composition in what was a very creative year for the poet, and why many regard it as his single best poem, if for no other reason because of its extraordinary structural and formal characteristics. Never before or since, I think, has so much movement, rhythm, sound and emotion been so masterfully orchestrated within the confines of an Italian sonnet. A paraphrase of the poem's literal action is quite ordinary: an exuberant narrator admires the graceful flight and sudden descent of a kestrel. The poem's dedication, "To Christ Our Lord," however, provokes the reader to see the flight of the small bird with the same symbolic significance and accompanying excitement as the narrator:

> I caught this morning morning's minion, kingdom
> of daylight's dauphin, dapple-dawn-drawn Falcon, in his riding
> Of the rolling level underneath him steady air, and striding
> High there, how he rung upon the rein of a wimpling wing
> In his Ecstasy! then off, off forth on swing,
> As skate's heel sweeps smooth on a bow-bend: the hurl and gliding
> Rebuffed the wind. My heart in hiding
> Stirred for a bird,—the achieve of, the mastery of thing!

If one insists upon reading this poem only as an extraordinary nature meditation, echoes of "Meditation 56" might be heard, though not significantly, as in "When the eagle- falcon, or ger-falcon, or any other kind of long-winged hawk, hath flown a high pitch, and skimming through the air hath mounted up to the clouds . . ." (ix, *Meditations*) From this description may have been derived the more striking "rung upon the reign of a wimpling wing" or the sweep of a skate's heel. But Hopkins, himself a keen observer of nature, would need no primer on how to describe a hawk's flight.

If, on the other hand, one follows the prompting of the poet's dedication "To Christ Our Lord" and understands the flight as representative of Christ's own mastery of his destiny and humanity's, the potential significance of Fray Diego de Estella's "Meditation 56" as translated by Robert Southwell and published by Morris may be seen and heard in earnest. The passage from the meditation which Morris quotes in his Preface is as eloquent a summary of the religious meaning of "The Windhover" as any ever rendered:

> O Princely Hawk! which comest down from Heaven into the bowels of the Blessed Virgin, and from her womb unto the earth, and from the earth unto the desert, and from the desert unto the Cross, and from the Cross unto hell, and from hell unto Heaven, and madest those turnings to pursue our souls which Thou wert losing, and which without Thy helping hand had perished, is it much that Thou requirest our heart for reward of the travail and pains that Thou hast done to work our redemption? What hawk ever made such a brave flight, or lost so much blood in the pursuit of her game, as the salvation of our souls hath cost Thee, our God and our Lord? (*A Hundred Meditations*, ix–x).

"O" we wait for Diego, via Southwell, to declare "my chevalier!" For the parallel imagery between the two passages includes, not just the comparable flights of the hawks, but the awe at the hawk's regality and the consequent recognition of Christ's own kingship in the masterful flight. The essential spiritual movement of the two passages, in fact, is identical: the brave and redemptive life of the princely Christ witnessed in the flight and fall of a hawk, prompting the consequent stirring of the observer's heart.

The climactic spiritual awakening in Hopkins's poem, the inexplicably lovely fire which breaks from the kestrel at the moment of buckling, also has a precedent in Fray Diego's "Meditation 56." Consider first the opening three lines of Hopkins's sestet by which he arrives, in the last three words, at his famous version of "O Princely hawk!"

> Brute beauty and valour and act, oh, air, pride, plume,
> Buckle! AND the fire that breaks from thee then, a billion
> Times told lovelier, more dangerous, O my chevalier!

Now consider what might pass for a prose paraphrase of these very lines rendered into English by Southwell some two hundred and eighty years earlier:

> And is it much, O Lord, that I should offer unto Thy Divine Majesty my heart inflamed in Thy holy love, seeing that Thou, my God, didst so burn upon the Cross with the fire of infinite love, whereon Thou didst put Thyself for my sake and for love of me, insomuch that there sprinkled out so many flames of fire from the sacred breast as there were wounds in Thy most sacred body? (*A Hundred Meditations*, 282).

The inflamed heart and the fire are themselves conventional religious images, but the "sprinkled out . . . flames of fire" within the context of the hawk's flight bear a persuasive resemblance to Hopkins's "fire that breaks from thee then" (line 10), which becomes in the poem's provocative final line: "blue-bleak embers" which "Fall, gall themselves, and gash gold-vermillion" (13–14). The strangeness which the reader confronts in the imagery of blue embers falling to gold-vermillion is made less strange and more poignant when we hear how Southwell describes the receiving of the Blessed Sacrament in his poem "Unworthy receaving": "Christ shrined hath him self within my mortal chest / And shoured his vermilion bloud within my brest" (McDonald-Brown, 110).[28]

Since the above passage from "Meditation 56" does not appear in Morris's Preface, Hopkins would have had to turn to the meditation himself, prompted, if he did so, by the passage in Morris's Preface,

28 The use of "vermilion" by the two authors is in all likelihood an artistic coincidence. McDonald and Brown include "Unworthy receiving" in their edition of Southwell's works (1967) among poems of "Doubtful Authorship" on the basis that it only appears in the F manuscript. This seems no reason to doubt Southwell's authorship of the poem that bears his familiar traits. What is doubtful is that Hopkins would have ever seen "Unworthy receiving" since the poems in the F manuscript were not published by McDonald until 1937. If somehow Hopkins was made aware of the poem he would have assumed Southwell's authorship.

and believing that the words which he read there were those of Fr. Robert Southwell, a predecessor English priest and poet.

It may be that the comparison of the redemptive life of Christ to the flight of a hawk, though novel to us, was in Hopkins's day a somewhat more conventional part of religious imagery which has since been lost, leaving behind a poem which seems more eccentric and original than it is. It is likewise possible that the imagery and the embedded spiritual argument of "The Windhover" are entirely the product of Gerard Manley Hopkins's experience of observing a kestrel in Wales and his own poetic fancy. Yet all works of art, and especially great ones, are, in some fashion, an imaginative compilation of certain things which have come before them. In the exclamation "ah my dear," of the poem's second-to-last line, for example, Norman White hears Hopkins borrowing from George Herbert (White, 283). My own suggestion is that the poem contains a much more substantial borrowing than these three words. Unbeknownst to Gerard Hopkins or Mother Eleanor, "The Windhover" owes its origins to a sixteenth-century Spanish writer via two of Hopkins's brother Jesuits, Fr. Southwell who accomplished this, his most significant work of translation, under extraordinary circumstances,[29] and Fr. Morris who worked in

---

29 There are several possibilities as to when Southwell actually accomplished this translation. It is possible, of course, that he completed it prior to departing for England, and then brought it with him with the intention of using it in his ministry or perhaps reprinting portions of it. He may have brought the Italian version and translated it in England. In either of these cases we have to recognize that he would have been very careful and very limited in packing for his trip to England. Space would have been at a premium, and transporting any potentially incriminating text would be unwise. It is just as likely therefore that Southwell discovered the volume in the private collection of a recusant household and translated as time and circumstances allowed; his translation would have served three important purposes: private religious meditation, sharpening his English prose style and fashioning a text that might be used for the inspiration or conversion of others. Of course, this work would also have passed the time when it was not safe for him to move outside of the household. In any case, the work represents an extraordinary investment of time.

immediate proximity to his future pupil, Gerard Hopkins, to bring to publication what he believed to be the original work of an important English poet and Jesuit predecessor.

The implications of the above case of influence should be of some interest to readers of Hopkins. In the first place, if Hopkins did read "Meditation 56," he may also have read some, though likely not all, of the other *Hundred Meditations* in Morris's edition which numbers 538 pages. Certainly the first two meditations, stirring canticles to creation and the creator, would have engaged Hopkins's sensibilities and drawn him in, and Diego's Franciscan-inspired love of nature, which is apparent in the imagery of nearly all the meditations, may well have had particular appeal to Hopkins. Since Hopkins never mentions *A Hundred Meditations* specifically in either his journals or correspondence, any other cases of influence must rest upon the external evidence I have presented here and any notable similarities between the two authors' texts. One other implication of the above argument is that Gerard Hopkins, as Jesuit poet, may have found in the example of Southwell and the encouragement of Morris something of a respite from the artistic isolation in which his religious life seems to have placed him.

Before we turn to other specific comparisons between Southwell's and Hopkins's poetry, it is important to keep in mind that Southwell, as an innovator of sacred parody in English verse, was determined to demonstrate how the poetic techniques of his contemporaries could be used to depict religious subject matter. Most of his poems, therefore, were written in the conventional "loom" of his age; many are transparently Petrarchan in tone and most exhibit an obvious Elizabethan aesthetic in music, imagery and form. Even so, for all his efforts at poetic demonstrative proof, Southwell was not entirely English. He had, after all, spent over a decade of his short life on the continent and there are instances where his verse exhibits a baroque quality of the kind that Crashaw latched onto; times when certain passages sound more medieval, or even modern, than conventionally Elizabethan. The poetically sensitive ears and imagination of Hopkins, I believe, discovered in Southwell's poems several innovations and eccentricities, not just in imagery, but auditory effects of the kind that he would employ in developing his own sprung rhythm: spondaic declarations, monosyllabic lists, odd juxtapositions and compound nouns, peculiar nominalizations, and subverted grammar and syntax.

In considering the connection between these two poets, it is also important to observe their common aesthetic and shared poetic qualities, independent of any probable influence. Poems such as Hopkins's "Barnfloor Winepress," "New Readings," and "Easter Communion" belong to his Anglican period, having been written prior to his becoming either a Catholic or a Jesuit. The influence of Southwell upon these poems is therefore unlikely. The similarities that some of the lines and images in these poems share with Southwell's poetry therefore indicate a poetic sensibility as a religious poet that Hopkins shared not only with Southwell, but with Herbert, and perhaps Crashaw as well. Consider, for example, Southwell's poem "Christ's bloody sweate."

> Fat soyle, full springe, sweete olive, grape of blisse,
> That yeldes, that streames, that powres, that dots distil,
> Untilled, undrawne, unstampde, untouchd of presse,
> Deare fruit, cleare brooks, fayre oyle, sweete wine at will:
> Thus Christ unforc'd preventes in shedding bloode
> The whippes the thornes, the nailes the speare, and roode (1–6)

Knowledgeable readers unacquainted with the works of Robert Southwell are likely to attribute these lines to either Hopkins or perhaps George Herbert.[30] What people hear in the lines that prompts such identification are the bold spondaic and monosyllabic imperatives associated with what Hopkins called "sprung rhythm." They also recognize the odd adjectives that characterize many of Hopkins more familiar lines and poems; in tensive phrases like "full spring," "faire oile," and in the peculiarly impossible image "Fat soile" readers may hear a voice which they had previously thought peculiar to Hopkins or those seeking to imitate him.[31] So too in the insistently negative

30 I have conducted this unscientific experiment of "name the author of these lines" numerous times over the years, and have often received the quick and emphatic reply of Hopkins. One exception was from a very knowledgeable Hopkins scholar who seemed to recognize the lines, but couldn't place them with a specific poem, and suggested that though they sound like Hopkins's work, they must be Herbert.

31 Hopkins's impact upon the century that came after him is as significant and complex as that of Southwell upon the seventeenth century,

string of iambic adjectives: "Untild, undrawne, unstampt, untoucht of presse." As the poem falls into more conventional, Petrarchan-like paradoxes and accompanying iambic arrangements, things sound more Elizabethan, but in the declarative opening lines of the second stanza one may hear something suggestive of Hopkins's poetry: "He Pelicans, he Phenix fate doth prove / Whom flames consume, whom streames enforce to die." The reversed syntax here suggests at first read the iconic Pelican and Phoenix are being deployed as verbs, but this is soon remedied (7–8). Hopkins, in his interpretation of Aquinas's famous hymn to the Holy Eucharist, uses the trope of the Pelican, though by then it had become rather anachronistic: "Like what tender tales tell of the Pelican" (l. 21).[32]

"Christ's bloody sweat," offers a conglomerate set of images that we reasonably attribute to Ignatian-style meditation. Christ is presented as an agricultural composite of untilled soil, undrawn Spring, unpressed olives and unstamped grapes which nonetheless yield dear fruit, clear brookes, faire oile and sweet wine. Prior to any Ignatian

and a great deal more substantiated. In 1985 Richard F. Giles performed a significant service to Hopkins scholarship by asking selected scholars to examine Hopkins's impact upon other poets. The contents of Giles's volume include essays on Robert Bridges, William Yeats, James Joyce, William Carlos Williams, Edwin Muir, T. S. Eliot, Ivor Gurney, Hugh MacDiarmid, E. E. Cummings, David Jones, Hart Crane, A. J. M. Smith, Day Lewis, Patrick Kavanagh, William Empson, W. H. Auden, Theodore Roethke, Randall Jarrell, Dylan Thomas, Thomas Merton, Robert Lowell, Elizabeth Jennings, Sylvia Plath and Seamus Heaney. And Giles's volume, which ends with an essay on Nigerian poets, some of whom "regard Hopkins as a disease," is by no means exhaustive. Giles regrets, for example, the exclusion of Robert Graves, Wallace Stevens and John Berryman. One notes as well the absence of Elizabeth Bishop and James Dickey as well as, more recently, Desmond Egan and Robert Pinsky. See Giles, Richard F., *Hopkins Among Poets: Studies in Modern Responses to Gerard Manley Hopkins*. The International Hopkins Association Monograph Series, 3. The International Hopkins Association, 1985.

32 Kermode records the uncancelled variant: "Bring the tender tale true of the Pelican" (333, GMH *Works*).

influence, and quite possibly before ever having read Southwell's poetry, Hopkins fashioned a similar composite of images in "New Readings": "I read the story rather / How soldiers platting thorns around
CHRIST'S Head / Grapes grew and drops of wine were shed" (3–5)
and "From wastes of rock He brings / Food for five thousand: on the
thorns He shed / Grains from His drooping Head" (11–13). Similarly,
in "Barnfloor and Winepress," also likely preceding any close acquaintance with Southwell, Hopkins describes Christ as grain "Scourged
upon the threshing-floor" (6) and "The wine . . . racked from the
press" (18). Jerome Bump notes that the editors of the fourth edition
of Hopkins's poems cite Herbert's influence on these poems: ". . . Hopkins's representation of Christ's thorns as grapes in 'New Readings,'
for instance, recalls Herbert's 'The Sacrifice' (ll. 161–63), and the basic
form of a series of interpretations of passages from the New Testament
is a favorite of Herbert's" (309). The lines from Herbert's "The Sacrifice" to which Bump refers are spoken by Christ in the first person:
"Then on my head a crown of thorns I wear:/ For these are all the
grapes Sion doth bear,/ Though I my vine planted and watred there."
Herbert's influence may very well be present in these two Hopkins
poems, but the similarity in tone, imagery and voice that they share
with Southwell's "Christ's bloody sweat" suggests the possibility that
Herbert's own poem may have been influenced by Southwell, in which
case Hopkins may have unwittingly been the recipient of Southwell's
influence secondhand.

Even without contemplating such a complex connection, however,
we may acknowledge the shared religious aesthetic of these three
poets, and appreciate even more Hopkins's own ripeness for influence
when he did encounter more fully the poems of Southwell. For in reading Southwell he may have been discovering an earlier, if less talented,
source of much that he admired in Herbert. After all, "the basic form"
of a series of New Testament interpretations, which Bump calls one
of Herbert's favorites, would become for Hopkins, as it was for Southwell, not just a literary form, but a prescribed and ritually practiced
discipline. In keeping with this prescribed, meditative sequence, in fact,
Southwell's "Christ's bloody sweat" is followed by "Christ's Sleeping
Friends." Herbert's influence upon Hopkins is not diminished in any
substantial way, I think, by contemplating an important literary predecessor of both men who, as a Catholic and Jesuit, may ultimately

have been a more significant and intimate influence upon Hopkins than was Herbert.

As an Ignatian meditation, "Christ's bloody sweat" moves from the above contemplation of the nature of Christ's blood as a physical and spiritual phenomenon to a recollection of the biblical precedence in Elias's "fire of wondrous force/ That blood and wood and water did devour" (14–15). "Such fire is love," the poet resolves, preparing us for a shift in the poem's final stanza to the first person, or more fundamentally, the turning of the meditation into a prayer.

> O sacred Fire come shewe thy force on me
> That sacrifice to Christe I maye retorne,
> If withered wood for fuell fittest bee,
> If stones and dust, yf fleshe and blood will burne,
> I withered am and stonye to all good,
> A sacke of dust, a masse of fleshe and bloode (19–24).

As I have noted earlier, this kind of personal prayer is unusual in Robert Southwell's verse, the first person plea being typically reserved for a more famous persona—Magdalene, Peter, Joseph, or even Mary Queen of Scots. That the above passage arrives at a personal declaration is quite in keeping, however, with the movement of Ignatian meditation described above. The exercitant progresses from a generic contemplation upon a biblical object, event or spiritual revelation, such as Peter's or Magdalene's recognition, the arrest in the Garden of Gethsemane, Christ's bloody sweat, Hell, the road to Emmaus, to a personal response to this event or phenomenon.

By contrast, George Herbert offered to Hopkins a less Ignatian and less Roman Catholic approach to the divine, an approach in which the meditation upon a biblical revelation comes *after* a personal, first-person declaration. Consider that of Herbert's 169 poems, more than half of them begin with an address by the speaker/poet directly to God. These declarations often come, like Donne's, in a dramatic fashion. For example: "Kill me not every day/ Thou Lord"; "Oh King of grief! (a title strange but true)"; "Broken in pieces all asunder, Lord hunt me not"; "Lord I confesse my sinne is great." Of Robert Southwell's seventy-five poems, on the other hand, only one begins with a first-person address by the speaker directly to God, where the speaker is not identifiable as a person separate from the poet. He begins "Sinne's Heavy Load" speaking, apparently as himself: "O Lord, my sin doth overcharge Thy breast."

What then of Hopkins's meditative structure? If the manner of beginning meditative poems is any indication, his works far more resemble those of his Ignatian predecessor. Of Hopkins's 140 poems and fragments, only a handful begin with a direct address to God, such as the conventional, "Thee, God, I come from, to thee I go" and "Thou art indeed just Lord, If I contend"; or the eccentric, "Let me be to Thee as the circling bird,/ Or a bat with tender and air-escaping wings." Then there is the extraordinary stanza of poetry that eclipses Herbert and Southwell altogether, the stunning opening of his masterpiece: "The Wreck of the Deutchland":

> Thou mastering me
> God! giver of breath and bread;
> world's strand, sway of the sea;
> Lord of living and dead;
> Thou hast bound bones and veins in me, fastened me flesh,
> And after it almost unmade, what with dread,
> Thy doing: and dost thou touch me afresh?
> Over again I feel thy finger and find thee (1–8).

One may perhaps sense in this powerful, personal declaration some echo of Southwell's rare first-person outburst at the end of "Christ's bloody sweat." Southwell's speaker is reduced to "a man of flesh and blood," Hopkins's to "bound bones and veins"; Hopkins's speaker describes himself as "fastened flesh," Southwell's as "a sack of dust." The near despair of Southwell's speaker, "withered . . . and stony to all good" is something Hopkins's poetry will not approach until his later sonnets (1885). Whether during his time in Ireland Hopkins retained any copy or access to Southwell's works we cannot be sure. Certainly memory of it would have offered him the great comfort of a fellow exile. In any case, the sacred fire that concludes Part I of "The Wreck" is not the consuming sacrificial flame of Southwell's poem, but rather that of the Creator as blacksmith fashioning the speaker: "And with fire in him forge thy will . . . melt him but master him still" (10: 2–4).

While I would not insist with any stubbornness upon possible echoes of Southwell in "The Wreck" we should recall the strong probability that in the very year that Hopkins fashioned this extraordinary poem, which has martyrdom as its central theme, he had also, by way of Father Morris, likely become more closely acquainted with Southwell's life and writings. It is possible that during his final years of Jesuit formation, as Hopkins blossomed as a mature poet, Southwell's influence on his poetry eclipsed that of Herbert's and other poets.[33] Poetic influence, whatever else it is, is an imprecise composting whose results are only sometimes discernable; but attentive readers ought at the very least to recognize the common Ignatian elements and patterns in these two poets' works, and particularly the meditative movement from a biblical passage or spiritual phenomenon towards, ultimately, the invocation of a personal response. Just as it is unusual for either poet to begin by calling upon God, it is practically inevitable that, like Herbert, each arrives at some resolution concerning the relationship of the speaker—and by extension humanity—with God revealed in Christ, though rarely to such effect and with such succinct simplicity as the final line of Hopkins's "Pied Beauty" (1877): "Praise him."

With this in mind let us turn to several other instances where Southwell's poetry might be heard to echo in Hopkins's; echoes like the one W. H. Gardner, a pioneer of Hopkins studies, heard long ago in Hopkins's "The Bugler's First Communion." Hopkins's description of the Eucharist as "Low-latched in leaf light housed his too huge god-head" so resembles Robert Southwell's description, "The God of hoastes in slender hoste doth dwell" in "Of the Blessed Sacrament of the Aulter," observed Gardner, that the line is either "reminiscent of Hopkins's early reading or a remarkable coincidence" *(Poetic Idiosyncrasy,* 169). Given the two poets' shared vocation, and deployment of poetry for religious purposes, it is perhaps not such a remarkable coincidence, but Gardner may well be correct that the compressed metaphysical lesson of transubstantiation here is an instance of direct poetic influence.

---

33 Hopkins the trained classicist claims in his letters to admire Milton as well as the Neoclassical poet Dryden. While Milton's influence is discernable, few readers by themselves would connect Hopkins's poetry with that of Dryden.

Southwell's poem "Mary Magdalens Blushe" offers another instance. The poem is a specimen of sacred parody, turning a scriptural narrative into a conventional Petrarchan complaint. In stanza three, for example, Magdalene declares: "All ghostly dynts that grace at me did dart,/ Like stubborne rocke I forced to recoyle" (13–14). The next line, however, contains a small but unusual ingredient found elsewhere in Southwell and frequently in Hopkins, the grammatical conversion of a verb to a noun: "To other flights *an ayme* I made my hart" (15, italics mine). In stanza five of this same poem this technique, combined with the creation of a peculiar compound noun, the use of alliteration and the choice and arrangement of other words results in poetry which, even in its conventional meter, might easily be mistaken as Hopkins's own:

O sence o soule o had o hoped blisse
You woe you weane you draw you drive me backe
Your crosse-encountering, like their combate is
That never end but with some deadly wracke
When sence doth wynne, the soule doth loose the field
And present happ makes future hopes to yelde (25–30).

The peculiar declaration "o had" in the opening line of the stanza can carry over as a past-perfect verb whose object is blisse, as in "Oh had blisse and Oh hoped for blisse," or, stated simply "Oh past happiness and future happiness." The curiosity of the syntax is that grammatically and metrically "o had" can argue its place as a noun in a list of four others, each preceded by the declarative "o": "o sense, o soule, *o had*, o hoped for blisse." The arrangement of a simple verb or article to function ambiguously with noun-like properties is a recognizable grammatical eccentricity, among the many in Hopkins's poetry. I offer but four examples from his poems: the use of "have" and "get" in "Spring"(1877), "Have, get, before it cloy,/ Before it cloud, Christ, lord, and sour with sinning" (11–12); the use of "any" and "some" in the riddled opening lines of "The Leaden Echo," (1882), "How to keep—is there any, is there none such, nowhere known some, bow or brooch or braid or brace, lace" (1–2); the stirring "let me be fell" (l.8) from Sonnet 65 (1885); and finally the memorable, haunting final words of Sonnet 66: "This to hoard unheard,/ Heard unheeded, leaves me a lonely began" (13–14).

The almost excessive alliteration of the first three lines of the above stanza from "Mary Magdalen blush"—sense, soule, had, hoped, wooe, weane, draw, drive, crosse, combate—punctuates the grammatical force of the first three lines which then give way to a more prosaic and less disruptive declaration in the final three lines. Besides the use of the word "had" in the stanza's opening line, the stanza's alliteration also highlights another innovation that gives a reader of Hopkins pause. Line three "Your crosse-encountering, like their combate is" relies upon the unusual and powerful compound noun, "crosse-encountering." The sense which this noun carries in the context is conventional enough, something like, "My sense, soul, memory and hopes all fight unsuccessfully against your cross when they encounter it." Such paraphrase, of course, diminishes the effect which Southwell achieved with the conversion of "encountering" from a present participle into the second half of a compound noun. The resulting "cross-encountering," as with the adjective "Self-blaming" in "S. Peter's Remorse," would likely have stayed in the mind of Hopkins, the relentless purveyor of compound words, who gives us such nouns as "martyr-master," and "starlight-wender,"[34] and who uses the very same grammatical conversion by which Southwell created "cross-encountering" to construct compound adjectives like "world-mothering," "widow-making," "Cuckoo- echoing," "Blue-beating," and "day-labouring-out."[35]

The word "wrack," while it contributes to the Hopkins-like sound of this stanza, does not, in fact, appear in Hopkins's poetry except in "shipwreck" from "The Wreck of the Deutschland." The final two lines of the stanza, in contrast to the first four, are less striking, having been deliberately woven like most of Southwell's poetry upon a conventionally Elizabethan loom. There are, however, several other instances in Southwell to be considered in which the nearest kindred verse to the sound and sense of a particular Southwell passage is found in the poetry of Hopkins.

34 From line 7, stanza 21 of "The Wreck of the Deutschland" and line 101 of "The Loss of the Eurydice" respectively.

35 From, in order: line 1 of "The Blessed Virgin Compared to the Air We Breathe," line 8 of stanza 13 of "The Wreck," line 2 of "Duns Scotus's Oxford," line 5 of stanza 26 of "The Wreck," and line 4 of "The Caged Skylark."

Consider for example Southwell's striking poem "A Vale of teares" which, for a sixteenth-century poem, contains unusually detailed descriptions of nature. The opening stanza reads:

A Vale there is enwrapt with dreadfull shades
Which thicke of mourning pines shrouds from the Sunne
Where hanging clyftes yelde shorte and dumpish glades
And snowye fludd with broken streames doth runne (1–4).

Only Henry Vaughan, it seems, appears between this poem and the nineteenth-century indulgence in the sublime that admittedly has little place in Hopkins's poetry. Southwell's sorrowful valley of repentance brings comfort to the world-weary soul because "sorowe springes from water, stone and tree" and "everie thing with mourners doth conspire" (59–60). By contrast, Hopkins's "Penmaen Pool" is the quaint guest-book poem which it is intended to be, and his "In the Valley of the Elwy" a forgiving landscape: "Lovely the woods, waters, meadows, cobes, vales," a place where "God, lover of souls" completes his creatures where they fail. "Binsey Poplars" and "Inversnaid" are inviting Romantic landscape meditations, not the terrifying locus of Southwell's "Vale." Nonetheless, there are, in lines like Southwell's "Where waters wrastle with encountering Stones" (16), some vague suggestions of Hopkins's descriptions of nature as well as his verbal playing. This is evident in the odd compound noun "eyerome" ("Where eyerome is from rockes to cloudye skye" (5), or "the crushed waters frothy frye" (7) of stanza two, and in the phrases "an onely boure" (33), "a dumpish moode" (34), or "the pible stones" (39), as well as in the declaration of the poem's final stanza: "Let teares to tunes and paynes to playnts be prest" (73). While specific words like crushed, froth and pressed are used by Hopkins in his verse, none of these lines constitutes a specific case of influence, only a verbal and imaginative style that we associate with Hopkins.

Those who have in recent decades argued with deconstructive insistence for the shocking spiritual despair of Hopkins's sonnets of desolation,[36] seem not to have read and regarded as Hopkins did the Book

36 See in particular Daniel A. Harris's book *Inspirations Unbidden: The Terrible Sonnets of Gerard Manley Hopkins.* Berkeley: University of

of Psalms, the poetry of Herbert, or the poetry of Robert Southwell. Southwell's "A Phansie turned to a sinners complaint," for example, contains all of the spiritual forlornness and emotional distress of both Herbert's and Hopkins's similar laments. In Chapter Three I examined this poem's potential influence upon Herbert's Affliction poems. Here let us consider how some of its particular stanzas may have served as well a source for Hopkins:

> O thoughtes, no thoughtes but wounds,
>   Sometyme the seate of joy,
> Sometime the store of quiet rest
>   But now of all annoye (45–48).

Any number of moments in Hopkins's poetry may be suggested in the disrupted syntax of the stanza's opening line and in the emphatic resolution of thoughts as wounds, punctuated by the verb "annoy" used as a noun in the stanza's final line. Echoes in Hopkins's Dark Sonnets are by no means exact, but we might consider, for example, the jolting: "I wake and feel the fell of dark, not day" (67, 1), or "No worst, there is none . . ." (65, 1). As Southwell's poem continues, he inaugurates an agricultural metaphor of a bad harvest to describe his spiritual despair:

> I sow'd the soyle of peace,
>   My blisse was in the springe;
> And day by day the fruite I eate,
>   That Vertues tree did bringe.

> To Nettles nowe my Corne,
>   My feild is turn'd to flynte

California Press. Harris, the first one to have a close look at the sonnets in manuscript form, argues for a narrative sequence which shows Hopkins's descent into irreversible spiritual despair. I offered a response to Harris's argument, as well as my case built upon a narrative arrangement of these poems, in the essay "What Gets Said In a Narrow (10 X 14) Room: A Reconsideration of Hopkins's Later Sonnets" in the *ELS* volume, *Recent Studies in Hopkins*, 1996.

> Where I a heavie harvest reape,
> Of cares that never stynt (49–56).

How much more concisely and powerfully does Hopkins utilize this very metaphor for the same purpose in "Carrion Comfort": "Why? That my chaff might fly; my grain lie, sheer and clear" (9). As noted in Chapter Three, "Phansie" contains the use of simple verbs as nouns, peculiar syntax, a stark statement of spiritual despair, and human paradox, all of which combined, suggest particular influence upon Hopkins:

> In was, stands my delighte
>   In is and shall my woe
> My horrour fastened in the yea
>   My hope hangd in the no (65–71)

Here, in any case, is a reasonable summary of Hopkins's *Dark Sonnets* whose "lonely began" and searching for "God knows when to God knows what" (69, l. 12) belong very much to both a poetic and spiritual convention which his Jesuit predecessor quite evidently shared.

I offer as a final sampling of Southwell's possible influence on Hopkins a stanza from "*Saint Peter's Complaint*":

> I was I had I Coulde
> Are wordes importing wante
> They are but dust of dead supplies,
> Where needfull helpes are scant (41–44).

The lines contain again the surprising conversion of three verbs into nouns as the syntax unfolds. The reference to these words, and perhaps words in general, as "dust of dead supplies" hints at the ultimate futility of language—even eloquent language—in the face of stark, overwhelming spiritual or worldly realities. Southwell's legendary eloquence would, in the end, not be enough at his perfunctory trial to preserve him from the inevitable end of his "counterpoise." His "words importing want" would be read in secret by his contemporaries and by the likes of Donne and Herbert through the controversial aperture of "pseudo-martyrdom." Crashaw would regard his work sympathetically and admiringly, and yet his most empathetic reader and important literary descendant was Gerard Manley Hopkins. For while Hopkins may have profited from the poetry of each of these men, in Southwell he discovered a literary predecessor as well as a brother Jesuit whose own suffering far surpassed his own, and from whom, across the centuries, he could derive not just a certain poetic affect, but spiritual consolation and empathy.

The incidents of possible influence that I have presented here are certainly not exhaustive. However, if it is the case, as I hope this study has demonstrated, that Southwell's prose and poetry provided "needful helpes" to Hopkins, as well as to the sixteenth- and seventeenth-century religious poets I have considered in these chapters, then it is also true that his voice still lives in their works more than four centuries after his gruesome end at Tyburn. The determined young priest could not have conceived of such literary longevity when he stepped upon that beach near Folkestone in 1586, effectively tripping an alarm, the immanent or eventual sounding of which would result in his capture and death. Nor, when he composed his dedicatory verse to "W.S." at the beginning of *Saint Peter's Complaint* and called upon "heavenly sparkes of wit" to "License [his] single penne to seeke a pheere," could he have imagined that he would actually provoke peers like Shakespeare and Donne in whose works his own words still reverberate. But like Saint Peter, whose rise and fall and redemption in Christ he chronicled to enduring effect, Father Southwell would have appreciated the peculiar paradox of his small triumph and rejoice in his place as a minor poet and a lesser known saint.

Afterword
What Remains When Disbelief Is Gone

In 1939 T. S. Eliot prepared a lecture on English religious verse that he was going to give on a tour through Italy, a plan that had to be abandoned with the outbreak of World War II. In his written lecture Eliot repeated his familiar criticisms of the poetry of Gerard Hopkins for its *Wordsworthian* sensibilities and eccentrically personal style (Bush, 34). However, in the same lecture he now referred to Hopkins as "perhaps the greatest poet of his generation because of the universal philosophy that tempered his romanticism" (Bush, 34). Even more surprising than Eliot's reconciliation to this major religious pre-Modern poet was the prophetic view that he offered in the conclusion of his undelivered remarks. He wrote of the future of religious poetry, and his prediction brings us at "the end of all our exploring" to "where we started," or, in any event, to where this book started. The place we know "for the first time" is, in Eliot's mind, the place known long ago by George Herbert. But as he describes this place we recognize the pleadings of the outlawed Jesuit priest and poet who preceded and provoked Herbert.

Compare the by now familiar words of Southwell's famous prefatory epistle with Eliot's unheard and unheeded lecture to his own generation:

> The probable direction of religious poetry in the immediate future is towards something more impersonal . . . It will be more interested in the dogma and the doctrine; in religious thought, rather than purely personal feeling (Bush, 34).

Eliot foresaw a revival of the religious lyric "deeply influenced by Thomism, and to some extent by Karl Barth and Kierkegaard." This new kind of poem, he believed, would be "concerned

primarily with giving poetic form to theological thought." It "will,"
he wrote,

> tend to have more kinship with . . . the seventeenth century,
> than with that of the nineteenth . . . content to meditate
> upon the central mysteries of the Incarnation and the Eu-
> charist" (Bush, 34).[1]

Sans Barth and Kierkegaard, one could not find a more apt description
of the poetry that Robert Southwell composed and urged his countrymen to imitate at the end of the sixteenth century.

The religious poetry that Eliot is forecasting, of course, is his own.
As Ronald Bush says so aptly, "*The Four Quartets*, whatever else it
might be, is Eliot's own meditation upon the central mystery of the Incarnation" (224). So too one might say of all of Southwell's work, and
the work of those who felt his influence most keenly, especially Crashaw
and Hopkins. The central mystery of the Incarnation and the Eucharist
is the meditation to which Southwell's life was vowed and with which
his writings are preoccupied. Eliot's attention to Herbert and Donne
notwithstanding, no poetry in the English language is more "interested
in the dogma and the doctrine; in religious thought" than that of Robert
Southwell. Certainly no other poet, save Hopkins, treats as successfully
the incarnational mystery of the transubstantiation in verse.

Eliot never spoke the above words in Italy or anywhere else, and
the war that prevented his lecture carried with it horrors equal in scope
and worse in kind than those of the century's first war that had provoked Eliot's *Waste Land,* a poem far more imitated and admired by
other poets than any portion of *The Four Quartets* or *Ash Wednesday.*
In the end, therefore, discussion over the quantity of first person self-
consciousness or the expression of sacramental imagery in the religious
lyric is a conversation that yields to a far greater matter—namely, the
virtual disappearance of the religious poem itself. For, Eliot's vision of
the future of the religious poem notwithstanding, most readers of

1 I have taken Eliot's words as cited by Ronald Bush's book *T. S. Eliot,*
   p. 224. Bush takes the words of the undelivered lecture for the type-
   script called "Types of English Religious Verse" in the T. S. Eliot Collection at King's College, Cambridge University.'

religious poetry today stand in "awkward reverence" like the fellow in Philip Larkin's cleverly named poem "Church Going." The speaker has stopped his bicycle and, only once he is "sure there's nothing going on" inside, he walks into "Another church." He browses amidst the familiar religious artifacts, donates "an Irish sixpence" and concludes that "the place was not worth stopping for." Yet stop he did, and to this small mystery the poet devotes another forty-five lines of verse, pondering what will become of these increasingly empty churches whose "shape is less recognizable each week" and whose purpose is "more obscure." Will such structures become museums to be visited (as not a few already have), or "unlucky places to be avoided?" Belief becomes superstition and superstition becomes disbelief, but "what," the solitary church visitor asks, "remains when disbelief has gone?" And "who," he ponders, "will be the last, the very last, to seek / This place for what it was"? It may be a "Christmas-addict" or it may be someone like himself: "bored, uniformed," visiting "a serious house on serious earth . . . gravitating . . . to this ground" if for no other reason than "so many dead lie round."

The English religious lyric strikes me as an artifact facing a similarly diminishing relevance. It is hard to say who will be the very last to seek it for what it was. In his provocative poem "A Note to the English Poets of the Seventeenth Century" the recently deceased contemporary American poet Miller Williams offers a litany of poets that includes Herbert, Donne and Crashaw, but not Southwell or Alabaster as he observes mournfully:

> most of you will be gone
> from whatever pass for
> books in years to come /
> and some
> reading the three or four that make it through
> will shake their heads and say,
> as even now we do
> (having I think already turned back a few),
> "They didn't have many poets, but they were great."
>
> Of course they were.
> You've lost the ones that were hopelessly only good,

saying things that nobody else could say
and lucky to be heard in their own day.[2]

In this instance Robert Southwell belongs to those "already turned back" from books for being, alas, "hopelessly only good." It is a sobering and somber thought. And one can understand how easily Southwell's inferred vanishing might occur without proper vigilance from the present small band of Southwellians. After all, there is plenty to behold and admire upon walking into the poetry of Hopkins or Herbert or Donne, whether in shared belief, leftover superstition or resolved disbelief. Southwell—his thin canonical presence hanging upon the thin gossamer leaf of "The Burning Babe"—is a harder case. As churches go, his is a very "serious house" on very "serious ground," the poetic plume of imaginary incense still hanging in the air, lest the pursuivants catch a whiff of the real thing.

In a contemporary intellectual culture that poet and critic Dana Gioia calls "consciously anti-Catholic"[3] there is yet something that did not exist just a few decadess ago: serious attention being paid to Catholicism in Tudor England. When Alan Hager assembled and edited a Bio-Bibliographical Critical Sourcebook of *Major Tudor Authors* in 1997, he noted in his introduction his surprise at "the number of Roman Catholic authors" (xi). In his remarks in a Southwell Session at the 45th International Congress on Medieval Studies at Kalamazoo in 2010, John Watkins offered observations about what he termed "a revolution in our thinking about the Catholic Church in later Tudor England"[4] in the past several years. "The old Dickensian tale of a nation permeated by Lollardy and waiting only for the catalyst of Henry VIII's divorce to spring fully into its destined Protestant identity," he said, had been laid to rest by Christopher Haigh and Eamon Duffy. "There are . . . plenty of reasons to suspect that the old man on the road to Tyburn who cried out to Robert Southwell 'God in heaven

2   From *The Ways We Touch*, University of Illinois Press, 1997.
3   "A Conversation with Dana Gioia," *Image,* No. 73 Spring 2012.
4   John was serving as a respondent in the second of four annual sessions on "Southwell at Kalamazoo" arranged by Frank Brownlow. I quote his remarks here with his permission.

bless and strengthen you' expressed a sentiment shared by many more people than we used to think."

Even more poignant in Watkins's observations was his description of our present world that was permitting such a reassessment of the past. It is instructive to consider his remarks upon the current state of things:

> Hegel famously quipped that the Owl of Minerva flies at midnight to suggest that we can only make sense of a historical moment once it has passed. We are in a better position to understand the English martyrs, and more generally to make sense of the sixteenth-century Reformation, because we are witnesses to the end of Protestant England. This culmination of a half-millennium of history is not exactly taking the form that men like Southwell and Campion would have liked to see. Catholicism is thriving in the U.K., but so are Hinduism and Islam. The religious profile of Europe has changed in ways that the sixteenth-century Jesuits could never have predicted. But one thing is clear: for the first time in five hundred years, historical forces have severed the longstanding connection between Protestantism and English nationhood. Did Tony Blair really have to wait until he left office before he announced his conversion [to Roman Catholicism]?

In this surprising new world, reassessments of the Catholic presence in the Tudor and Stewart eras have continued, and Robert Southwell's fragile bark may, after all these centuries, actually be rising with a general tide of interest in what I recently heard one scholar call "Shakespearean Catholics."

Lest we become too enthusiastic, however, let us step back into the daylight with Larkin's touring bicyclist and recognize that it is not just the Church which is "going" towards obscurity and "a shape less recognizable each week." It is poetry itself. Consider that when Robert Southwell wrote his fiery epistle in 1593 calling poets to reform the kind of verse they wrote, the content of poetry mattered enormously, even more perhaps than most prose. It was a significant part of the mass media of its day. In Hopkins's age this was still true, though far,

far less so. Today, the content of poetry is of little consequence to the broader culture. "The time of minor poets is coming," Charles Simic (major or minor?) announced in his 1989 award winning book *The World Doesn't End*. So perhaps it is already here. "Welcome you whose fame will never reach beyond your closest family and perhaps one or two good friends gathered after dinner over a jug of fierce red wine" (58). It may not yet have come quite to that, but we may already ponder, standing unsteadily upon the slippery ground of cultural studies, with our fingers stuck in favorite pages of Eliot, Hopkins, Herbert, Crashaw or Southwell, "who will be the last, the very last, to seek / This place for what it was?"

So, this is the counterpoise of our century. But in any era recognizing the extraordinary in the ordinary and pointing it out is still the essential work of the poet, major or minor. Naming the extraordinary in the ordinary as divine remains still the essential sacramental work of the priest, illegal and disguised, lonely and obscure, or, like the priest in Graham Greene's the Power and the Glory, "poised in a chair . . . like a black question mark."

It may be, as Southwell insisted so long ago, that "the vanity of men cannot counterpoise the authority of God." Be that as it may, the weight of the priesthood certainly counterpoised each word of his poems. What counterweight Robert Southwell's poetry has been or still is to English poetry is a question to which I hope this book has offered at least the beginnings of a meaningful answer. Meanwhile, I offer this modest hope for his work: that, in the words of Larkin's Church-goer, "someone will always be surprising / A hunger in himself to be more serious / And gravitat[e] with it to this ground."

Bibliography

Primary Works

William Alabaster. Edited by G. M. Story and Helen Gardner. Oxford University Press, 1959.

Unpublished Works by William Alabaster (1568–1640). Edited by Dana F. Sutton. University of Salzburg, 1988.

The Complete Poetry of Richard Crashaw. Edited with an Introduction and Notes by George Walton Williams. New York University Press, 1972.

Donne, John. *The Complete Poetry and Selected Prose of John Donne.* Ed.

Charles M. Coffin. Random House Inc., 1994.

Drayton, Michael. *The Works of Michael Drayton.* Ed. J. William Hebel. Oxford: The Shakespeare Head Press, 1961.

——. Matilda the faire and chaste daughter of the Lord Robert Fitzwater, the true glorie of the noble house of Sussex. Publication date: 1594.

Ellman, Richard and Robert O'Clair. *The Norton Anthology of Modern Poetry.* New York: Norton, 1973.

Estella, Fray Diego. *Meditaciones devotissimas amor Dios.*

Gerard, John. *The Autobiography of an Elizabethan.* Trans. Philip Caraman. New York: Pellegrini and Cudahy, 1952.

Herbert, George. *The English Poems of George Herbert.* Ed. C. A. Patrides. London: J. M. Dent and Sons, 1974.

Hopkins, Gerard Manley. *The Correspondence of Gerard Manley Hopkins.* Three Volumes, ed. Claude Colleer Abbott. Oxford University Press, 1935.

——. *The Poetical Works of Gerard Manley Hopkins.* Ed. Norman Mackenzie. Oxford: Oxford University Press, 1986.

Shakespeare, William. *The Complete Signet Classic Shakespeare*, ed. Sylvan Barnet, 1963.

Southwell, Robert, Saint. *An Epistle of Comfort*. Ilkley: Scholar Press, 1974.

———. *A Hundred Meditations on the Love of God*. Edited with a preface by John Morris, S.J. London: Burns and Oates, 1873

———. *The Poems of Robert Southwell*. Ed. James H. McDonald and Nancy Pollard Brown. Oxford at the Clarendon Press, 1967.

———. St Robert Southwell, *Collected Poems*. Ed. Peter Davison and Anne Sweeney. Manchester: Carcanet Press, 2007

———. *The Prose Works of Robert Southwell Containing Mary Magdalen's Funeral Tears, The Triumphs Over Death and An Epistle of Comfort from the Editions of 1593*. Ed. W. Jos. Walter. London: Keating, Brown & Co., 1828.

———. *The Triumphs Over Death*. London: Manresa Press, 1914.

———. *Two Letters and Short Rules of a Good Life*. Ed. Nancy Pollard Brown. Charlottesville: University of Virginia Press, 1973.

Spenser, Edmund. *The Yale Edition of the Shorter Poems of Edmund Spenser*. Ed. William A. Oram, Einar Bjorvand, Ronald Bond, Thomas H. Cain, Alexander Dunlop, and Richard Schell. New Haven: Yale University Press, 1989.

Walton, Izaak. *The Lives of John Donne, Sir Henry Wotton, Richard Hooker, George Herbert and Robert Sanderson (1670)*. London: Oxford University Press, 1927.

Secondary Works

"Books Belonging to Hopkins and His Family." *The Hopkins Research Bulletin*, 5, 1974.

"Books Hopkins Had Access To." *The Hopkins Research Bulletin*, 6, 1975.

Anonby, David. "The Sacred Pain of Penitence; The Theology of John Donne's *Holy Sonnets*" in: Nelson, Holly Faith (ed. and intro); Szabo, Lynn R. (ed.); Zimmerman, Jens (ed.) *Through a Glass Darkly: Suffering and Sacred, and the Sublime in Literature and*

Theory. Walterloo, ON: Wilfrid Laurier University Press, 2010. xxvii.

Bacigalupo, Massimo. *"Hopkins Among the Moderns."* Gerard Manley Hopkins, Tradition and Innovation. Ravenna: Longo, 1991, 273–78.

Baker-Smith, Dominic. "John Donne's *Critique of True Religion"* in *John Donne, essays in celebration*. London: Methuen, 1972.

Bald, R. C. *John Donne, A Life*. Oxford University Press, 1970.

Bassett, Bernard. *The English Jesuits: From Campion to Martindale*. New York: Herder and Herder, 1968.

Berthelot, Joseph A. *Michael Drayton*. New York: Twayne Publishers, Inc., 1967.

Bewley, Marius. *Masks and Mirrors*. New York: Athenaeum, 1970.

Bizup, Joseph. "Hopkins' Influence On Percy's *Love in the Ruins*." Renascence, 46:4, 1994.

Bloom, Harold (ed.). *John Donne and the Seventeenth-Century Metaphysical Poets*. New York: Chelsea House Publishers, 1986.

Bouchard, Gary. "Robert Southwell, The Original Metaphysical Poet." *Explorations in Renaissance Culture, (Fall) 2000*.

——. "The Curious Case of Robert Southwell, Gerard Hopkins and A Princely Spanish Hawk." *Renascence* 51.3 (Spring) 1999, pp. 181–89.

——. "The Roman Steps to the Temple: An Examination of the Influence of Robert Southwell Upon George Herbert." *Logos, A Journal of Catholic Thought and Culture*, 2007.

——. "Resurrecting the Dust of Dead Supplies: The Poetry of Robert Southwell and Gerard Manley Hopkins." *Studies* (Spring) 1997.

——. "What Gets Said in a Narrow (10 X 14) Room: A Reconsideration of Hopkins' Later Sonnets" in *Hopkins: The Person and the Poetry, New Essays on Gerard Manley Hopkins*. English Literary Studies Series, 1996.

——. "Who Knows Not Southwell's Clout? Assessing the Impact of Robert Southwell's Literary Success Upon Edmund Spenser." *LATCH A Journal for the Study of the Literary Artifact in Theory, Culture or History*, v. 3, 151–163, 2010.

———. "Gerard Manley Hopkins: The Incarnational Work of Priest and Poet." *The American Benedictine Review,* 44:2, 1993.

Boyle, Robert, S.J., *Metaphor in Hopkins.* Chapel Hill: University of North Carolina Press, 1960.

Brooks, Helen M. "When I would not change in vowes, and in devotione": Donne's "Vexations" and the Ignatian Meditative Model. *John Donne Journal,* 19, 2000.

Brown, Nancy Pollard. "Robert Southwell's Mary Magdalen." Recusant History, 31: 1 (May 2012), 1–12.

—— "Paperchase: "The Dissemination of Catholic Texts in Elizabethan England." English Manuscript Studies 1100-–700, vol. ed. Peter Beal and Jeremy Griffith. Oxford, Basis Blackwell, 1989.

Brownlow, Frank. *Robert Southwell.* New York: Twayne Publishers, 1996.

———. "John Donne: 'The Holy Sonnets'" in *Donne and the Resources of Kind,* edited by A. D. Cousins and Damian Grace. Madison & Teaneck, NJ: Fairleigh Dickinson University Press (2002) 87–105.

—— "Southwell and Shakespeare." *KM80: A Birthday Album for Kenneth Muir.*Liverpool: Liverpool University Press, 1987.

Bush, Ronald. "Eliot and Hopkins: Through a Glass Darkly" in *Hopkins Among Poets: Studies in Modern Responses to Gerard Manley Hopkins.* Richard F. Giles, ed.,The International Hopkins Association Monograph Series, 3. The International Hopkins Association, 1985.

Carey, John. *John Donne: Life, Art and Mind,* Oxford University Press, 1991.

Cefalu, Paul. "Godly Fear, Sanctification, and Calvinist Theology in the Sermons and 'Holy Sonnets' of John Donne." *Studies in Philology,* 100 (2003) 71–86.

Charles, Amy M. *A Life of George Herbert.* Ithaca: Cornell University Press, 1977.

Clegg, Cyndia Susan. "Justice and Press Censorship in Book V of Spenser's *Faerie Queene.*" *Studies in Philology,* 95:3 (1998 Summer) 237-62.

Covington, Sarah. *The Trail of Martyrdom, Persecution and*

Resistance in Sixteenth-Century England. University of Notre Dame Press, 2003.

Cunnar, Eugene and Jeffrey Johnson. *Discovering and (Re)Covering the Seventeenth-Century Religious Lyric.* Duquesne University Press, 2003.

Delvin, Christopher. *The Life of Robert Southwell, Poet and Martyr.* New York: Farrar, Straus and Company, 1956.

—— "Robert Southwell and Contemporary Poets – I." *The Month,* 1950, 169–180.

—— "Robert Southwell and Contemporary Poets – II." *The Month,* 1950, 309–19.

Downes, David A. *Gerard Manley Hopkins: A Study of His Ignatian Spirit.* New York: Bookman Associates, 1959.

Dilworth, Thomas. "David Jones and Gerard Manley Hopkins" in *Hopkins Among Poets: Studies in Modern Responses to Gerard Manley Hopkins,* Richard F. Giles, ed. The International Hopkins Association Monograph Series, 3. The International Hopkins Association, 1985.

DiPasquale, Theresa M. *Literature and Sacrament: The Sacred and the Secular in John Donne.* Pittsburgh: Duquesne University Press, 1999.

Duncan, Joseph. *The Revival of Metaphysical Poetry, 1872–1912.* PMLA (v 68, no. 4) 1953.

Eleanor, Mother Mary, S.H.C.J. "Hopkins' 'Windhover' and Southwell's Hawk." *Renascence* (v 15), 1962.

Ellrodt, Robert. "The Search for Identity: Montaigne to Donne." Confluences XI. Paris: Centre de recherches sur les origines de las modernite et les pays anglophones, 1995. 12.

Ellsberg, Margaret R. *Created To Praise.* Oxford: Oxford University Press, 1987.

Endean, Philip, S.J. "The Spirituality of Gerard Manley Hopkins." *Hopkins Quarterly,* VII, 3.

Evetts-Secker, Josephine. "Consolatory Literature of the English Recusants." *Renaissance and Reformation* 6:2 (1982): 122–41.

Flynn, Dennis. *John Donne and the Ancient Catholic Nobility.* Indiana University Press, 1995.

Fraser, Antonia. *The Gunpowder Plot*. London: Weidenfeld & Nicolson, 1995.

Frye, Northrop. *Anatomy of Criticism*. New Jersey: Princeton University Press, 1957.

Gardner, W.H. *Gerard Manley Hopkins: A Study of Poetic Idiosyncrasy in Relation to Poetic Tradition*, 2 vols. London: Oxford University Press, 1949.

Gee, John. *Foot Out of the Snare*. Ed. T. H. B. Harmsen. Nijmegen: Cicero Press, 1992.

Giles, Richard F. *Hopkins Among Poets: Studies in Modern Responses to Gerard Manley Hopkins*. The International Hopkins Association Monograph Series, 3. The International Hopkins Association, 1985.

Gioia, Dana. "A Conversationwith Dana Gioia." *Image*, 73 (Spring 2012) 65-80.

Guiney, Imogen Louise, ed. *Recusant Poets, Saint Thomas More to Ben Johnson*. New York: Sheed and Ward, 1939.

Hager, Alan, ed. *Major Tudor Authors, A Bio-Bibliographical Critical Sourcebook*. Greenwood Press, 1997.

Hamrick, Stephen. "Tottel's Miscellany and the English Reformation in *Criticism.*" 44:4 (Fall 2002), 329–61.

Heale, Elizabeth. "Spenser's Malengin, Missionary Priests, and the means of Justice." *Review of English Studies*. 41:162 (1990), 171–84.

Heuser, Alan. *The Shaping Vision of Gerard Manley Hopkins*. London: Oxford University Press, 1958.

Hinchcliffe, Peter. "Hopkins and Some Poets of the Thirties." *Vital Candle: Victorian and Modern Bearings in Gerard Manley Hopkins*. Proceeding of the International Conference, March, 1981, "Gerard Manley Hopkins: The Poet and His Age," University of Waterloo and Wilfrid Laurier University, ed. by John North and Michael Moore. Ontario: University of Waterloo Press, 1981.

Hollahan, Eugene. "An Anxiety of Influence Overcome: Dickey's *Puella* and Hopkins' *The Wreck of the Deutschland*." James Dickey Newsletter, 1:2 (Spring, 1985) 2–12.

Janelle, Pierre. *Robert Southwell, The Writer; A Study in Religious Inspiration*. NY: Sheed and Ward, Inc., 1935.

Jens (ed.) *Through a Glass Darkly: Suffering, the Sacred, and the Sublime in Literature and Theory*. Waterloo, ON: Wilfrid Laurier University Press, 2010.

Kerrigan, William. "The Fearful Accommodations of John Donne." *English Literary Renaissance,* 4: 3, 1974.

King, John N. "Recent Studies in Southwell." *English* Literary Renaissance 13:2 (1983).

Klause, John. *Shakespeare, the Earl and the Jesuit*. Klause, John. Fairleigh Dickinson University Press, 2008.

—— "Donne and the Wonderful." *English Literary Renaissance* 17 (1987).

—— "Hope's Gambit: The Jesuitical, Protestant, Skeptical Origins of Donne's Heroic Ideal." *Studies In Philology* 91:2 (Spring 1994), pp. 181–215.

——. "New Sources for Shakespeare's *King John*: The Writings of Robert Southwell." *Studies in Philology* 98:4 (2001).

—— "Politics, Heresy, and Martyrdom in Shakespeare's Sonnet 124 and *Titus Andronicus*" in *Shakespeare's Sonnets: Critical Essays*, ed. James Schiffer. New York: Garland, 1999, pp. 219–40.

Kuchar, Gary. "Petrarchanism and Repentance in John Donne's *Holy Sonnets*." *Modern Philology: Critical and Historical Studies in Literature, Medieval Through Contemporary* 105 (3), 2008, pp. 535–69.

—— *The Poetry of Religious Sorrow in Early Modern England*. Cambridge: Cambridge University Press, 2008.

Law, Thomas Graves. *Jesuits and Seculars in the Reign of Elizabeth*. London: David Nutt, 1889.

Lahey, G. F. *Gerard Manley Hopkins*. London: Humphrey Milford, for Oxford UP, 1930.

Leggio, James. "The Science of a Sacrament." *Hopkins Quarterly*, iv, 2.

Lewalski, Barbara. *Protestant Poetics and the Seventeenth-Century Religious Lyric*. Princeton: Princeton University Press, 1979.

Lichtmann, Maria R. *The Contemplative Poetry of Gerard Manley Hopkins*. New Jersey: Princeton University Press, 1989.

Low, Anthony. "Absence in Donne's *Holy Sonnets*: Between Catholic and Calvinist." *John Donne Journal*, 1, 2004, pp. 5–115.

MacKenzie, Norman H. "Yeats and Hopkins" in *Hopkins Among Poets: Studies in Modern Responses to Gerard Manley Hopkins*. Richard F. Giles, ed. The International Hopkins Association Monograph Series, 3. The International Hopkins Association, 1985.

Manning, Roger B. *Religion and Society in Elizabethan Sussex*. Leicester England: Leicester University Press, 1969.

Mariani, Paul. "The Sound of Oneself Breathing: The Burden of Theological Metaphor in Hopkins." *Hopkins Quarterly*, iv, 1, 20.

Marotti, Arthur. "Southwell's Remains: Catholicism and Anti-Catholicism in Early Modern England." *Texts and Cultural Change in Early Modern England*, ed. Cedric Brown and Arthur Marotti. Basingstoke: Macmillan, 1997.

——. *Catholicism and Anti-Catholicism in Early Modern England*. London: Macmillan Press, 1999.

Martin, Catherine Gimelli. "Unmeete Contraryes: the Reformed Subject and the Triangulation of Religious Desire in Donne's Anniversaries and Holy Sonnets," in *John Donne and the Protestant Reformation; new perspectives*, 2003.

Martz, Louis. "John Donne In Meditation: The Anniversaries." ELH (December) 1947.

—— *The Poetry of Meditation*. Yale University Press, 1954.

——. *The Paradise Within: Studies in Vaughn, Traherne and Milton*. Yale University Press, 1964.

Meyers, Russell J. "Webster, Two by Two or One by Four, the Structural Dilemma of Spenser's *Fowre Hymnes*" presented at "Spenser at Kalamazoo" at the International Congress of Medieval Studies, Kalamazoo, Michigan, 1982.

Miller, Hillis, J. *The Linguistic Moment*. New Jersey: Princeton University Press, 1985.

Miller-Blaise. "Priests and Yet Prophets? The Identity of the Poetic

Voice in the Shorter Religious Lyric of Robert Southwell and George Herbert." *Les voix de Dieu; litte rapture et prophetie en Angleterre et en France a l'age baroque.* 65, 2008, pp. 13–14.

Milward, Peter, S.J. "Sacramental Symbolism in Hopkins and Eliot." *Renascence*, XX, 2 (Winter 1968), 109.

——. "Shakespeare and the Martyrs." *Recusant History.* 31:1 (May 2012), pp. 13–22.

Monta, Susannah Brietz. *Martyrdom and Literature in Early Modern England.* Cambridge University Press, 2005.

Murphy, Elaine. "Gerard Manley Hopkins: A Legacy to the Twentieth Century." *Studies*, 85:338 (Summer 1996), pp. 99–107.

Murray, Molly. "'Now I ame a Catholique' William Alabaster and the Early Modern Catholic Conversion Narrative" in *Catholic Culture in Early Modern England.* Ed. Corthell, Ronald, Dolan, Frances E., Highley, Christopher and Marotti, Arthur. University of Notre Dame Press, 2007.

North, John and Michael Moore, ed. *Vital Candle: Victorian and Modern Bearings in Gerard Manley Hopkins.* Proceeding of the International Conference, March, 1981, "Gerard Manley Hopkins: The Poet and His Age" University of Waterloo and Wilfrid Laurier University. Ontario: University of Waterloo Press, 1981.

Peterson, Douglas L. "John Donne's *Holy Sonnets* and the Anglican Doctrine of Contrition," *Studies in Philology* 65 (1959): pp. 504–18;

Pick, John. *Gerard Manley Hopkins.* London: Oxford University Press, 1942.

Pilarz, Scott R. "To Help Souls: Recovering the Purpose of Southwell's Poetry and Prose" in *Discovering and (Re)Covering the Seventeenth Century Religious Lyric.* Ed. Eugene R. Cunnar and Jeffrey Johnson. Pittsburgh: Duquesne University Press, 2001.

——. *Robert Southwell and the Mission of Literature, 1561–1595: Writing Reconciliation.* Ashgate, 2004.

Raspa, Anthony. *The Emotive Image: Jesuit Poetics in the English Renaissance.* Fort Worth: Texas Christian University Press, 1983.

Roberts, John R. and Lorraine. "'To Weave A new Webbe in Their

Owne Loome': Robert Southwell and Counter-Reformation Politics." In *Sacred and profane: Secular and Devotional Interplay in Early Modern British Literature,* ed. Helen Wilcox, Richard Todd and Alasdair MacDonald. Amsterdam: VU University Press, 1996.

Rust, Jennifer R. "Malengin and Mercilla, Southwell and Spenser: The Poetics of Tears and the olitics of Martyrdom in *The Faerie Queene,* Book 5, Canto 9" in *Redrawing the Map of Early Modern Catholicism,* ed. Lowell Gallagher. Toronto: University of Toronto Press, 2012.

Scallon, Joseph D., S.J. "The Poetry of Robert Southwell, S.J." *Elizabethan and Renaissance Studies.* 11th ser. Salzburg: University of Salzburg, 1975.

Schweers, Gregory. "Bernard of Clairvaux's Influence on English Recusant Letters: The Case of Robert Southwell, S.J." *American Benedictine Review* 41:2 (June 1990).

Shell, Alison. *Catholicism, Controversy and the English Literary Imagination, 1558–1660.* Cambridge University Press, 1999.

——. In *Catholicism and Anti-Catholicism in Early Modern England,* ed. Arthur Marotti. London: Macmillan Press, 1999.

Stachniewski, John. "The Despair of the *Holy Sonnets, ELH* 48, 1981.

Strier, Richard. "John Donne Awry and Squint: The *Holy Sonnets,*" *Modern Philology* 86 (1989).

Stinson, John J. "The Gratitude for Influence: Hopkins in the Work of Anthony Burgess." *The Hopkins Quarterly,* 27:1-2 (Winter Spring 2000), pp. 18–43.

Stubbs, John. *John Donne, the Reformed Soul, a Biography.* New York: WW Norton & Company, 2006.

Swardson, H. R. *Poetry and the Fountain of Light.* Columbia: University of Missouri Press, 1962.

Thomas, Alfred, S.J. *Hopkins the Jesuit: The Years of Training.* NY: Oxford University Press, 1969.

Walker, Julia. "The Religious Lyric as Genre." *English Language Notes* (ELN) 25, 1987, pp. 39–45.

White, Norman. *Hopkins: A Literary Biography.* Oxford: Clarendon Press, 1992.

Wilson, Richard. "A Bloody Question: The Politics of *Venus and Adonis.*" *Religion and the Arts* 5:3, 2001.

Yearwood, Stephanie. "Donne's Holy Sonnets: The Theology of Conversion," *Texas Studies in Literature and Language* 24, 1982.

Index